TEA WITH DEMONS

THE PLUNGE:

"I had a bad dream," I answered noncommittally. I didn't tell Stan about the jester or the mad calf or dancing our last wedding dance. I didn't tell him how frightened and fragmented I felt, how my world was suddenly crumbling like a stale cookie, how I couldn't find the batter to make a new batch.

THE DEPTHS:

For the first five minutes of my talk, all was well. My stone is protecting me, I thought as I proceeded. Then suddenly, the stone turned on me. It became hot, scorching the flesh of my right hand. I clutched it more tightly, and it became a piece of burning coal. The pain that had begun in my hand now began to travel up my arm. I was on fire.

THE RETURN:

The parting from my hospital friends was like telling childhood chums goodbye. We talked of writing and of meeting again, but I knew that it was a youthful illusion. They belonged to that time and no other, like friends made at summer camp or on vacation in some foreign place. I knew I must choose between their society and that of the world, and for all its imperfection, I chose the world.

TEA
WITH DEMONS

CAROL ALLEN
with Herbert S. Lustig, M.D.

BALLANTINE BOOKS • NEW YORK

To protect the privacy of those involved, the names of all persons mentioned in this book have been changed, with the exception of Dr. Herbert S. Lustig, Dr. Milton Erickson, and the author's friends Elaine, Mimi, Carol, and Sally.

Library of Congress Catalog Card Number: 85-5066

ISBN 0-345-33560-0

This edition published by arrangement with William Morrow and Company, Inc.

Manufactured in the United States of America

First Ballantine Books Edition: August 1986

To my children and my family for their sustaining love

C.A.

For the young child to whom I made that special promise many years ago

H.S.L.

Author's Note

One of the most satisfying prerogatives of moving on in life is the shedding of our former selves. Sometimes I look back at the Carol on these pages and puzzle over her. It is difficult to encounter former selves in so public a medium as print. While the Carol presented on these pages is not the Carol I am now, I have chosen to let her be. Beyond some minor editing for this paperback edition, I have resisted the impulse to rewrite her because she is true to that time. I join Lillian Hellman in joyfully proclaiming myself an unfinished woman.

—CAROL ALLEN

Acknowledgments

While this is a personal account, written from my point of view, Dr. Herbert Lustig, my psychiatrist during the time of these events, played an invaluable collaborative role in helping me reconstruct portions of the therapy conversations presented. I was able to remember our interactions in broad outline, with highlights and conclusions firmly etched in my mind. When my memory grew dim over details, Herb and I sat together with my notebooks and his clinical notes and re-created our conversations to recover the specifics, sequences, and flow that lend authenticity to the work. He also thoughtfully and methodically reviewed the manuscript. I am most deeply indebted to him, however, for vigilantly directing me toward sanity and self-respect throughout the course of my therapy, and for his enthusiasm in working on this project as a friend.

For reading the work in progress and offering encouragement and insights that added immeasurably to the finished work, Dr. Lustig and I wish to thank Lindy and David High, Dick and Judy High, Nancy and John Zelnick, Mort Maimon, Margaret Maule, Carol J. Agnew, Mary Mercurio Scheip, Michael Scheip, Michi Ishida Rose, Dick Rose, Barrie Van Dyck, Claire Fitzgerald, and Martin Goldberg, M.D. For their support and thoroughgoing critique of the final draft, we are especially grateful to Patrick S. Pasquariello, Jr., M.D., and Paul J. Fink, M.D.

Our special thanks to our editor, Maria Guarnaschelli, for the spirit and enthusiasm she brought to this project and for her critical insights, which guided our revisions of the manuscript.

Our thanks also to Renee Davis, for the professionalism, care, and patience she displayed in preparing the manuscript. We would also like to thank Minerva Rosa for her early help in this respect.

For their support, we are indebted to many friends and colleagues in our private and professional lives. We would particularly like to acknowledge Nathaniel Branden, Gerard McCauley, Sharon Lustig, Dan and Margo Polett, Gordon Wyner, Linda Kurtz, Sandra Schultz Newman, Sid Waldman, and Kay Reed. I would also like to thank Susan Schwartz McDonald for teaching me the discipline of writing in the workplace.

For their unhesitating acceptance and many kindnesses during the time of this story, I will always remain grateful to my friends and neighbors, Mimi Mortimer, Martha Wintner, JoAnne Zanin, Margo Cairns, Judy Goldberg, Wendy Gollub, Jerry Gollub, Earlene Sloan, Marty Dickson, Madeline Gutwirth, Sylvia Glickman, and Eleanor and Sam Gubins.

Finally, my special thanks to Elaine Maimon for her critical judgment and illumination of the craft of writing, and for her unqualified loyalty and friendship throughout the past fifteen years.

—CAROL ALLEN

Contents

	Author's Note	vii
	Acknowledgments	ix
	Introduction: The Cave	xiii
PART I:	Blinded by the Fire	1
PART II:	Journey Out of the Cave	79
PART III:	Blinded by the Sun	127
PART IV:	Journey Back to the Cave	211
PART V:	Looking in a New Direction	251
	Psychiatrist's Note	282

Introduction
The Cave

Plato tells a story about how we are all prisoners in a cave under the ground. We are bound and shackled and stand facing a wall of the cave, so that we can see only what is directly in front of us on that wall. Behind us is a rampart upon which puppets move—not just wooden dancing men, but figures of rivers and rainbows, and trees, and all the other things in the world.

Behind the figures is a fire that casts its light onto the figures, projecting their shadows onto the wall. It is these shadows that we see; it is these shadows that we think are real. We have fun and debates over these shadows. We play shadow games and have contests over them, and praise or blame the prisoner who can pick out this or that shadow quicker or better than the rest of us.

Plato asks us to imagine that someone frees us from our shackles and turns us around, so that we now face the fire. At first our eyes would be so confused by the light that we could discern objects only dimly. But as our eyes grew stronger and accustomed themselves to the light, we would begin to pick out the puppets and then the fire, and thereby know the shadows for what they are.

What if, Plato asks us, a wise person were to lead us on a journey up the tunnel and out of the cave? The journey would be difficult, with much prodding and stumbling. And if we succeeded, and came out into the sunlight, we would once again be blinded, but even more strongly this time. Our eyes would be so filled with light that we would see nothing. In order to adjust our eyes, we would first have to look at the objects in the light of the moon or look at their gentle reflections in the water, until our eyes became so accustomed to the sunlight that we could finally look directly at the things themselves. Then we would know that the shadows in the cave are actually copies of puppets, which are copies of reflections, which are copies of real things in the world above.

If we should come so far, Plato says, we would want to remain in the sunlight and nevermore enter the darkness of the cave. But it would be our task and our obligation to go back, in the hope of leading others out. But if we should enter the tunnel to the cave once more, our eyes would again be confounded by the darkness.

Plato says that our eyes become confused in two ways: by going from darkness to light, and by going from light to darkness. And if we should return to the prisoners below and begin to tell them what we have seen, they would not understand us, for how can one tell shadow people that their shadows are not real?

If we should return to the cave and compete in the games once again, we would be clumsy and awkward, and ridiculed as fools. Then, says Plato, we would fall silent, unable to speak about our different vision. We cannot put sight into blind eyes, or knowledge into people's heads. We can only turn the prisoners around, so that they look in a different direction. Or so Plato says.

PART I

Blinded by the Fire

Chapter 1

I sat for the first time on a hard deacon's bench in the doctor's narrow waiting room. Opposite me, too high to give me back my own image, was a large oval mirror with a polished black frame. It reflected the framed photograph hung above my head, a picture of the world, whose cloud cover formed the shape of an embryo. I stared at the disturbing reflection for some time until the world gave up its image. Now dancing demons marched mockingly around a pond of mirrored ice. Splinters of nightmare broke off and pierced me. Waves of pain stripped me of my strength.

Dr. Lustig came out of the inner office, and I saw his lips move as he motioned me to come in. I walked quickly past him, too caught up to notice him. When I did look at him, I was startled to see him looking back. We were like two shopkeepers on opposite sides of the street, who one day simultaneously lift the shades of their shops, only to as quickly drop them back into place.

Then I was past him and into the room, where browns and oranges and golds formed lines and straight angles. Raw mineral crystals with sharp contours through muted colors—pale gold and purple and rose—stood on a table to my right. On the opposite wall a prehistoric fish fossil, solidly placed in its rock, seemed certain of its own history.

In the center of the room, near one wall, were two comfortably upholstered armchairs facing each other. Between them was an upholstered ottoman. Around the perimeter of the room were a few smaller, movable chairs. Dr. Lustig sat down in one of the armchairs and motioned me to sit in the other.

I sat down without words, pressing my hands together to insist on a unity, to join the pieces.

"Would you like to get yourself together before you begin?"

I nodded and fumbled for the pieces of myself. It took several minutes.

"My reality problem" was what I gathered to present. "I have a reality problem, and it has been denied for a long time...." I stopped there. My words were frightening me. I took a deep breath and for the first time spoke the worst.

"I think I'm crazy."

I waited for the barely perceptible intake of breath, the composed and serious expression of concern, the carefully modulated voice probing my childhood.

"Congratulations! Some of the most creative people in the world think they're crazy ... and sometimes they're right. What's your claim to craziness?"

I was too startled to reply. Somewhat defensively I finally answered, "When I was a child I had this way of knowing things, this power..." My voice gave out and I could not go on.

He asked me what sort of things. I didn't know how to talk about the odd experiences that I had had of late or of the demons in the mirror. I began talking about intuition.

"Many people have intuition of the heart," I said, "which allows them to know what other people feel. But other people have intuition of the eyes, which lets them see what other people can't see." I talked at random now, groping for common ground.

"And which is it that you have?"

"I have them both," I said with some drama. "It is a terrible thing to know too much."

"That's been a problem of artists throughout the ages. In which creative medium do you use it?"

I was again taken aback and thought the question over for some minutes.

"I don't know how to use it," I finally said, and I was very sorry as I said it. "I just feel that I am being overwhelmed with information that I don't know what to do with."

"You probably are," he said softly. "There's no other thing that I can think of that will so rapidly ... *immobilize* a functioning person."

I felt the suggestion of hope. "What shall I do?"

"What did you do here today, after you sat down and before you began to speak? Because when you sat down you were very distraught, but by the time you spoke you were much more collected. What did you do then?"

"I don't know."

"Fair enough. Even though you don't know what it was that you did, could you do it again?"

I said I didn't know, but I would try.

"Fine indeed. Will you try now?"

I nodded tentatively.

"Let yourself get a *little* overwhelmed. Not too overwhelmed, not so overwhelmed that it really becomes burdensome, but just a little overwhelmed." He paused a moment until his eye caught the lamp on the table near his chair. "Perhaps about the lamp over there. You know, it comes from driftwood. As a matter of fact it is constructed of pieces of driftwood. Now I don't know its history, except that it is made of driftwood. But perhaps intuition of the eyes gives you some information about its origin and travels that I don't have. So could you get a little overwhelmed about this lamp, and then do whatever it was that you did at the beginning of today's session to get yourself collected and functioning?"

I tried, but after a few minutes I was getting more than a little overwhelmed, so I stopped.

"The lamp is falling apart," I said.

"As a matter of fact the lamp *is* falling apart, if it were not for two or three *very real facts* of nature." He took his time over the words "very real facts," stretching them out, giving them time to seep in.

"Those facts are nails. You can see one of them right from where you are sitting."

I looked, but couldn't see anything holding it together. I didn't say anything.

"The thing about this lamp is that if it were not for those nails, gravity would cause the whole thing to fall down."

"In other words, the laws of nature?"

"You might say that. From the imposition of a minimal amount of order caused by the rigidity of the nails comes a beautiful structure."

"What are the nails that hold a person together?" He seemed to understand so well that I could afford to be direct.

"The thing that holds us together is not nails," he slowly replied. "It's more like . . . an invisible shield. A skintight invisible shield that envelops us, that keeps the outside out and the inside in. Except when we want an interchange between the two."

I felt the lump of fear diminish in my stomach and the pain in my limbs ease, and I took a deep breath. We sat for some time in silence of the comfortable kind, until my hands could finally rest quietly together on my lap.

The familiar image of Plato's cave came into my mind. I was one of the prisoners chained in the half-light, watching shadows move on the rough wall. I looked at Dr. Lustig again, and for a moment he was the wise person who would lead me out of the cave into the sun.

"I am going to take a long journey and you will be my guide," I told him. "I can see the beginning of the journey and the end, but not the middle."

"Where are we going?"

"I had a dream a few days ago that I was bitten by a mad calf—by madness. That's how it begins. Two days later I had a second dream. I was standing with a psychiatrist in his office and he was holding me by the shoulders and gently rocking me back and forth. Everything bad had come out. I was filled with an indescribable peace, the kind that I've never had in my life. That's how it ends."

"That's certainly a dream worth having again," he replied.

Then the magic began to crowd in on me again. It came like a sorcerer out of nowhere, keeping to the shadows, everywhere making its presence felt. It cast its spell over the ordinary and mundane, so that background leaped forward into sudden prominence, insignificance caught in a sudden light. I thought of the items on my grocery list, even the dust on a bowl of rose leaves, and they were no longer indifferent, would not stay in place. I was defenseless against so much surplus significance. So I fastened it onto Dr. Lustig, that it should be less terrifying, that it should have a place.

"There's one thing I need to know before I start," I said. I was still talking about the journey, but the focus had shifted, and the wise man had become the sorcerer.

"I know you'll deceive me along the way," I said, "but will it be the deception of the thrush?"

He asked me what that was, so I began to quote T. S. Eliot. I wanted him to know I really did have something in mind, that I was not making it up.

"Footfalls echo in the memory," I began and went on until I came to the question:

> "Round the corner. Through the first gate,
> Into our first world, shall we follow
> The deception of the thrush?"

I finished and waited expectantly, not realizing that the meaning of my quotation was obscure. Dr. Lustig, however, did not seem uncomfortable with my strange literary reference.

"Ahh . . . *that* kind of deception," he said. "Yes, I can promise you it won't be anything more than that."

"I know you are going to use magic," I went on insistently. "Will it be good or bad magic?"

"I *only* use good magic. Bad magic gives me headaches." I laughed.

"Yes," he said with satisfaction, "it will be one hundred percent organic good magic—no artificial preservatives."

It was almost time to go, but I had one last question.

"At home my children have a small blue puzzle that's shaped like a cube. It's made up of smaller shapes joined together in different combinations and angles, and the idea is to form the pieces into one large cube. But I don't know how to put the pieces back together."

He was thoughtful for a moment.

"The first thing we're going to do *here* is to put the cube back together any which way. It won't matter if the pieces are in the wrong place. Then, after the cube is stuck back together again, we'll take the pieces off one by one, and put each one back into its proper place."

I smiled and he smiled back.

We talked several minutes more. Then Dr. Lustig wrote down some background information, gave me a regular appointment time, and saw me out the door with a warm handshake. I left reluctantly.

I pulled my collar up against the wind and felt the warmth on my back. Neither the gray November day outside nor the magic within could have their way with me now. I had found an ally who could sit down to tea with demons in the afternoon, and still sleep soundly at night.

Chapter 2

It had begun suddenly eight days before I saw Dr. Lustig. That was the strangest thing of all. One moment I was who I was—a thirty-year-old wife, mother, and part-time philosophy professor at a Philadelphia college. The next moment I was spinning through a dreamlike void, swept into some primordial chaos whose dimensions made me very small, whose currents gave me a different name.

It began with a dream. I remember it clearly. It was the night of November 10, and it was the first dream I had remembered in twenty-five years.

I am in a modern, many-angled house that sits on a hill overlooking the ocean. It is light and airy with ceiling-high windows looking out on the water. In this house I am about to be remarried to my husband, Stan, and my relatives have gathered to prepare a wedding feast. I wander through the house looking for Stan. I cannot find him. I begin to run. I run faster and faster. I am out of the house, running down a ramp from the door of the house to the roadway in front.

I cross the road and find myself in a country fairground, such as those I remember from the late summers of my childhood. Directly in front of me is a wooden fair

9

booth, the kind that you would expect women to sell pies from. In this booth, a play is being performed. The grass in front of the booth is divided by an aisle into two sections. All of the audience members sit rigidly in stiff-backed chairs arranged neatly in rows on the right-hand side. I cross over to the left-hand side of the grass, assuming a reclining position to watch the play.

On the right side of the booth, to the back, stands a king, the central character of the play. He is beating time with two sticks. On the left side of the booth, to the front, is a small platform where a jester stands. He is also beating time with sticks, mimicking the rhythm of the king. Although the jester is supposed to maintain the tempo by following the king, I begin to realize that he is slowly and subtly shifting the rhythm. Finally the two are in discord. The jester is undermining the king. No one else in the audience notices this. I am the only one who understands.

I leave the fairground and wander through some desert grass, until I come to a corral where beautiful wild horses are galloping around the perimeter. As I approach the fence, I notice a number of cowboys crowded around. Leery of them, I step back and keep my distance. Suddenly the men shout, the corral door bursts open, and all the wild horses gallop out and away. The cowboys yell and wave to me frantically to get out of the horses' way. I am not frightened. I do not move, and in a kind of trance watch the horses sweep by.

Through the cloud of dust raised by the horses I see a small calf following the horses out of the corral. It stands between me and the fence. Once again, but even more frantically this time, the men wave to me to get out of its way. I pay no attention, however, because it seems so harmless. Suddenly the calf lunges at me and bites me on the right hand with a jagged tooth. Pain shoots down my left side and I realize that the calf is rabid and that I am dying. Bitten by madness, I stagger back toward the road that I have crossed, where a stranger, a kindly man, comes to my assistance. He takes my wounded arm and helps me back to the house.

I run through the rooms, looking for someone, until I find my friend Marion. We are standing at the door of a *totally dark room. I point to the room and say in terror, "I must interpret my dream." She makes no reply.*

I enter the pitch-black room alone and redream the dream. As I am leaving the room, Stan appears and we dance the last wedding dance. Stan then disappears. I leave the house and go to the shore of the ocean. I stand at the bottom of a hill of sand that is strewn with baby blankets. I struggle through the sand trying to get to the top of the hill, where my mother stands with a wedding cake.

I lay in bed in the dark, holding my breath, frozen in that instant before full consciousness returns. Beside me I could hear the steady breathing of my husband, Stan, and I wondered that his sleep should be undisturbed. For me the dream images filled the room, driving out my rationality and the safety it had brought all these years. I could feel again the bite of the calf. My fear was as dark as the room in my dream.

Some time passed, I could not tell how long, and then I reached out and switched on the bedside lamp. The sudden light brought me back to the present, but my body still shook from the memory of the dream. As if compelled, I began to look for a pencil and paper, for I felt I must record my dream. After living so long without a dream dimension, I felt the importance of what had happened, even as I did not grasp its sense.

My hands shook as I wrote. When I looked down I could not recognize my own writing. The marks resembled chicken scratchings in the dust, as if mysterious forces were at play with a private language and script all their own.

By an effort of will I finished. Gingerly, I put the paper away in a drawer, awed by the magic now trapped in the words. Then quietly, without waking my husband, I gathered a blanket around myself and trailed through the house. I turned on every light as I passed it. I got to the living room and sat on the couch, huddled over, with my feet pulled up under me in a posture of defense. So I sat through the night.

I must have looked tired the next morning, because Stan said to me over breakfast, "Were you up last night?"

"I had a bad dream," I answered noncommittally. I didn't tell Stan about the jester or the mad calf or dancing our last wedding dance. I didn't tell him how frightened and fragmented I felt, how my world was suddenly crumbling like a stale cookie, how I couldn't find the batter to make a new batch.

"Oh," he replied distractedly, as he shuffled his lecture notes for the day's economics classes. He went back to his reading and made no further comment.

Why is this happening to me, I wondered, just when I thought everything was safe? I have a husband, far from perfect but still a source of stability; I have two beautiful children and a profession. Why, then, do I feel this confusion surrounding me, blanketing me, clouding my mind and my judgment? Is it a diversionary tactic of the self, designed, perhaps, to smother the failure I feel in so many directions: Failure not of acting, for I have always been responsible, but failure of focus, as if in trying to do too many things at once (and each, of course, perfectly) I am inevitably confronted with partial results, lingering and sometimes totally preoccupying uncertainties: how to be a good mother when all of my time is not devoted to my children; how to be a professional when my children take energy away from my work; what to do with a husband who tolerates but does not love me, what to do with myself when I fail to meet my own expectations. I am always running out of time, I thought, and now time is running out on me.

If the children noticed anything unusual about me that morning, they didn't indicate it. My three-and-a-half-year-old daughter, Elizabeth, carried on her usual morning chatter. My son, Daniel, who was nearly one, contributed a combination of words and noises. Our routine of breakfast, baths, and dressing went slowly, but otherwise much as usual.

As soon as possible after Stan left for the day and the children were settled, I called Marion, who had been next to the black room in my dream. I told her the dream, expecting her to interpret it. She was baffled but suggested that I call her therapist for a consultation.

Am I crazy? I wondered, as I dialed her therapist's number. I had never considered a psychiatrist before—

nobody in my family ever had. We solved our own problems. Marion had said a "consultation." That was only going once. Maybe that will be enough. Yes, I'll go and just get my dream interpreted. That won't mean anything; there's no stigma in that. I rested comfortably on that thought for several minutes, before the worry intruded again. But what if I really am going crazy? Is this the kind of thing you are the last to know?

I dialed her therapist's number and made the appointment. Then it all just seemed to slip out of my mind. In its place came tears shed throughout the day. I no longer thought of reasons why I should be crying, and the tears mostly slipped unnoticed down.

Elizabeth looked at me inquiringly several times during our walk to the duck pond that day, and as we painted watercolors while Daniel napped. But she did not question me. Daniel followed my footsteps more closely than usual. Once he patted my arm in a gesture of comfort.

At around five Stan arrived back home, and I became aware that the tears had stopped. There remained a shadowy haze, as if a filter had slipped between me and the world, lending an air of unreality to all that I experienced. When my children and my husband spoke to me, I found it hard to concentrate on what they said. I answered them absently. They did not seem to notice my distraction. Trying to focus my attention on them, I idly wondered why they were talking, or should want to disturb the stillness with their words.

I tied my daughter's shoes automatically, then warmed up the food for my baby's meal. But I kept returning to the window, as if the answer lay in that direction. Finally forcing myself back to the kitchen, I turned my attention to the kitchen clock. I was fascinated by its measured sounds, and searched its face for secrets. But it ticked on regularly, despite my scrutiny.

Unsatisfied by my encounter with the kitchen clock, I wandered slowly through the house, staring at the faces of all the others. It was then I noticed that all the clocks had gone awry. First they moved faster, then they stood still. Or perhaps, I thought, it is I who have stopped in the middle of a new dimension, where no clocks can be trusted, where proportion is as absent as in a clock without hands.

I shook myself and grasped the dining room table. I wanted the reassurance of hard smooth wood, that the real was real and could not be dispelled by my unruly imagination.

Chills swept over me and then I burned, but I managed to keep my hold on the mahogany. The urgency with which I needed to be steadied underscored the danger and made me afraid. I had read about people who had lost their grip on reality. I *am* going crazy, I thought. I grasped the table even harder. Some time went by and then, just as suddenly, it was over. The air in the room seemed to clear and I was out of the fog. I took some deep breaths and then shakily went to prepare dinner.

So it went that day and the next. I stumbled through the tasks of the hours alternately weeping, foggy, or frightened, confounded by the power of this visitation. Then, on the night of the second day, I had another dream.

NIGHT OF NOVEMBER 12, 1974

I am with a psychiatrist in his office. I am aware that he is a young man, although his face is indistinct. We are standing, and he is holding me by the shoulders and gently rocking me back and forth. I know everything that was hidden has come out; all the fear is over. I can hear him talking softly to me, but I cannot distinguish his precise words. I am exhausted. Lulled by his voice, I am filled with an indescribable peace of the kind I have never had in my life.

The next morning I tried to tell Stan about my dreams and my need to interpret them.

"I don't understand," Stan said when I was finished. "What exactly is the problem?" He spoke irritably, as if I were trying to confound him.

I sighed. It had become my response to most everything that Stan said. I really do want Stan to understand, I thought. Then, with more candor, I admitted that it might not be so.

The next day I saw the consulting psychotherapist. He did not interpret my dreams. He told me I needed therapy. He referred me to a young psychiatrist, Herbert Lustig. As he wrote down the name on the card for me, he noted how conveniently located Dr. Lustig's office was—only a block and a half's walk from my home, the first-floor apartment in an old stone house on Philadelphia's Main Line.

I phoned Dr. Lustig's office when I got home, but he was out. It was nearing five o'clock when Dr. Lustig returned my call. I remember because I was again preparing dinner. "This is Dr. Lustig," he said. "How can I help you?" Shock went through me when I heard his voice. It was exactly the voice of the psychiatrist in my second dream.

Chapter 3

The sense of security I had found following my first meeting with Dr. Lustig was still with me when Stan returned home that evening. I rushed eagerly to the door to meet Stan, excited by my strange encounter with Dr. Lustig and the relief it had generated. "Oh, Stan," I began, and then in a rush of words told him about my meeting that afternoon, how Dr. Lustig had seemed to know what I was thinking, how he had seemed to understand.

Stan looked vexed at what I said. "Calm down," he told me. "I can't follow you. Now, *exactly* what happened?" He spoke slowly and methodically and somewhat impatiently.

My enthusiasm dried up at his tone of voice. "Never mind!" I said with irritation, and gathering up the children, left the room.

But Stan was not finished with the topic. Later, at the dinner table, he asked me again how my therapy session had gone, curiosity and suspicion mingling in his voice.

My reply was brief and noncommittal. "It was helpful" was all that I said, feeling suddenly too tired to explain to anyone.

"Is that all you can say about it?" Stan prodded his food, exasperated.

"Yes," I answered softly, avoiding his eyes.

Neither of us spoke for several minutes. We continued pushing our food around, without much evidence of appetite. It seemed to me that Stan sat at a great distance that could not be traversed with simple words. But as the silence between us deepened, it seemed to shout at us with a third voice.

"It's too hard to explain," I finally began, wanting to rob the silence of its alienating power. But my words did not break the barrier that Stan and I had so unwittingly built.

"Well, are you going to continue or what?" Stan's words were doing no better at reaching me.

"Yes," I replied, suddenly knowing I was committed to therapy with Dr. Lustig.

"Okay," Stan replied, sensing my determination. Then, focusing on the financial issue, he added, "How much did he say it would cost?"

"I don't know," I said, feeling foolish. "I forgot to ask."

"Well, you'd better find out. Let's just be clear," he continued deliberately, "that *you* will have to pay for most of this out of your teaching money. We can't afford it out of my paycheck." So saying, he turned his attention to the children.

After dinner I washed the dishes and cleaned up the kitchen, then bathed the children and readied them for bed. Stan, meanwhile, retired as usual to the study immediately following dinner, to work on the book that was to assure his academic future at the college where he taught. He generally worked until about midnight, so it was not unusual that at bedtime I should find myself in the bedroom alone.

It was about 11 P.M., as I prepared for bed, that I sensed another presence in the room with me. I froze, and then, as if directed, slowly turned my head toward the closet door. No one was near it that I could see, so it was with horror that I watched it slowly creak open. The secrets must go back into the closet, I told myself. I cannot bear this. Then the invading forces gathered in my head. Terrifying disconnected thoughts intruded, pounding out a pulsating, portentous rhythm, swirling through my brain with recurring urgency. Round and round.

Madness.

Death.

What I know is terrible.

Extra Y chromosome.

A childhood house on Eleventh Avenue East. Basement of the house, playing house, blankets draped like houses, something wrong. Did I do it?

"Mommy, Mommy, you've got to help me!"

My sweet baby brother. Did I do something terrible to him?

"He went after me with a butcher knife. I really must have made him mad."

Our dog Vicky, gentle and kind, in my dream turning into a rabid animal with yellow and green stripes and foaming mouth.

I am going mad.

My mother saying, "Your brother Daniel was born kind."

My son Daniel's eyes, looking at me.

Thirty-one months between my brother Daniel and me.

Twenty-seven months between my children.

The numbers must mean something.

I must stop this, or I will die.

Stan came in while these thoughts were whirling, but we did not speak. It was then that I began the pattern that was to last me for some time. Unwilling to confirm my madness before audiences, I dissembled and pretended to be perfectly all right. I learned that I could shroud my turmoil in a cloak of normalcy, and few would be the wiser except for me.

Although we did not speak, I was reassured as always by Stan's physical presence. Perhaps he is petty about details, I thought. At least he is grounded in the real world. Devils would not dare disrupt his dreams.

"I need a hug," I said coaxingly. Stan came over to the bed and put his arms around me.

"I really have been afraid," I confided softly.

"Of what?" he asked calmly, secure as always when I showed my need. Then, seeing the look on my face, he tried to be comforting.

"Don't worry," he said. "It'll be all right, honey." He got up from the bed and finished undressing for the night.

"Now," he said, climbing into his side of the bed, "let's get some rest, okay?" Clearly he thought everything was settled. Reluctantly I switched off the bedside light.

"Good night, Stan," I said. His answering "Good night" was muffled, for he was already half asleep.

"Good night," he muttered again, reaching over to pat my shoulder.

"Good night, Stan," I whispered.

I lay still in the bed for many minutes, listening to the steady sound of Stan's breathing. I was now alone in the dark with the forces of my mind. The terror began to overwhelm me again. I kept a lonely vigil, born out of desperation. If I kept my eyes open and my senses alert, no harm could come to me or entirely have its way.

As the hours passed I thought about Dr. Lustig, and he seemed to be my only recourse. He had given me his home number the day before, and I considered carefully how early in the morning I could call him. The hours ticked on. It was 4:30 or 5 A.M., at that hour known to the diseased and desperate and lonely, when the will to continue begins to atrophy and the clowns have a cup of coffee in the kitchen, that I determined that I could call him at 7 A.M. Then it was just a matter of counting out the minutes, second by second, for I had put an arbitrary time limit on my undoctored pain.

Chapter 4

At seven o'clock on the dot I dialed Dr. Lustig's number. I could hear him answer groggily, then almost instantly snap to attention. Afterward, I could not remember exactly what he had said. I remembered only his tone of voice and the way he had spoken. He was not sympathetic. Rather, he spoke tersely, in a decisive, commanding tone—in a voice that imposed control and demanded order and coherence. He told me to write down my terrifying thoughts. When I hung up the phone, I felt an enormous sense of relief. He has told me what to do, I thought. He has told me how I must talk to myself, what tone of voice to use.

I wrote the words down and then practiced speaking to myself firmly. I found that this exercise shored me up. Enough, anyway, to go about the business of my day, which, that Tuesday, was teaching my two midday philosophy classes. I prepared breakfast for the children, and got them and myself dressed. Then at ten o'clock the babysitter came to my house to watch the children, so that I could go to work. Driving to the nearby college, I steeled myself for the ordeal of facing my students. I concentrated my attention on behaving as normally as possible.

20

Walking up the hill that led from the parking lot to the main campus, I regarded the near perfection of this picture-postcard scene. The sun beamed down brightly on the colored tapestry of fall. The academic spires and towers that rose in the distance seemed to point heavenward, as if they had direct access to some higher authority and were never plagued by confusion or troubled by doubt.

The faces on the passing students were equally confident, revealing burdens no greater than late term papers or poor exams. Most of them were laughing, their faces alternately playful and earnest, suggesting preoccupation with the latest basketball score or the proper dress for an upcoming dance. They communicated health and life and happiness. Or so I romanticized them, as we are apt to romanticize those younger than ourselves. They seemed to be at home in this academic sphere, accepting the gifts of the mind as naturally as they accepted a plate of supper—some out of hunger and some because it was there and had been offered. Not here, tormented intellects or Heideggerian angst.

I arrived at my classroom and reluctantly opened my text to begin the class. In what seemed to me like an enormous irony, I was teaching the philosopher Descartes that day. I turned the pages of my book to the first meditation, "Concerning the Things That Can Be Doubted," in which Descartes, using doubt as a philosophical method for arriving at the truth, determines to "make a serious and unimpeded effort to destroy all my former opinions," and to "abstain from belief in things which are not entirely certain and indubitable."

I tried to teach my first class with my usual objectivity but I found my mind racing out of control or going blank over certain passages, as I interpreted these abstract hypothetical statements literally.

"Nevertheless, I must remember that I am a man, and that consequently I am accustomed to sleep and in my dreams to imagine the same things that lunatics imagine when awake...."

I flushed hot and then cold, and felt my face redden. They must know, I thought. It must be as obvious as the mark of Cain. I pushed the thoughts aside and kept on teaching.

"I realize so clearly that there are no conclusive indications by which waking life can be distinguished from sleep...."

My dream. The rabid calf. Mustn't think about the dream now. I continued reading in a literal way.

"How can I be sure that God has not brought it about that I am always mistaken when I add two and three or count the sides of a square...."

The numbers. What do they mean? Two—divided. The Pythagoreans said four was the number of justice.

"I will therefore suppose that, not a true God, but a certain evil spirit, no less clever and deceitful than powerful, has bent all his efforts to deceive me. I will suppose that the sky, the air, the earth, colors, shapes, sounds, and all other objective things that we see are nothing but illusions and dreams that he has used to trick my credulity. I will consider myself as having no hands, no eyes, no flesh, no blood, nor any senses, yet falsely believing that I have all these things...."

What did I just read? I can't rememember. My mind's gone blank. Must continue, so nobody knows.

"Even though there may be a deceiver of some sort, very powerful and very tricky, who bends all his efforts to keep me perpetually deceived, there can be no slightest doubt that I exist, since he deceives me...."

Small consolation, I thought. Small solace in my presient world.

*   *   *

I glanced at my watch and the hour was over. Somehow or other I had gotten through the class. I suppose I taught by habit, much as one sometimes drives a car, on a sort of mental automatic pilot. I was aware of little as I walked out of the classroom, but the students joining me suggested by their manner that all had gone as usual, so I guessed there had been nothing untoward in my conduct.

I taught a second class in the early afternoon in much the same fashion. Finished for the day, I started across campus to have my usual cup of coffee. As I walked, all the colors and sounds jumped out at me with double intensity, as if I was witnessing them with a heightened, unnatural clarity.

As I walked, I became aware of the intensity of the sun. It seemed to focus itself into a single narrow beam, targeted directly at the top of my head. I physically felt it pierce my skull. And then it happened. In a moment of blinding light and excruciatingly sharp pain, I felt my head split into two pieces, with the cut dividing the right side from the left. In that instant all the sights and sounds faded, and the scene became a black-and-white motion picture with the soundtrack switched off. I slipped out of the action and became an observer, located behind the movie camera that was filming the scene. I was separated from my surroundings as surely as a piece of film is separated from life.

I wasn't aware of what happened next. I just found myself walking robotlike in the direction of my car. My body obeyed the forces of long-standing habit and I found myself driving home. There, I dismissed the babysitter, and with the children trailing me, I moved unhesitatingly to the phone. I dialed Dr. Lustig's office number. When he answered, my internal soundtrack switched back on and I could hear clearly what he said. "I have a terrible headache," I murmured. "Is there any medicine I can take?"

He told me to come over at the beginning of the next hour. I took Elizabeth by the hand and, carrying Daniel, walked directly to Dr. Lustig's office.

When he came out into the waiting room between appointments, I silently handed him a piece of paper on which I had written the thoughts of the night before. He closely regarded my face, then quickly read what was written. He took me and the children into the inner room and handed me a small bottle of medicine. Then he sat down and wrote out a prescription for me. He gave me the instructions for taking it, then told me to call him the next morning.

I was in a daze, so much so that when Daniel, my baby, grabbed at one of the crystals on the side table, I did not move. Dr. Lustig intervened and pulled Daniel's hand back. Then he asked me how much help I had with the children. I told him my schedule and how I could not focus my attention on them. He asked me for Stan's number and said that he would phone him. Then he spoke sharply and decisively to me.

"You must get all the babysitting help that you need, but when you're with the children, you must focus your attention on them, even if it's only for one half hour a day. When you're with them, you must be there for them."

I nodded mutely. Something else was weighing on my mind. Finally, my thoughts coalesced.

"I'm terrified of remembering something now," I said, my voice cracking. "Something that I just can't bear." My hands tore at one another as I spoke. And then with seeming irrelevance, but utter conviction, I voiced an idea that just seemed to materialize out of nowhere.

"You must hypnotize me," I said. It was the first magical solution that occurred to me.

I made the suggestion with no knowledge that Dr. Lustig had, in fact, studied hypnosis with one of its foremost practitioners, Dr. Milton Erickson. I had always doubted the legitimacy of hypnosis and had certainly never expected to plead for its use with me. But some uncanny instinct guided me in making my request, some primitive knowledge of how the healing should occur.

Dr. Lustig did not appear particularly surprised at my strange request. He told me later that patients often came to him knowing what they needed. "Sometimes a person will carry a book under their arm with the diagnosis of their problem in the title," he said as if awestruck by the wonder of the human mind. "Very little surprises me anymore," he added, "especially about the capability of the human heart and mind to get itself into trouble and then to find a perfect solution for it."

So when I made my impulsive request for hypnosis that day, he gave a brief nod. "I'll be glad to use hypnosis with you, but there's something I'd like to know first. Will whatever it is that you're afraid of remembering stay locked inside you, until after you've taken the children home and have returned to this office."

"I think so," I replied hesitantly, thinking to myself, I've kept myself from remembering so far. I guess I can continue for a little while longer.

Dr. Lustig instructed me to take the children home and let Stan watch them, and to return to the office at the next hour, between his regular appointments.

I did as he suggested. When I returned at 6 P.M., he had us both sit in our usual chairs. He told me that he was going to teach me hypnosis.

"Carol," he said, "here's what I want you to do. Sit back comfortably in the chair, get your body and feet and arms relaxed, and pick a spot on the ceiling to look toward. It can be any spot, in front of you or even slightly in back of you on the ceiling, and keep on looking right toward it and pay *close attention* to my words. It's not necessary that you *hear* all of my words, nor is it necessary that you *see* the spot very clearly . . . but just *do* the best you can in paying attention to the sound of my voice, and at paying attention to the precise area of the ceiling where the spot is located." The tempo of his speech slowed and his voice deepened.

"Focus all of your attention on the sound of my voice and on the spot on the ceiling, so that you can enter into the state of altered consciousness that we commonly call hypnosis." He paused, waiting expectantly.

"That's right . . . just let your eyelids close . . . and become familiar with how *comfortable*, and *calm* . . . and *confident* you feel, and how *proud you are* with what you've been able to accomplish here today.

"Hypnosis is a *skill in focusing attention*, and because it is a skill, you can *practice* it and become better at using it. Hypnosis can serve for you, when you're outside this office, the same lovely function that it serves for you now . . . to give you a moment's healing, to allow you to have this period of peace and comfort and calm and restoration, in the midst of what has been a very hectic day."

When I was relaxed and fully aware of his words, but listening with more attentiveness than usual, he addressed my concerns.

"The mind is very powerful in each of us. It causes us to experience feelings of pain and pleasure; it causes us to remember events and to forget them; it causes us to create beauty and to unveil illusion.

"Now, there's something that a part of your mind, the front of your mind, does not want you to remember. The back of your mind will not allow you to remember anything that is terrifying or unpleasant, until your ordinary mind, the front of your mind, is ready to accept it and to deal with it comfortably. The back of your mind will just keep it locked safely inside, calmly waiting for its time."

He waited until the words had sunk in, and then added, "You have a very powerful mind, Carol. Are you willing to let it work for you?"

I nodded yes almost imperceptibly. "Then let it begin now," he intoned.

Slowly, I gathered my thoughts, blinked my eyes, and stirred in my chair. I felt as if an enormous burden had been removed from my shoulders. I breathed more easily.

He observed me closely and then spoke again gently. "If you have any more bad thoughts, write them down, and then let them go out of your mind. You don't have to remember them—the paper will. You can just let them go."

Then he smiled, as if to let me know that everything would be all right.

Fortified and reassured, I returned home, stopping by the pharmacy on my way to fill the prescription. I took the prescribed dosage that evening. About half an hour later, my head began to clear, and I found it was easier to focus my attention on my immediate surroundings. Some of the color had returned, although everything still had a grayish cast. But I was vastly reassured to be able, with considerable concentration, to hear my children and understand their words.

Stan came out of the kitchen just then, carrying a bunch of yellow and white mums that he sheepishly presented to me, as if he was afraid they might be too little, too late.

"I spoke to Dr. Lustig," he said, as I sniffed the flowers and smiled for the first time in days. "I'll take care of the children this evening," he continued. "You just get some rest."

"Thanks," I replied, starting toward the bedroom.

"Honey," he called after me. "I really am worried about you. I really do want you to be all right." He held out his arms to me and I walked into them, clinging to him, too weary to speak.

"I'll help you as much as I can," he whispered. "Now, get some rest."

He walked me to the bedroom. Wearier than I had ever been, I went to sleep.

Chapter 5

Something about the hypnosis calmed me at the deepest level. It had really seemed so simple—an inner state of intense concentration akin to meditation; peace and stillness seeping in, replacing fear and angst—but its effects were far-reaching. My deepest terror, the terror of remembering something, something so terrible that I would forever go insane—that terror was gone. I was still foggy from time to time, still confused and upset. But I was no longer in an irrevocable nightmare, a nightmare from which I could not wake up.

In the days following the hypnosis session, I found it easier to perform my daily tasks. Because it had relieved so much of my inner strain, some of the attention that I had turned inward could now be directed to events outside myself, providing me with the energy to play a more active role in the world.

As I continued to practice the skill of focusing my attention, I found that I could concentrate better, focus better on things other than myself. It showed in my interactions with the children, with Stan, with my friends. My mind was less apt to float away from them during a conversation. I focused more on what they said; I was more present in our daily activities. Strange as it might seem, hypnosis, an intensely inner state, acted like a glue to bind me to the world outside myself.

My children accepted my renewed focus as a matter of course. Although the difference in me was subtle, Stan appeared to notice it and to take comfort from it. I found him scrutinizing my face from time to time, trying to read there some clue to my recent mysteriousness, some evidence that I was still solid, that he could count on me, that he needn't be afraid.

The effects of the combination of medicine and hypnosis were also apparent the next time I saw Dr. Lustig. I found the walk from my home to Dr. Lustig's office, in a small shopping center, invigorating. I entered his office building, climbed the flight of stairs, and walked down the chilly corridor. Stepping from the sterile, harshly lit hallway into this thickly carpeted, softly lighted waiting room was like entering a cocoon where all the elements had been spun together to achieve a delicate warmth and balance. Something in me relaxed, as I sat there and waited for him to appear at the door.

By the time I sat down in the chair opposite him for my therapy session, I found myself noticing details about him and the room that had escaped my attention earlier. The room looked like a reflection of a real person, with small, odd personal touches, rather than some decorator's vision of office finery.

"Your room isn't what I expected," I said.

"What did you expect?" He spoke good-humoredly, as if he was pleased that he had avoided some stereotype.

"I don't know exactly," I answered hesitantly. What was a psychiatrist's office supposed to look like? "I guess I expected something more formal—a desk or an analyst's couch—something like that. I didn't expect it to be so homey and comfortable."

He nodded. "That was my purpose in choosing the decor," he told me. "I wanted it to be comfortable for me and for the people who visit me."

My attention fastened onto the rather large, square picture that hung on the wall between our chairs. It looked like a sun with multicolored rays emanating from it. In the center of the design stood a stylized American Indian figure surrounded by several Indian symbols.

"What's that?" I asked him, pointing to the picture.

"It's a Navajo sand painting, one that an Indian medicine man uses when he heals a sick child." His tone seemed to compliment me for having noticed it. "When I first picked it out, I didn't know anything at all about it. I just knew that I liked it. Later I learned what it's used for." He smiled to himself, as if pleased with the appropriateness of his instincts.

"What about the fish over there?" I asked, turning my attention to the fish fossil hanging on the wall opposite the sand painting.

"Oh, that's for me," he answered. "It helps me keep things in perspective. That fish is forty million years old. When I look at it, I can appreciate where people's problems fit into the overall scheme of things. And," he added, "it happens to be a very pretty fossil."

I didn't say anything more for a while. I just looked around the room, noticing again the table lamps whose bases were made out of gnarled driftwood, the subtle harmony of the multishaded beige chairs we sat on, the abundance of natural surfaces and textures: plants, stones, crystals, and woods. Finally, my examination of the surroundings completed, I turned my attention to Dr. Lustig himself.

I noticed for the first time how young Dr. Lustig seemed. I guessed that he was no more than my age. How could anyone that young know what he was doing? I wondered.

"You look very *young!*" I said challengingly.

He nodded in agreement. "Compared to that fossil, we both are," he said. "I'm thirty-one," he added, answering my implied question.

"Exactly how much experience do you have?" I continued. "Have you been in practice long?"

"I've been in private practice here for a year and a half," he answered casually.

I retreated from my challenging tone and became apologetic. I was afraid I might have offended him by questioning his credentials. And if I offended him, maybe he would throw me out. "I'm *sorry* I have to ask you these questions," I said miserably. "It's just that..." I couldn't continue.

"It's perfectly all right," Dr. Lustig replied good-naturedly. "I'm glad that you *are* asking these questions, since *you're* the person who has to decide whether you can ultimately benefit from my services. What else would you like to know?"

I had trouble formulating my concerns.

"Well, where did you go to school?" I asked at last.

"Do you want me to start with grade school?" He was smiling. Perhaps it was the absurdity and unexpectedness of the question that made me laugh.

"Medical school will do," I said.

"I went to Albert Einstein College of Medicine in New York, and then interned in pediatrics at Montefiore Hospital."

"In New York too?"

"Yes," he replied. "Then, I trained in adult psychiatry at The Johns Hopkins Hospital in Baltimore, and finally came to Philadelphia to take my child psychiatry training at the Philadelphia Child Guidance Clinic. After that, I opened this office in July, 1973. It was a momentous day in my life," he continued. "It was the first time I was totally on my own."

I was glad to know about his professional credentials, but something else was still nagging at me. I tried to think how to express my real concern. "When I asked you about your schooling," I said at last, "I guess what I wanted to know was not about your professional training, although I am glad to know it. What I really want to know is whether you're any good at what you do and whether I should trust you."

"Good question. The truth is, you don't know whether you can trust me and you won't know that for a decent period of time. The only thing you do know, about me and my professional skills, is that you left here on the last two occasions feeling a heck of a lot better than when you walked in."

I nodded.

"The real question," he continued, "is whether it can be done again. That's the true test of my ability as a therapist. If it can't be done on a regular basis, then I'm not the one for you."

I stared impassively into the distance, feeling the fog slip over me again. I had to be certain that he was a good therapist—how could I turn my mind over to anyone who was less?

He regarded me in silence for a few moments and then continued, as if he was still thinking over my question and how to answer it.

"*I* know I'm a good therapist," he continued slowly, "and *you'll* be able to find that out in due time. For now, I'm glad that you're a person who trusts her intuition. But don't use that as the sole basis for making your decision about my professional skills. Combine your intuition with the facts of the results that you obtain from our appointments here. Then you'll be on solid ground."

I tried to think. He seemed to be talking about "facts" and "results." The way he had said "solid ground" was like a command for me to focus my attention and come down to earth. I took a deep breath and focused my attention on his face.

"The ultimate determiner of my usefulness to you," he continued in a soothing voice, "is whether you improve in your ability to function effectively in the outside world, and improve in your ability to function comfortably inside your mind."

I continued staring straight ahead. I was intently trying to think. Even though I did not know how it would be accomplished, I could appreciate the goal that he had articulated.

"You know," I said musingly, thinking about my meetings with him, "I really did feel better after seeing you. It was amazing the way you could read my mind."

"Well," he said, "I'm glad you felt better. But I must admit that I flunked mind reading in medical school." I was confused: There was something uncanny about the way he seemed to know what I was thinking.

"I *know* you're using magic," I insisted, remembering my earlier instinctive conviction that he was a sorcerer.

"No," he replied calmly. "I am *not* a magician. But there is something that I do very well. I pay very careful attention to all that people say and to all that people do and to all the meanings of their words and actions when they are in this office. Some people who are not accustomed to this kind of attentiveness might mistake it for mind reading."

"But how did you make it work, then?" I asked him. "Why did I feel better?"

"I don't know why you felt better because I can't read minds," he replied with just the faintest hint of irony. "But I'll tell you what you accomplished while you were here. You practiced the skill called getting yourself back together. And anytime a person practices a skill, they get better at it. The skills that you practiced here, at our last two meetings, are probably the most fundamental of all the mental skills."

"What skills are you talking about?" I asked him, puzzled. I had always thought of skills as being things like playing baseball well, or being good at schoolwork, or being able to paint or play a musical instrument. And I had always been rather good at that sort of thing. I couldn't understand what other kinds of skills he meant.

"You learned and practiced *two* skills at these last two meetings—two ways to use altered states of consciousness for your own betterment. If you're in an altered state of consciousness that is not very comfortable and not very pleasant, your first session's skill teaches you how to *leave* it, so that you can function much more comfortably in the real world. And in the second session, with the hypnosis, you learned how to *enter* an altered state of consciousness, in which you can feel comfortable and relaxed and whole, despite what is going on in your real world.

"And I'm sure there'll be some other important, but probably lesser, skills that you'll also have to learn along the way, about how to get along in the real world, and possibly even how to get along in your own inner world. But you'll learn them as you encounter them."

I sat very still. I felt dazed. What he said was very reassuring. But another part of my mind clung to my former impressions of magic at work and was confused by this altogether practical slant on things.

Dr. Lustig seemed to sense the inner turmoil behind my passive facade, because when he spoke a few moments later, it was in a different vein.

"Last month," he said, "a third-grade boy was brought to me because he was misbehaving in the classroom and wasn't doing his schoolwork. Whenever the children were supposed to be working quietly at their desks, he was always jabbering to his neighbors.

"His parents said he was a bright boy and, in fact, he was. When I asked him about his jabbering, he said that his friends whispered to him during the silent work periods, and that he couldn't ignore them. So he would answer back, and then get caught by the teacher."

I was listening intently to Dr. Lustig while he talked, even though I couldn't understand why he was telling me about this particular boy.

"So," Dr. Lustig went on, "I asked the boy whether he knew how to turn his ears off. Of course, he said no. I told him that I would teach him. I took out a book, brought the boy into the waiting room, tuned the radio to a rock music station, and explained how he could turn his ears off. Then, I told him to start reading the book, which was an interesting one for boys his age, and to turn his ears off so that he couldn't hear the music. He practiced in the waiting room with louder and louder rock music, and he became very good at ignoring the radio. Before he went home with his parents, I instructed him to read for half an hour at bedtime every night, with loud rock music turned on and with his ears turned off."

Dr. Lustig paused for a moment in his story, registering in a glance my absorption in his words. "The next time, we played a game," he continued in the same even voice. "The boy was to read the book and ignore all of the distracting sounds that I made. While he was reading, I made all sorts of noises and grunts and clanged all sorts of things together, in order to distract him. He won the game, though. I was not able to divert his attention. The boy continued to practice at home, until he had mastered the skill of maintaining his concentration whenever *he* wanted to, and both he and his teacher were pleased with his new behavior at school."

By the time Dr. Lustig had finished the story, I was beginning to grasp what he meant by skills. But it still seemed to me that this therapist had an uncanny ability to know what was wrong with people.

"How did you *know* that the boy didn't know how to turn his ears off?" I asked.

"That's very simple," he replied. "You think I knew *intuitively* what the problem was, don't you?"

"Of course," I said. "You're a psychiatrist, aren't you?"

"Well, I'm not as intuitive as you are," he replied. "So what I had to do was to *imagine* what it would be like for me to be a normal third-grader surrounded by talkative friends, and to not be able to concentrate on my school-work. Then I figured out what *skill* I needed to learn in order to allow me, as the third-grader, to get along better. And, of course, I had the advantage of being able to use my adult mind when I imagined my experience as a third-grader."

I decided that Dr. Lustig knew what he was doing. Something about the boy's story appealed to me, maybe because it didn't seem so strange, but was just an ordinary sort of problem.

"Then you don't just see crazy people here," I concluded.

"I see people who have problems and people who are falling apart and all those in between. They have one thing in common, though—they all have a problem that they don't know how to solve. *My* job is to provide them with a fact or a skill or an experience that will solve it. *Their* job is to practice the solution and become good at it."

"But I thought what was done in therapy was to probe the past, in order to uncover hidden traumas, that sort of thing." What he was saying did not seem to fit with everything I had ever heard before about therapy.

"Most people live in the present. And when they do have problems in the present, they want to be able to solve them in the present.

"That's what I help them to do. And the way that I help them to solve their problems is to arrange for them to partially experience those problems in an altered state of consciousness. While they're in that altered state of consciousness, they can practice changing the situation, and therefore find a solution themselves. Then, when they're back in their real life in the present, they'll be able to take the steps that are necessary to implement the solution that they've already experienced and approved of. I usually leave the past for historians. I'm a healer, not a historian."

His focus on finding solutions in the present made me want to laugh in sheer relief. I stirred in my chair, as if shaking off my earlier confusion. What he said seemed so sensible—staying in the present, learning skills. I didn't feel so frightened about the craziness that took me over from time to time. I sat enjoying a more rational calm and the simple pleasure of being in his presence. As I sat there, I surreptitiously looked him over out of the corner of my eye, although I was careful that our eyes did not meet. I noticed his hands for the first time, and that he wore no wedding ring. Gathering up my courage, I looked him full in the face.

"Are you married?" I asked.

"No," he said. "Not yet."

I looked at him again, consciously registering for the first time how attractive he was. He was a trim, short man, about five foot six, two inches shorter than I. He had a beautiful short, full, reddish-brown beard and a slightly receding hairline of darker color. He was stylishly dressed in a conservative wool suit. I found that these elements, combined as they were with his large, brown, and exceedingly clearsighted and direct eyes, carried substantial charm.

Well, well, I thought, and then, embarrassed by my thoughts, quickly turned my attention to more neutral subjects.

"How often should I see you?" I asked, looking down at my shoes.

"I think, for now, twice a week would be adequate," he said. "Later on, when you're functioning better, once a week should do just fine."

"How long do you think it will take?" I asked him, not knowing whether we were talking in terms of weeks or years.

"Two years . . . maybe a little more" was his answer.

I thought over the estimate. It wasn't going to be an overnight cure. But then again, neither did two years sound like forever. I was satisfied with what seemed to me to be a realistic optimism.

"There's one thing we haven't talked about yet," he said, "and that's my fee."

"How much do you charge?" I asked quickly, realizing that I had forgotten about the money issue involved.

"Fifty dollars for each fifty-minute appointment," he replied.

"Isn't the standard fee forty dollars?" I asked. It wasn't that I wasn't willing to pay him; it was just that fifty dollars seemed like so much money to spend on a regular basis.

"Yes, it is, but I'm worth it."

"When do I pay you?" I asked him.

"At the end of each month. I'll give you a bill," he said, adding, "If you have insurance, I'll be glad to fill out the forms so that you can be reimbursed."

"What shall I tell my husband?" I asked, remembering Stan's resistance to the idea of therapy and to its cost.

"Tell him that you're fighting real hard to not have a nervous breakdown. Tell him that I'll do my best to see that you don't, and that he can contact me anytime he wants. I probably will want to see the two of you together sometime soon," he added.

"Okay," I said. The practical details arranged, I glanced at the clock, saw that my time was over, and stood up to go. He again gave me a warm handshake as I left. I did not feel the droplets of rain on my face as I made my way home, wrapped as I was for the moment in the protective cloak he had given my mind, focusing me on skills in the present, reining in bad memories until such time as I could comfortably recall them and understand their place.

Chapter 6

That evening I talked to Stan again about my therapy and its cost. I explained its necessity for me, using Dr. Lustig's words. Even though Stan was initially reluctant to pay for the therapy out of his salary, I hoped he might be persuaded otherwise.

"I need your help, Stan," I said. "I just can't afford the therapy out of my part-time salary."

"All right," he agreed as if making a great concession. "I'll pay for it now, but don't expect me to pay forever."

I said thanks, realizing that this was the best I could do. I wasn't angry at Stan, but there was an edge to my gratitude. I knew he was doing the best he could, that even his grudging support was a concession, for it required him to admit that something might be wrong. He felt my mind drifting away from him, out windows he could not look through. He did not know how to reach out and bring me back. I knew that underneath somewhere he was as afraid as I was, that from his viewpoint controlling the money was a means of containing the situation. But I was angry at myself for having to ask. I wished again that we could recapture the camaraderie and understanding of our early marriage, the small details of kindness that had marked our days—a small love note left on my pillow, a bunch of roses picked from our back garden and carefully arranged in a rose bowl, the encouragement he had given me about my career, the charming way he could tell a story and make me laugh. Now the emptiness, the drawn-out silences, the alienation. I hoped my therapy would not turn into a new battleground.

Feeling unsettled in spite of our tentative accord, I went into the bathroom to apply a fresh coat of makeup to my face. I had adopted this form of protection lately, from the day of my first dream. Each day I would apply heavy facial makeup, whitish and icy in hue, complemented by a dark purple lipstick.

The effect of this makeup mask was a subtly exaggerated one, suggesting something between the disguise of a clown and the appearance of a Japanese courtesan. But it served to protect me in the most primitive sense, or so it seemed to me at the time. It stood like a sentinel at the gate, guaranteeing that no distorted thought should slip unnoticed through the door of my face and out into the larger world. I felt safe behind my second face because it helped me hold my anguish in as, at the same time, it effectively kept other people at bay. I could hide and, by hiding, rest from the constant monitoring of my inner distortions. My mask protected me from the world, and it from me, or so I thought.

As I stood before the mirror applying my makeup that late November day, I did not perceive how ashen and cold it made my face look. Although highly dramatic in its contrast of dark lipstick against pale skin, it must have hovered somewhere within the bounds of normal, because neither Stan nor any of my friends, whom I saw regularly during that time, mentioned much about it. One of my friends, our neighbor Mimi, the wife of one of Stan's colleagues, did look at me strangely one afternoon when we were having coffee in her kitchen.

"You look different," she commented, shaking her head slightly, as if she was perplexed by the elusiveness of her impression. "Did you get your hair cut or change your lipstick or something?"

"It's just that I haven't been feeling well lately," I replied.

"Well, I guess that explains it," she answered with less

than total conviction. "You do look pale," she continued, clearly groping for an explanation that would put to rest the unease that still nagged at her.

Our children's squabbling in the living room interrupted us. By the time we had settled the dispute and gotten the children to play peacefully again, it was time for me to return home and get supper ready. By then, the topic of my changed appearance had been forgotten.

Only Dr. Lustig seemed to take my makeup into account.

I had been in therapy for about two weeks when he gave me the gift of a new face. One day, after I had sat down in my usual chair and we had talked for a few minutes until I was adjusted to being there, he told me that he had some homework for me to do.

"I want you to go out and buy some new makeup," he said, "in a warmer shade to match your skin. I also want you to buy a new lipstick in a pretty shade of pink or orange."

I sank down protectively into my chair, curving my shoulders inward and clutching my arms with my hands. "I can't," I whispered. "I just can't."

"But," he continued as if he hadn't heard, "first I want you to take this paper and pencil and write what I tell you." He handed me a pad of yellow, legal-sized notepaper and a pencil, and I obediently wrote as he dictated:

I, Carol Allen, do solemnly swear to buy a warm shade of lipstick for my lips, only when I am ready. I do further swear that I shall not wear the new lipstick publicly until I have worn it privately in Dr. Lustig's office.

CAROL ALLEN
December 2, 1974

I relaxed and we talked until the session was over. But Dr. Lustig's simple command had its effects. Carrying all the force of a legal contract between us, our agreement demanded that I assume a normal and healthy demeanor. At the same time it quelled my fear of losing my protective covering, since I had been instructed to wear new makeup only when I was ready. And I found myself ready sooner than I had thought.

Only two days later I went out and bought new face makeup and lipstick. I approached the cosmetics counter intent on my task. I carefully examined all the options, but I found that my right hand, as if propelled by an outside force, kept selecting lipsticks that were purplish or brown in tone. The others, the pretty reds and pinks and oranges, looked vulgar to me. Finally, in a gesture that was a triumph of rationality over instinct, I utilized my knowledge of mixing colors and grabbed a lipstick with my left hand. Reassured by its name that it would count as a "pretty pink" lipstick, I hastily bought it. Then, with the saleswoman's help, I established the correct shade of face makeup to match my skin tones.

I took my new purchases home and hid them in a drawer, frightened by the possibilities they represented. But on the day of my next therapy session, I dutifully took them out and carried them to Dr. Lustig.

He told me to go to the rest room down the corridor and completely wash the old mask off my face. Then I was to return to the therapy room without any makeup on. Only years of being, first, a dutiful daughter and, then, a dutiful wife could have made me go through this painful exercise. I was so panicked that I could scarcely breathe. My face, stripped of its protective coating, looked naked and ugly to me. But I steeled myself to go back and face him without my integument. I opened the bathroom door a crack and, assured that no one was presently in the hall to see me, ran back to the safety of Dr. Lustig's office.

I walked back into the therapy room embarrassed. But Dr. Lustig acted as if nothing was wrong. In fact, he smiled and nodded approvingly, and told me how nice I looked. As I continued to endure our conversation, my discomfort grew by leaps and bounds. It became a kind of extreme mortification. Several times, with my body uncontrollably shaking, I had to sit on my hands to stop them from reaching up to cover my face. Dr. Lustig continued to behave as if everything was normal. I wondered how he could just sit there like that, seated across from such an ugly person.

Toward the end of the hour when my discomfort had become unbearable, Dr. Lustig told me to go back to the rest room and put on my new makeup. It was such a relief to have *any* protective coating for my psyche that I barely noticed the way in which the new makeup transformed me. This time when I returned, his face positively beamed, and he told me again how nice I looked. "And human," he added. Thus encouraged, I told him that I thought I would be able to wear my new makeup home, and I did.

On the way home I stopped off at the supermarket to buy some bread. As I stood in the express checkout line, the woman standing next to me glanced at me briefly, and then smiled. It was a simple, ordinary gesture. But it startled me and, at the same time, was greatly pleasing. I smiled back.

I discovered in the days ahead that my warmer complexion touched a responsive humanness in the people around me, and in these newfound and simple bonds, I experienced brief moments of connectedness and peace.

My friends, in particular, responded affirmatively to the newfound warmth in my face. A week or so after the makeup change, I was having lunch with one of my best friends, Elaine. We had taught together several years before, at the same small liberal-arts college—she in the English department and I in philosophy—and we had discovered in each other kindred spirits. Our friendship had continued, even after she left the college where we had met. Although she now lived about an hour's drive away, we still kept in frequent contact by phone and usually managed to arrange a monthly meeting. Lunch, that day, was the first occasion I had seen her since I had dreamed my dreams and begun therapy.

Over lunch, Elaine listened to my dreams with interest and some concern. But she accepted the fact of my therapy with pragmatism, and spontaneously commented on my appearance.

"That's a very pretty lipstick you're wearing," she said. "It really accents your attractiveness. I never noticed, till now, how pretty your mouth is."

"Thanks," I said. "It's a new color I've started wearing recently."

"Well, it does wonders for you," she confirmed.

I was very pleased by her comments and the progress that they seemed to indicate. Even Stan noticed I was looking better, although he did not acknowledge this as a positive effect of my therapy, but rather a confirmation of his original judgment that there was nothing really wrong with me.

In spite of these reassurances, however, sometimes the loss of my old protection was too much for me. Catching a glimpse of my new face in a passing mirror would send waves of pain sweeping through my limbs. Then I would be pulled down into the dark windswept places beyond loneliness, where the gods of my imagination demanded payment for my presumption in possessing a moment of ordinary happiness. Later the pain and nausea would ease, leaving me with a gray cloud that settled on my head, heavy with moisture, but unable to yield any portion of healing rain.

Meanwhile, in the weeks that followed, Dr. Lustig began teaching me new and "healthy protections" to use in place of my maladaptive mask. One such conversation with him took place several days after I had put on my new makeup. We were talking about protections, and I was telling him how naked and vulnerable and defenseless I felt without my old makeup on.

"Even though my new makeup sometimes makes me feel good," I was saying, "it often at the same time terrifies me, because I feel so transparent and vulnerable."

"That's absolutely correct," Dr. Lustig said. "That's how everybody feels when they don't have any self-protection. But how did your old makeup protect you, *really* protect you? How was it a protection against the unpleasantness that was occurring in your ordinary life, and the unpleasantness that was occurring inside of you? How was it protecting you—really?"

"It covered up the . . ." I paused, and then started over. "It made me feel safe, like I could hide, and what was bad about me inside wouldn't come out and harm anybody. People wouldn't be able to read my thoughts."

"The old makeup certainly did provide you with that illusion, didn't it?" he equably replied. "There are some things in life that are absolutely true. For instance, that our thoughts stay locked inside our heads until we communicate them, and that no one can read another person's mind. You don't need makeup to have them be true."

"But people must be able to see it in my face," I replied.

"You do have a very expressive face," he confirmed. "What it conveys is *your reaction* to what's going on in your everyday life and to what's going on inside of you. If what's going on is very pleasant, whether inside or out, then your face is a very relaxed one. But if what's going on inside or out is very unpleasant, then your face is a face that very dramatically demonstrates the distress."

"But don't you see," I said, "that's just what I'm afraid of. That I'm going to show that I'm crazy. And I just can't let people see that. How can I teach my classes if my students can see it? How can I care for my children if they can know?"

Dr. Lustig settled back in his chair a bit, as if his answer would not be a brief one. "Well, I'll tell you something," he finally said, drawing his words out very deliberately. "If you want to *really hide* behind something, then hide behind pleasantness and ordinariness, so that if another person were to glance at you briefly, they would not see anything unusual in your appearance or mannerisms. That would be a far more powerful protection for you, against whatever is going on inside, than bizarreness."

"You mean my old makeup was like a road map of my madness—the visible expression of it, rather than a protection?" I asked. "Is that what you're saying?"

"Your face makeup was a road sign that indicated that there was danger ahead," he replied, subtly adjusting the metaphor to his own satisfaction. "However, there's no need for there to be danger ahead. There's no need for that particular road sign. The danger can be contained. It can be contained inside you safely, and comfortably handled.

"You see," he continued, sinking even further into his chair, "the first order of business for people is to ensure their own physical safety, their actual physical survival. The second order of business is to ensure their mental or emotional well-being. You do whatever you have to do to make sure that your physical integrity and your mental integrity continue. If it's a thought or a book that disturbs you, put it away. If it's a movie that causes you distress, walk out. Even if it's a conversation or an interaction that becomes uncomfortable for you, remove it—not the person but the interaction. It's not 'if thine eye offends thee, pluck it out'; it's if a sight offends thee, close thine eye, or move thy gaze."

"But," I objected, "aren't defenses by definition bad? That's what everyone seems to think. All people talk about nowadays is 'openness' and 'honesty,' about 'expressing your feelings' and not being 'defensive.' "

"This attitude ignores the laws of survival, which supersede everything else," he answered. "The laws demand your continued healthy existence. Protection of both your physical and emotional integrity, therefore, becomes the first order of business. Communication becomes secondary. But once you're ready to communicate, you must *decide* how much to keep private and how much to make public about what's going on inside of you. It's your right to *keep private* as much as you want to."

Dr. Lustig paused for a moment, as if lost in thought. I also sat deeply absorbed, thinking over what he had said. I had been listening intently to his words, and in the silence that followed they seemed to wash over me again, seeping into the furthest reaches of my mind. I have a right to protect myself. I have a right to my privacy. Survival is the first order of business. I felt my fears slipping away.

After a few minutes, Dr. Lustig resumed the conversation, as if he was rethinking the whole issue. "Let's go back for a moment," he said. "There were two purposes that your icy makeup served for you. One was to make the physical distinction for you between your inside and your outside worlds, and the other was to communicate the distress that you were experiencing inside. Now that you have, in fact, communicated that distress, it's no longer necessary for you to use makeup to send that message to me anymore. I understand that you're in distress. And I understand a bit about its magnitude and its character.

"Your purpose is different now. Now your purpose is to continue to protect yourself, but to do it in a more effective way. And the most effective protection is the illusion of no protection at all. It's like the martial arts master who appears to be unarmed, even though he or she can immediately, correctly, and appropriately respond to any situation. So too can you present to the rest of the world the illusion that you have no protection, when, in fact, you can be constantly imposing protective actions and mechanisms on your own functioning and on the world's intrusion upon you. In this way you can ensure your functional integrity and well-being."

What he said calmed me somehow, but the idea was still a new one. Finally, I voiced my one remaining objection. "How will an ordinary, transparent face protect the world from *me*?"

"As a representative of the rest of the world, I want you to know how much I appreciate your concern," he replied in a parody of seriousness. I laughed.

"But it's not a humanitarian act on your part to wear icy makeup. It only serves to isolate you from the rest of the world, so that you're truly alone." He thought for a moment. "The concept is correct. You have to keep what's inside in, and maintain the boundary between inside and out. It even makes sense to coat yourself, so that you have a constant tactile and visual reminder of where that boundary is. But there's no law that says you have to coat yourself with something that's bizarre. You can protect yourself better with an ordinary covering. Yes," he continued, as if pleased with this image, "protect yourself so that you still can maintain contact with the rest of the world.

"Your humanitarian instinct to warn the world of the danger within Carol can be handled in another way. The world is not in any real danger. Carol may be, but the world is not. Life will be better for you if you stop trying to save the world, when all you really need to do is to start taking better care of Carol. I, as a representative of the rest of the world, will do all that I can to ensure that the dangers you perceive yourself to embody will become neutralized, or else channeled in such a way that they become functional and contributory rather than destructive."

I nodded, feeling better, sure now that I had a right,

perhaps even an obligation, to effectively protect myself, more confident that I posed no danger to others.

In the days that followed I began to wear my new, more human face with greater ease and more satisfaction. I began, for brief moments, to feel better about myself, and the improvements in my casual interactions with other people only served to reinforce this newfound pleasure.

But there were still times of great price, when my infant, struggling liking for myself confronted other forces inside me that were less charitable, if no less resourceful, and certainly of longer habit. Then I instinctively knew that for every movement, however slight, toward a more positive conception of myself, my inner demons would extract an exorbitant fee. But I endured those times as best I could, and kept returning to Dr. Lustig. It was part of our implicit agreement that he would nurture and foster in me whatever was healthy and strong—that however much discomfort I experienced from trying on a new identity, he would help me fight my internal demons in such a way that the victory would be decisive and I would be whole.

For every forward movement, however, there was the occasional slipping back. But the direction in which I was proceeding was at least clear to me. In order to move forward I had to place my trust in Dr Lustig, because he was my only hope, and because it is always easier to do something when it is the only choice.

Chapter 7

DECEMBER 18-25, 1974

One day I woke up and realized that Christmas was a week away. I had been so caught up in clinging to the edge of sanity, as a small child clings to the hem of its mother's skirt, that Christmas caught me quite by surprise. Forgotten were my usual ways of welcoming it—buying gifts for friends and family, lavishing thought and care on the details of giving, wrapping presents in bright bits of silver and red and green, mailing cards to people I had known in other times and in other places, decorating the house with sprigs of holly and berry and branches of long-needled pine. This year it was as if an unexpected death in the house had postponed the rituals of the living.

We were expecting guests. My parents were coming from Idaho to celebrate Christmas with us, and my sister and her husband from New York were joining us too. Also expected was a favorite friend of a favorite aunt. But even their imminent arrival could not spur me to activity or preparation. I could not fix my attention on any date. I drifted through the calendar days of late December much as a novice deep-sea diver drifts past underwater formations and creatures, caught off guard by the pressure of water on his body, more conscious of his limited time underwater and that it might run out than with the details of the passing scene. I drifted, I floated, I clung, I survived, but nowhere was there room for celebration. My sole gesture toward the season was to go out and buy a Christmas tree. It was a blue spruce, elegant and full-branched. I brought it home and, then otherwise absorbed, set it aside in a living room corner, where it stood leaning against the wall inconspicuously, as if it had settled in to wait for the day of its dress.

On December 19, the day before my guests were to arrive, I returned home from teaching to find an empty house and absent children. In the kitchen I found an urgent message from Stan to call him at the local hospital. Terrified, with my imagination leaping ahead to disaster, I dialed the hospital number. After being passed through several connections, I finally located Stan. Briefly he recounted what had happened.

Daniel had suddenly begun gasping for breath and choking. The frightened babysitter had phoned Stan, who was working nearby. He had raced home and rushed Daniel to the emergency room. A surgeon had been called in, and X rays were taken, which seemed to show a blockage in Daniel's throat. Before performing an emergency tracheotomy, however, the doctor had once again examined Daniel. Unable to feel any foreign object or obstruction, the doctor had ordered new X rays. These showed no blockage and the surgery had been canceled. Daniel was now thought to be having a severe asthma attack, and had been put, minutes before, in an oxygen tent.

I hung up the phone and stumbled blindly to the car, automatically turning the ignition and starting it up. I was numb; I was stunned. Although I thought I had left my early fundamentalist-Christian upbringing far behind, on that drive to the hospital, I bargained with God.

Please, God, let him live. Please make him safe. If I've brought this harm upon him because of my misdeeds, then punish me instead. I'll do anything, suffer anything. Only please, God, let him be all right.

I somehow made my way to Daniel's hospital room and found him standing wide-eyed in a hospital crib, surrounded by a transparent oxygen tent. His breathing was a bit raspy, but he appeared calm and unconcerned. When he saw me and put out his arms to me, I silently began to weep. The invisible cord that connects the flesh of mother to child at even ordinary times was intensified that day, cutting through the plastic wall that separated us. I asked the nurse if she could pull the oxygen tent aside for a moment, so that I could hold him. I needed to touch him to know that he was safe; I needed to touch him to make my love tangible. The nurse kindly complied.

Stan and I stayed with Daniel for some time. Then we were told to go. I asked to stay with him overnight, but for some reasons that I couldn't grasp, I was told that this was not allowed. Forced to leave his presence but unwilling to leave his proximity, I walked several corridors away and waited in the hospital waiting room. Stan returned home with Elizabeth.

It is strange how in times of crisis or intense emotion, odd, incidental details become etched in your mind. I still remember things about that waiting room (where I spent the better part of the next three days) that I do not remember about houses where I lived for years. I can still see the cover of the *Good Housekeeping* magazine, showing a smiling hostess beside a gaily decorated tree. I remember the funnel shape of the plastic coffee cups laid out beside the Christmas napkins that somebody had kindly brought. I can see the plastic holly of the nurses' corsages, standing out in stark contrast to the starched white of their uniforms. I remember the small Christmas tree standing by the window, gaudily wrapped in someone's idea of finery, looking slightly embarrassed at its overdress, its blinking colored lights reflecting eerily off the sterile white walls.

I was overwhelmed by a sense of unreality. Hospitals had always struck me as otherworldly, but on this occasion, I felt transported. I would think about Daniel and my mind would recoil, unable to bear the thought that somehow it was my fault, that somehow or other I had brought this malady upon him.

The feeling was magnified by my sense of helplessness. This hospital domain clearly belonged to the doctors and nurses scurrying around in their brisk, professional way. It did not belong to the mothers, fathers, relatives, or friends who sat in the waiting room and loved and waited. I felt useless, except for the time I actually spent with

Daniel, because then I could see that he liked my being there. Otherwise the task of waiting seemed futile and detached. Although one part of me knew that my son was in no danger, another part of me was filled with doom as I sat and waited.

I was also filled with memories of other times in other hospitals. How large and white everything had looked the first time I was brought to a hospital for minor knee surgery, when I was ten years old. How metallic and scary-sharp the instruments had seemed on that occasion, how the brush had sounded as it scrubbed inside the wound. My mind took me back three months, to the memory of my own recent hospital stay. Doubled over with abdominal pains about a year after Daniel's birth, I had been admitted to the hospital with a uterine infection caused by my IUD. For three days and nights a fever of 105 degrees had raged within me, until a new combination of antibiotics had finally worked. I remembered one night of delirium, when a nurse had sat beside me and bathed me in ice.

Thinking back on it as I sat and waited, it seemed to have been the beginning of my coming unhinged. I remembered the aberrant thoughts that had flickered across my mind, seeming to be apart and unconnected to me, tied instead to burning sensations, feeling on fire, fire—what was there about fire that was so disquieting? I remembered the nurse's soothing voice as I had rambled. What had I said? Disconnected, that was all I could recall. Fever ravaging the wholeness of my mind, so that what was left was random pieces, broken thoughts that made no sense. Had the fever and delirium sparked the madness, caused a chemical imbalance, uncloaked buried memories, uncovered an innate tendency hidden within my genetic structure, snapped some synapses, burned away the mental glue by which our ordinary perception of the world is held together? What after all do we really know of the mysterious connection of body and mind?

Death—I remembered I had thought about death. I had thought not that someone else but that *I* would die, and I remembered that I had not faced death bravely. Sitting there now in the waiting room, waiting to see Daniel, I recalled just how afraid I had been. Then I pushed the memory aside, wondering idly as I did so just why Roosevelt had said that there was nothing to fear but fear itself.

My relatives arrived on the second day of Daniel's hospital stay, but I saw very little of them. I left to them the task of overseeing Christmas, and they carried on as best they could. On December 23, the day before Christmas Eve, Daniel was discharged from the hospital. My joy at bringing him home was overwhelming and was shared by everyone who welcomed him.

On Christmas Eve, we sang carols and drank toasts and performed the usual holiday rituals. We were all happy that Daniel was well, but a pall hung over our celebration in spite of that, because of the less comprehensible nature of the illness that visited me. My parents felt the presence of the powers that had stolen my well-being and perspective. They saw the strain on my face and the terror in my eyes. And they did not know what to do. They stood helpless before the nature of my complaint, wanting to take away my pain like good parents, but stymied by the unfathomable regions into which my mind had wandered, away from them into places where they could not follow.

Later that evening, when the children were in bed, I tried to tell my parents of the strangeness that was surrounding me, of my sense of loss, of the unreality at work. My mother tried to listen, but her mind kept turning away from my words. The pain and guilt they caused her were evident because she kept interrupting, offering anxious reassurances, minimizing the difficulties of which I spoke.

"I'm sure it will pass, honey," she said. "There's no reason to worry—everything will be all right."

I spoke of my fever and how it might have thrown off my chemical balance. I tried to explain that they were not responsible, that my childhood had been good. But my words bounced off them like balls against a net, thrown back at me, untouched.

I looked across at my mother, wanting to touch her, but it seemed to me that she stood at a great distance, as far away from me as I was from the Great Depression, which had colored her youth. Like others of her generation who had suffered that indignity, she struggled to put a positive face on all things, believing as she did that the negative aspects of life were a matter of private sorrow, that to give them voice was to admit defeat. I knew that she could not accept what was happening to me. I knew that her understanding was what I most wanted. So we stood there, separated by different histories, love on both sides but a gap in between.

My father listened intently as I spoke, and when I had finished made no reply. His face showed bewilderment that such irrationality should so suddenly impinge on his rational world. He remained standing silently for a minute more, as if unsure what response to make. Then he quickly stepped up to me and put his encompassing arms around me, to let me know of his love in any case. My mother joined us and we silently embraced.

Later that evening, preparing for bed, I tried to break the silence between Stan and me, perhaps because it was Christmas, perhaps because of the ordeal we had shared with Daniel.

"I'm terrified," I said, "of what's happening to me."

Stan's response surprised me, for he seemed very angry. "Why do you keep staring out of windows?" he asked accusingly. "Why are you so distant and uncaring about me? Your lack of attention is really disturbing. Why can't you be yourself, for heaven's sake?"

I said nothing further. There was nothing more to say. What has happened to us? I wondered for the umpteenth time. We had started out so bright just six years before. We had loved each other, and we could talk. We had gone on for hours about philosophy, politics, literature, always leaving the conversation with something more to say. Stan had such a good sense of humor. I do believe I married him because he could make me laugh.

I thought about the Stan I knew now, foolish, irritating, ponderous Stan, who still charmed me in public with his wit and laughter, who lectured me in private as if I were one of his slower students who could never grasp the obvious. Stan, who was solid and sensible by his own lights, grounded. Stan, who defined me as his extension— or rather, I thought, perhaps I am his shadow. Somewhat defensive, somewhat pompous Stan, who gave me a public persona, who cast me in a particular light by the simple fact of wedlock, who made me half of a couple but not a whole anything.

Our first few years had been good, I thought, or so it seemed in retrospect—although they did not, for all that, bear close scrutiny, because of the other women I chose to ignore, because of the uncertainty Stan had about the whole "married" business, as if he regretted turning our harmonious living together into a union that weighed on his spirits like too many loads of dirty laundry, that robbed him of his lightness and private laughter. "Marriage," he repeatedly told me, "is nothing but responsibility." The way he said "responsibility" it could have been "death," because it had the same sense of possibility extinguished.

I remembered a couple we had visited at Yale University during our first year of marriage. The couple, whose names I had forgotten, had fought with each other like trained guerrillas throughout the evening, never willing to step out of the underbrush and show their weapons outright, firing random shots in the dark, as if the enemy were always just out of sight. "Just wait until you've been married seven years," they had said over dessert. "The seven-year itch, you know."

Stan and I had smiled politely, arrogant and secure in our sense of marital superiority, certain that our marriage would never come to this. But now I was left wondering. Was it as simple as the seven-year itch? Would we outgrow it, say, in the eighth or ninth year? Would our silences with the sharp edges soften into harmonious ones?

"It takes two to make a marriage," my parents always said, but now Stan and I added up to less than one.

On Christmas Day itself, we opened our presents, prepared and had dinner, struggled through the rest of the day, trying to behave as if it were an ordinary Christmas. There was one brief respite that made me feel less alone. My sister and I took a long walk together. I could talk to her. She was not shocked at what I said.

"You know," she said, when I had finished speaking, "maybe it's really better this way. I know it must seem funny, but I'm almost envious—to have something vital and dramatic happening, so that once and for all you can straighten things out. As for myself," she continued slowly and thoughtfully, "I just go along doing the best I can.

But I sometimes wish that something drastic would happen to me, to shake me out of my lethargy and force me into action to make things better."

I listened carefully to what she said. I loved her for her understanding.

On the night of Christmas Day, everyone had become weary and retired early, so by ten o'clock I was alone. I walked through the house switching off the lights, knowing, despite the presence of loved ones, the special sorrow of a lonely Christmas. As I passed through the living room I glanced at the darkened corner where the silhouette of the Christmas tree could barely be discerned. There it stood, exactly as I had left it, naked and unadorned, leaning wearily against the wall. I stood and stared at it for a moment, then continued mechanically on my way through the house, turning off the lights as I went. No one decorated the Christmas tree, I thought absently, as I switched off the last remaining light.

Chapter 8

The days following Christmas continued in much the same manner. As Stan, the children, and I returned to our daily routines, I found myself for the most part blanketed by fog and fear, eclipsed by moments of illumination in Dr. Lustig's office. I would feel, after each therapy session, more cohesive, less afraid. But during the days between visits, my psychic pain would reassert itself, and once again I would drown in confusion and unreality.

I discovered, during that time, that it wasn't enough to learn a therapeutic lesson once. Often I had to have the instruction repeated within a variety of contexts, so that slowly new habits were built up, strong enough to supplant the old dysfunctional ones.

The self-hypnosis I had learned helped me in this respect. Sometimes when I was alone, I would sit on the living room couch and go into a trance where I would stay for some time, experiencing a timeless moment of peace and comfort. This private time was restorative and, along with my therapy, reinforced my fledgling belief that I could like myself.

By early January, my struggle to keep functioning— to care for my children, coexist with Stan, and teach my classes—in the midst of so much upheaval had left me exhausted and robbed of almost all emotion. It was then that a new feeling, anger, rose to the surface.

The day of January 9 started out gray and dreary. It was one of those early January days when winter seems the permanent season, leaving the imprint of its ashen face in the grime of the windowpanes and in the weariness of the soul. A steady drizzle of rain had made slush out of the mounds of dirt-streaked snow. Even the children hid indoors, unwilling to confront an atmosphere that could so unfeelingly make their once proud snowman weep.

During breakfast, I searched the morning papers for some glimpse of good news that would lift my spirits out of this winter gloom. But the paper, as might be expected, had only troubles to tell. Not even the horoscope, which was my last resort, could say a good word about a single sign. The children and I finished breakfast, and then I bathed them and got them dressed. At nine o'clock they were comfortably settled in front of the television, preparing to watch their morning programs. Meanwhile, I busied myself with my daily chores.

I was standing in the kitchen about an hour later, when the pain began. It started very slowly, as a tight band around my head, and it didn't seem to be attached to any specific thought or event. I was just aware one moment that it was there, where it hadn't been before. It was so strong that I was sure it must be coming from the atmosphere. I looked out at the sky and then at my children to see if the pain was encircling them too. But they played on unconcernedly, caught up in their games, undisturbed by any atmospheric visitation.

Ten o'clock turned to eleven, then twelve, and the pain droned on. By one o'clock, following lunch, it had moved to my chest, where it formed a small, hard sliver of anger. The infant anger gathered the pain around itself and suckled on it, and in this way grew, until it had become a ball of rage, burning out a place for itself in my chest cavity about the size of a heart.

From its thoracic perch the anger began to move. It burned its way up, down, and outward through my body, freezing and burning like dry ice. I felt the muscles of my face become rigid in response and my eyes freeze over.

At last it came to the walls of my flesh and pounded against them. But the walls of my body held fast, containing the enemy. So the alien inner growth turned back on itself to feed. But the only victim it could find was me.

Throughout the day, the anger continued to eat its way slowly through my psyche, but I vigilantly guarded against its escape. No visible expression of its presence passed through my face, although a trained observer might have sensed its presence from the rigid way that I held my body, or from the way that my hands periodically clenched and unclenched.

My dread was that I could not contain it, that this force would take me over and have its way. I stood clasping the latch of a Pandora's box, afraid that the slightest movement would unleash unimaginable forces and send them flying to wreak havoc across the world.

But my greatest fear was for my children. I could not pinpoint exactly what I was afraid of. It was more a kind of ungovernable anxiety that, somehow through contact with me, they would be harmed. What if my anger got loose and harmed them? What if I turned into a child abuser? But these thoughts were too terrible. I shoved them away.

By six o'clock I was exhausted from my guard duties. Stan, who would usually have been returning home by this time, was out of town at a conference. On this day particularly I wished he were home—to act as a buffer, or if necessary a safety zone. But instead I was alone with my children and my fears.

The evening dragged on, minute by minute. As I read Elizabeth and Daniel their bedtime stories, the mixture of anger and fear that I felt nearly choked off my voice. But I made myself continue reading. When the children begged for yet another story, it took all my strength to comply and push my anguish into the background.

Finally, it was bedtime. I had made it through the day. I tucked Elizabeth and Daniel into their beds and kissed them good night. As I bent over them, my fear for their safety was as large as my love.

Exhausted by the intensity of the day, I went to bed early, shortly after the children. But sleep, which often served me as an anesthetic, was elusive. I tossed and turned, fighting my internal battle. I still didn't know what to do about my anger. All I knew was that it terrified me. It made me feel evil.

After several hours of fitfully trying to sleep, I got up out of bed and began pacing throughout the house. Finally I stopped and stood in the middle of the living room. Unable to contain my anger any longer, I began to scream and scream.

Someone else might not have called it a scream, for the sound was a choked and garbled one. It did not flow out of me freely, cleanly, purely. But to me it was a scream, nonetheless—one long excruciating sound. It gathered together years of pent-up rage and gave them voice. I thought my cry must have been piercingly loud, because what I heard was the intensity behind it. I was surprised when it did not awaken the children.

When I was finished, I took several deep breaths. Some of the pain had gone, but left in its place was an even greater confusion. I was horrified at what I had done, at the enormity of my anger, at my loss of control. How can I ever trust myself again? It was then that I knew what was even more terrible than anger—losing control of my feelings; because then, I feared, I would lose control of my mind.

Chapter 9

JANUARY 10, 1975

I often asked myself afterward, and other people asked me, how I managed to continue functioning during that time. How did I care for my children, teach my classes, run my household in the grip of such anguish and emotional upheaval? I can only say that I led different lives. It was as if different persons inhabited one dwelling. Something in me seemed to know when it could rage and when it could not—when it could let go and slip into madness, and when it could not afford to give the slightest clue.

I would find myself switching, often within minutes, from one persona to another. I would, for instance, be talking normally to the children. Then I would put them down for a nap. During the ten-second walk from their room to my bedroom, another part of me would gain ascendency. Upon entering the bedroom, I would find my hands wringing each other and clutching after sanity, my mind so immobilized by fear that I could barely stand.

These aberrations, I found, would usually surface in moments when the context made it safe for them to appear—when I was alone, that is, or during the times when I saw Dr. Lustig. Some instinct for self-protection made me wait until these moments—even madness had to wait to have its time. When that time came, a part of me would watch, with fascination and horror, as another part would surface and completely hold sway. I found that the observing part of me, often helpless but ever present, could not stop the madness from gaining possession of me. But it could observe and record the onset of madness and struggle to limit its power.

It happened on the day after I screamed my midnight scream. I was switched into normal function during most of the day. I finished teaching my two classes at the college and drove directly to Dr. Lustig's office for a scheduled appointment at 3 P.M. But by the time I walked into his waiting room, another mental switch had been thrown. I found my anger and fear of the night before returning to my psyche and coagulating there, so that by the time Dr. Lustig came into the waiting room to greet me, I had no voice left in me to speak. I simply rose and walked stiffly past him, feeling the muscles of my face draw tightly, my cheekbones prominent, my eyes opaque. I sat down in the inner room and stared straight ahead of me, my eyes turned inward, unable to focus.

Dr. Lustig closely regarded me and then spoke. "Carol, what's going on?" he asked searchingly.

I sat motionless, making no response. I felt the sounds wash over me, but they were out of alignment and made no sense. Finally, in a kind of delayed reaction, they registered in my brain, and I understood that I had been addressed. I struggled to form a responding word, concentrating all my attention in an effort to answer his question. I took in a short breath and then struggled to open my mouth. I felt the tension in my jaw and in my neck as I tried to speak. But the power of speech eluded me. I found that I could not make a sound.

Dr. Lustig again broke the silence. "I don't know exactly what's going on with you, but I have some guesses about what it might be. For anyone to look the way you look here today, and to have made the effort to speak but to not have spoken as you did here today, usually means that the person is totally overwhelmed by some experience they are having at the moment or have just had. If, in fact, you are experiencing something like this now, I want you to understand that it will pass. And we'll just sit here together until it does. But if you had it earlier," he continued, "then you probably are feeling totally numb by now, which is a very safe thing to feel. Can you tell me which it is?" he asked.

I struggled to speak, this time with more success. In the barest cracking voice, I finally was able to articulate a few words. ". . . scream . . ." I whispered, and then, after another lengthy pause, ". . . last night . . ." I could go no further.

"Are you feeling safely numb now?" he asked. I made a slight movement of my head upward in assent. "Good," he said, seemingly glad of my response. "Keep on feeling that and use the numbness to *protect* you from the memory of last night's experience." He paused and then went on.

"And when all the feelings about last night's experience have been frozen by your numbness, could you tell me more about what happened last night?"

A feeling of safety slowly crept over me, the numbness forming a protective shield, encircling my fear and placing a limit on it.

Haltingly, I began trying to explain about my experience of the night before. ". . . angry . . . I was so angry. . . ." I stopped there; it was some time before I could say the worst. ". . . I am so evil. . . ."

When it was clear that I could not continue, Dr. Lustig spoke. "Did your scream last night let the evil out?" I nodded briefly. "All of it or just some of it?"

I tried to think. I was confused by the question and wondered why he asked it. I tried to answer anyway, because it had become my habit to follow his lead.

"I don't know," I finally answered. "Some of it, I guess."

"Then there might be some evil still left?" he asked. So horrifying was this possibility that I became mute and immobile again.

"Well, then," he continued heartily, "let's get it all out of you safely. Scream here for as long and as loud as you need, so that you can get all the evil safely out." I remained silent.

"But would you do me a favor?" he continued. "Could you please scream silently so that my ears won't be damaged? Would that be all right?"

I was relieved. This was easier to comply with than screaming out loud. It also made me curious. Will it really work to scream silently? I wondered. Then I imagined myself screaming a silent scream. "Will it work just as well?" I asked out loud.

"A scream is a scream," Dr. Lustig replied. "And the only thing that really matters is getting out of you whatever it is you don't want to keep. It's just a matter of expelling. It's as simple as coughing up a foreign substance that you've breathed in by mistake."

As I listened I was connecting his words with the sensation of relief I was beginning to feel. My earlier confusion seemed to have eased. Everything seemed simple again. I found I could talk more normally.

"It's funny," I said, "but I don't feel like I need to scream anymore. At least for right now," I qualified. I wasn't entirely convinced that my inner screams had been subdued. I was still concerned that the anger that had prompted my nocturnal outburst might reappear at any moment and once again I might be at its mercy.

"Last night I felt so out of control," I explained. "I was so afraid."

"Afraid of what?" he asked.

"Afraid that if all that force were released, I would disintegrate. Explode into a million pieces."

"That sure would be messy, wouldn't it?" Dr. Lustig answered cheerfully. He looked over to the wall across from us, motioned toward it with his hand, and continued, "You—splattered over the whole universe."

I hadn't intended my remarks to be taken quite so literally. Wait a minute, I wanted to say. You don't have to get quite so carried away. It was just a metaphor.

"Well, not really that," I said. "It was more of a *feeling*, really. The feeling that I wouldn't be able to contain the anger."

"Oh. . . ." he replied musically, as if he was understanding the issue in a new light. "Not able to *contain* it? Well," he said, "that's different.

"When a very young child becomes so angry that he cannot maintain control of himself, a good parent physically contains the child. The parent imposes control from

the outside until the child can regain control of himself
from the inside.

"Now," he continued, "when you, Carol, *as an adult*
become so angry that you begin to fear a loss of self-
control, I cannot always be present to impose control on
you from the outside. So I'll tell you what to do."

He took out his wallet as he spoke, and removing a
twenty-dollar bill, handed it to me. "I want you to take
this money and go out and buy yourself a sweater." He
glanced briefly at the navy-blue and red scarf that I had
tied tightly around my head that day. "Buy either a dark
blue or a red sweater. And make sure it fits very tightly.
Get a sweater that fits so snugly that you can feel the
edges of yourself—your physical limits. Then, anytime
you feel that you're about to lose control of your feelings,
or even if you *fear* losing control, go immediately and put
on the sweater. This will allow you to accurately perceive
your outer limits and to comfortably contain any emotion
that you are experiencing—even if the emotion is a very
frightening and powerful one."

I accepted his gift, gratitude mingling with amazement.
I didn't know psychiatrists made such personal gestures.
But it's such a right one, I thought, to address the fears
I'm feeling. I feel safer ready, safer and protected. He
really cares about me, or he wouldn't have given me the
sweater. I tucked the bill into my purse.

Dr. Lustig and I sat together quietly for several minutes. I was soaking up the calm, enjoying a moment's
rest. When he spoke again, it was in a different, more
conceptual vein, as if he understood that he was addressing a different person from the one who had entered his
office half an hour earlier.

"Sometimes, you know, intense anger is really a very
useful emotion to have. It so powerfully attracts our attention, even if it's in an uncomfortable way, that it allows
us to stay whole, rather than fall apart. Your anger last
night might very well have served that purpose for you."

I listened intently to what he said, captivated by the
originality of his suggestion. For the first time in my life,
someone had said that anger might be good, might indeed
even have some useful purpose. Relief flooded over me.
Maybe, in fact, I was using a *good*, self-protecting mech-

anism. Maybe, and this thought was the most radical one I had yet had, maybe there was something *healthy* about me after all.

We continued to talk, and soon our time was over. I thanked Dr. Lustig for his gift of the sweater. I did in fact go out and buy a tight, navy-blue sweater several days later. And on several occasions during the next month, I put it on to calm my alarm. But gradually I found that I didn't need it anymore. Dr. Lustig's words had given me some of the inner control that I sought. I no longer needed, for the moment at least, a symbolic container for my fears.

Chapter 10

LATE JANUARY, 1975

As January marched to a conclusion, the reality of my collapsing marriage began to take its toll, even as I denied the extent of the difficulty between Stan and me. The brief flares of anger that occasionally surfaced between us had, by late January, turned to marital ashes. As the winter snows piled up endlessly outside, the home fires quietly one by one died. Passion was extinguished; anger was put out. Left in their place were cinders and cold.

I felt numb; the feeling in me froze. My marriage had become a fragile shell, as if someone had pricked a hole in an egg and sucked out the yolk and the white. I learned how empty a marriage without its insides can be, a hollow echo chamber. Stan and I called across the open space and heard in reply only the distorted sound of our own voices. Words that no longer touched or communicated piled on top of silences that no longer touched or spoke. Frozen tears that could not be wept. Ashes and ice.

It was as if all desire to act had died with the feelings. We did nothing. To have done something would have taken too much effort. Our wills had atrophied. We drifted along lonely and cold but, oddly enough, with great politeness, as if the social amenities had replaced real connection.

"How would you like your eggs this morning?" "Whatever is easiest for you."

"Did you remember to call the garage about the car?" "No, it slipped my mind. Thanks for reminding me."

"Would you like me to carry out the garbage for you?" The politeness of strangers. Polished and cold.

After weeks of alienation, I told Dr. Lustig of the ever growing dissatisfaction between Stan and me.

"It's like a death by ice."

"What does Stan say about it?" he asked me.

"I don't know," I said. "We don't talk much."

After discussion, Dr. Lustig suggested a course of marriage counseling for Stan and me. It seemed like a good idea to me, and Stan agreed. So one of my weekly therapy sessions, from then on, was given over to the concerns of my marriage.

In the beginning, both Stan and I felt a sense of relief. At least we're trying, we told ourselves, feeling a shade less guilty for our mutual failures. At least we aren't throwing away a marriage without some effort to salvage it. It felt good to be doing something tangible, to be taking specific measures. It also felt good to be learning how to talk about our dilemma, which, paradoxically, we found easier to do in the presence of another than by ourselves.

That was our first "homework" assignment. We were to set aside ten minutes each day and talk with one another. It was difficult at first, and I felt very foolish. More awkward than on a honeymoon, we sat opposite each other across a table and tried to communicate. "What shall we do now?" I wanted to know. "Let's just try to talk," Stan replied, pausing, and then added, "You go first." After some more talk about talking and a few further fumbled conversational attempts, we did manage to have our first conversation in months.

"Why do you always seem so angry with me?" I finally gathered the courage to ask. "I want to tell you what's happening to me, about my confusion, but you always seem to resent it when I talk about it."

"I'm sorry," Stan said with genuine regret. "I guess . . . I guess . . . well, I'm just . . . afraid . . . of what might happen to *you*, of what might happen to *us*, of what might happen to *me*." He spoke softly, and I knew it was a great concession on his part.

"I know," I whispered, wanting to reach out and touch him. But something in me held back from physical contact. We both sat in silence for a while.

Then Stan voiced what I suspected had been bothering him all along. "You care about Dr. Lustig more than me," he said in an accusing way, and I could see how deeply his pride was hurt.

I wanted to tell him no, it wasn't as simple as that, that Dr. Lustig was my chance for mental survival, not a substitute for a husband, but somehow the words dried up in my throat.

"You don't understand," I said hopelessly, feeling exasperated at the attempt to try to explain anything to Stan. Then I calmed myself and tried again. "I need you too, Stan," I said softly. "I want our marriage to work out. I want to be well, and that's what Dr. Lustig is helping me with, but I also want to have a real marriage."

Stan seemed to understand. We began to talk, and then we talked and talked. I remember our euphoria. We became drunk on talk. We had become so accustomed to our perfunctory contact that our first simple communication in many months was an enormous relief.

After a few more evenings of practice, we began talking with each other better, although we were still often very general and vague. Once we had begun to converse, however, Dr. Lustig added to his original directive. He told us to be more specific in what we said about our emotional responses.

But as the weeks progressed and the initial euphoria wore off, we found ourselves very often in conversational dead ends. Neither one of us was very direct, and we both had a tendency to overanalyze the other person. We often used the seemingly direct language of our own emotional responses to indirectly critique each other's motives.

During one counseling session, we were talking about my unfocused behavior and my habit of staring out of windows when I was upset.

"I feel you're behaving that way just to be spiteful to me," Stan said.

"No, I'm not," I had replied. "I'm trying my best to be focused. And when I am not, I can't help it."

"The hostility that I feel coming from you is definitely there," Stan countered.

"No, it isn't," I insisted, and then continued with an imputation of my own. "And anyway, for you to say that what I'm doing is hostile to *you*, is in fact very hostile to *me*."

"No, it's not," Stan countered. And so it often went. After listening to several conversations of this kind, Dr. Lustig intervened.

"The primary purpose of communication," he said, "is to transmit facts about events in the external world. By only talking about your emotional responses to those events, or by talking about your *interpretation* of the other person's motivation, the two of you effectively subvert any useful communication between you."

He considered for a moment as if in search of a concrete example. "Suppose," he finally said, "that you're both hungry and can share a gorgeous piece of steak. But instead of using the steak for its *primary purpose* as food, the two of you decide that you'll save it as a work of art. By not eating it, you both remain hungry. And ultimately, the steak becomes unavailable even for a secondary purpose, because it decomposes.

"The mistake you're both making is that you're not using conversation to communicate about external reality, about the facts of whatever actually happened. Stan might say, for example, that he *considers* the overdone eggs that Carol gave him at breakfast to have been a hostile act. An important fact is that the baby vomited on the floor while breakfast was being prepared, and Carol was pleased to have been able to serve Stan anything at all. If Stan asks instead, 'Why are these eggs overcooked?' then Carol can tell him the facts about what actually happened. The two of you could then discuss the eggs and the baby, rather than just Stan's interpretation of Carol's motivation. Talking about your emotional responses to an external event or your interpretation of it, without any discussion of the actual event itself, is like not using the steak for food. It ignores the primary purpose of the communication."

Stan and I both listened to what he said in our own

way, and, over the next few months, we did from time to time communicate better. The icy climate that existed between us during the winter months thawed somewhat, due in large part to our new communion. But the ice did not melt into pure clean water. It resembled more a melted mound of grimy slush. Angers and hurts were expressed, but the conflict that lay behind them remained unresolved.

It always, in the end, came back to one thing. Stan told me that he did not love me, although I knew how much he wanted to love. "I just can't love you," he would explain mournfully each time we talked, rendering all other communications empty of healing. I knew that he found loving difficult within the confines of marriage, easy outside its context. I knew that it was the perceived burden of marriage itself, and not loving, that thwarted his attempts to reestablish a relationship with me. But in spite of this recognition, I would feel diminished each time he denied his love, believing that if he did not love me, it was because I did not deserve to be loved.

Still, we tried to save our marriage. It represented to both of us a commitment, independent of our personal feelings at the time. And at least through our marriage counseling we were talking, even though the talk rarely nourished, but became an empty form by which we maintained superficial contact.

But the attempt to save our marriage was itself reassuring, postponing as it did any need for more irrevocable action. Like Hansel and Gretel, we wandered through the woods, not knowing that we had stumbled into the witch's house. For the moment, we drifted on in the hope of a reconciliation.

Chapter 11

FEBRUARY, 1975

It was shortly after Stan and I had embarked on our course of marriage counseling that I began to have dreams about a figure in black.

NIGHT OF FEBRUARY 1, 1975

A spritely figure draped all in black is bending over a baby in the bedroom. The figure reaches toward the baby. At first I am frightened, because I think the figure wants to hurt the baby. Then, watching the way the figure moves, I realize that it only wants to hold the baby. As it bends over the baby, the figure sees me and, startled, rushes past me and out of the house.

The first dream about the figure in black alarmed me; the second, to follow some eight days later, left me terrified.

NIGHT OF FEBRUARY 9, 1975

I am in the upstairs bathroom with a friend. I am worrying

about teaching my philosophy courses, and she is reas-
suring me. I walk to the downstairs bathroom by myself
I am just standing near the bathroom sink when a figure
draped in black, with a black hood over his head, lunges
into the bathroom from the hallway. He grabs me. I try
to scream but no sound comes out. I am terrified that he
is going to do some violence to me—rape or kill me. He
puts his hand over my mouth and pushes me down.

The black-draped dream figure haunted my waking
hours. Especially disturbing was the implied violence in
the second dream. I had been rudely confronted with a
shadow. It reminded me of a plane trip that I had taken
not long before. It had been a sunny day, and idly looking
out of the window, I had been startled to see the outline
of the plane pursuing a parallel, if uneven, course on the
ground below. What struck me most, on that occasion,
was the way that the shadow had become a detached
reflection of the plane, an alter ego completely separate
from its source. I watched it as it dipped into valleys and
then elongated, as it pursued the contours of the earth
that it was following. It seemed an independent spirit,
although it had never completely lost its resemblance to
its originator. As the plane began its descent, the shadow
grew even larger, assuming awesome, detached proportions. I wondered, as I watched it, whether it would ever
join the plane in a peaceful uneventful merging, or whether
the price of togetherness would be a crash landing.

I instinctively recognized the figure in my dreams as
the same sort of shadowy presence, a reflection of myself
that held its own power, followed its own course. I was
afraid of it and startled by its presence, in the way that
an infant is afraid and startled the first time that it sees
its own reflection in a mirror. I too reached out a hand
to touch the stranger, only to be confronted with hard,
cold glass.

Where did these shadowy figures come from? I wondered. Surely not from my past. I thought over those early
years and all I saw was an all-American girl, raised in the
West with its traditional values of self-reliance and hard
work, with the love and guidance of an unusual family,
good at school, popular with my classmates. I saw no

shadows in the activities of my childhood—exploring caves, riding horses, taking explorations into the foothills near my grandparents' farm, pretending with my sister and other friends that we were pioneers exploring a new and untouched country. In winter we skied, in summer we played softball, and as the grade school years turned into adolescence, I felt myself becoming a lovely woman. I had many friends and I had many dates; I was president of my church club and was even elected junior prom queen. My academic performance won me a scholarship to Carleton College, a coeducational institution in Minnesota known for its fine academic traditions.

Here, perhaps, the shadows began? At least the smooth surface of my life knew some strain; here were the first rumblings of discontent. Attached as I was to my family, I felt transplanted, cut adrift from the bonds that had always steadied me. I chose philosophy as my academic discipline, reveling in its beauty and order and rationality, choosing it for itself and also because it pushed aside other gnawing fears that were so vague as to be nameless, reading philosophers like Kant who kept irrationality at bay— at least until I got to the existentialists.

Then, with Kierkegaard, I too saw the question of suicide as the ultimate philosophic question. I took the issue seriously, not just as an intellectual exercise, wanting so much to be good, and more than that wanting to have Truth with a capital *T* on my side, so that whatever I did would be justified. I found instead that I must take my chances like everybody else, though I wanted to die rather than be morally wrong. I finally decided that I would simply do the best I could and that no one, not even myself, could blame me for that.

I continued along the path of philosophy into graduate school at Bryn Mawr College, but even here the darker questions followed me. However, it was during these years that I met Stan, who was teaching at a nearby college where I was working as an editor for a major philosophic journal. I invested in him the same intensity and devotion that I had in philosophy. He was solid and steady and above all rational. He offered me safe haven from my darker side.

But now, it appeared, it could no longer be hidden. I found myself facing a dark figure in my dreams.

I didn't know what to do about my recent dreams, or about the haunting black figures in them. But the next time I saw Dr. Lustig, I told him about them. Terror was evident in my quavering voice, and in the difficulty I was having even saying the words.

Dr. Lustig listened intently to what I said, and then nodded. "I would like you to do something," he said. "I'd like you to go back over the second dream in your mind. Start from the beginning and imagine yourself in the upstairs bathroom. Then imagine yourself going to the downstairs bathroom, and the figure lunging at you. Go through the whole dream, recalling it in exquisite detail, until it is as vivid as when you dreamed it. Become completely immersed in the dream, so that you can feel the terror and all the other feelings that you felt then."

I looked at him askance. "You want me to imagine the dream again, to redream it here?" I asked. I couldn't believe it. "I don't think I can," I said. It was painful to even think about calling up such a terrible image—and purposefully at that.

"Yes, you can," he replied equably. "Just think yourself into the dream again—take your time and remember it from the beginning. When you come to the part about the figure in black lunging at you, when you can reexperience the terror, then stop and tell me."

So I began, feeling frightened and somewhat foolish. But I had trusted him before and he had helped me, so I took it on faith that there was a purpose to this exercise.

I focused my attention and slowly slipped back into the nightmare. I closed my eyes when I came to the part about the figure in black attacking me, as if I could ward off the image with this instinctive gesture.

Dr. Lustig must have been watching my face, because just as I was feeling the full extent of my terror, he spoke. "Can you see the figure coming at you now?" he asked.

"Yes," I replied.

"Now!" he said. "What are you going to *do* to him? How are you going to defend yourself?"

When I didn't reply, he continued, "Are you going to

strike him, or maybe stab him?" I still didn't reply, but I sank lower in my chair.

"Perhaps you would rather just kick him in the balls!" he continued. I put my hands to my face to cover my embarrassment.

"No, no, I couldn't do that," I replied in a small voice. Then, deciding that I had better pick an action quickly, for who could tell what preposterous alternative Dr. Lustig might suggest next, I said haltingly that I thought, well, *perhaps*, I *could* kick him.

"Fine," said Dr. Lustig. "Kick him somewhere."

I didn't even like *imagining* such violence, but I complied as best I could. Although I did not have the nerve to imagine kicking him in the balls, I finally did summon up a brief image of kicking the figure in the leg. Then I stopped, exhausted and overwhelmed by my audacity.

"What happened?" Dr. Lustig asked.

"He turned and ran away," I answered. *He turned and ran away.* I was truly astonished. The world had not disintegrated when I fought back. No bolt of lightning, no sign of the gods' displeasure. And although I was still a bit shaken, I was no longer terrified as I had been before.

I smiled at Dr. Lustig in a sheepish sort of way. "I did it, didn't I?" I said. I was pleased with myself, with the assertiveness of my gesture.

"Yes," he replied, and he seemed pleased too. "There's nothing in your imagination that you can't learn to handle, to control. The imagination is wonderful in that way. If you can *imagine* a particular dream of yours or a particular terror, you can also, just as easily, imagine a way of *achieving* that dream or of *banishing* that terror. If a gigantic bear is pursuing you, you can turn him into a mouse with a wave of your hand. If a witch casts a spell over you, use a counterspell and turn her into a glass of milk. It just takes practice," he said. "You have to develop the skills in that realm just as you're learning to do in the everyday world. It just takes practice, that's all."

My fears eased. From the way that he talked, the realm of the imagination seemed a less hostile and scary place. I felt less afraid of walking there, more sure that it, like other frontiers, could be explored safely with the proper amount of preparation and guidance.

"Thanks," I said, and I really meant it.

I was to remember his words in the days ahead, and slowly and cautiously I learned to put one foot and then the other into the waters of the imagination. And as for the figure in black, he was vanquished.

I was surprised when the figure in black did not return, and for many days afterward I half expected to see him in other dreams. But when he did not reappear, I began to grasp the power of the skill that Dr. Lustig had taught me—the power of the imagination to heal. It was a lesson that I never forgot. Demons that sprang from one's own untutored mind, I found, could be quelled by equal forces of a trained imagination. Imagined problems could be solved in the imagination itself. Nothing in that realm was so dark that it could not be confronted or, by a conscious act of imagining, robbed of its power.

It was this lesson about the skillful use of the mind that I began to teach my children. But that was later, of course, when they were a bit older and I had more fully mastered the lesson myself.

The first time Daniel had a nightmare, when he was about eighteen months old, at that age when it is common for children to have bad dreams, I was not alarmed. I talked him back to sleep. The next night, before he went to bed, he expressed fear about the return of the "monster." I asked him what he wanted to *do* to it. He didn't know, so I suggested some alternatives.

"You can hit him," I said, "or you can just tell him to go away and leave Daniel alone." Then we practiced. I can still remember Daniel's chubby little hand making a pushing-away gesture, and his small voice repeating, "Go away, monster, and leave Daniel alone!" It worked for my children, as it had worked for me. Neither of them was disturbed with nightmares again.

Several months later, following these lessons, Elizabeth came to me one morning and said with satisfaction, "I had a dream last night, Mommy."

"What was it about?" I asked her.

"Well," she said, "I was walking along a road with two other little girls, and we met a *giant* dinosaur. It was really scary," she said.

"What did you do?" I asked her.

"Oh, I just said, 'Get out of my way, dinosaur!' And guess what, Mommy," she continued. "The dinosaur went poof, and disappeared just like magic! Then we went on down the road."

I was glad that my children would grow up knowing how to move with ease and control in that timeless world where dragons can be conquered and fools can be king.

PART II

Journey Out of the Cave

Chapter 1

Looking back on it afterward, my first three months of therapy, from late November to my birthday in late February, had the quality and tone of a dream play—because they seemed to progress so effortlessly from confusion and chaos to some degree of order and control. As my marriage disintegrated into a shabby formality, my inner life blossomed and took on an exaggerated importance. My "cure" seemed to progress with lightning speed, confirming to me the nature and magnitude of the mystical dimension I had stumbled upon. Like Joseph, who was cast into the pit, I had been miraculously lifted up, and I did not yet know that a further and more devastating fall awaited me. That was to be later, when my marriage finally failed.

For the moment, I was caught up in the magic of therapy. So it scarcely surprised me when, on February 23, my thirty-first birthday, I woke to early sunlight. The gray psychic fog that I had been shrouded in since autumn had mysteriously lifted, giving way to simple sunshine and warming rays. Hope radiated from my chest and out across the otherwise unremarkable landscape. I felt like a fish that, beyond reason or expectation, had become unhooked.

I darted about excitedly, marveling at my exceptional reprieve.

I jumped out of bed and called eagerly to the children. I smiled at Stan for the first time in months, and hummed through the preparation of the bacon and eggs. I felt light and airy and released from a great draining weight. I talked; I gestured; I positively danced. I found the small crack in the breakfast dish enchanting, and the dusty clock in the corner profound. It seemed fitting that this should happen on my birthday. It seemed a good omen, a lucky charm.

I was especially glad that I would see Dr. Lustig the next day. I couldn't wait to tell him the news. I was as grateful as I was happy. I vowed to never again take ordinary happiness for granted. Then I promptly ignored my resolution, because when one feels most alive one expects the best. Rebirth has no memory for former deaths.

"I feel so much better," I told Dr. Lustig when I saw him.

"I can tell," he said smiling, and I could see how pleased he was.

Then I just sat and looked around, seeing the familiar room through lighter eyes. I noticed colors and tones I had never noticed before, and each object seemed altogether several shades brighter. My gaze particularly fastened on some perky-looking plants resting on the shelf behind Dr. Lustig's head. They're dressed in a particularly optimistic green, I thought, and I wondered why I had never noticed them before.

"Well, what do we do now?" I asked when I was through looking. I wondered what my therapy session would be about if I was not feeling a great deal of pain.

"Why don't we just take a vacation today?" Dr. Lustig replied. "There's no need to do any more work at the moment. You deserve a rest. Let's just enjoy the day."

So that was what we did. He asked me if I would like a cup of coffee, and then we sat back and drank our coffee together. We talked and laughed, and he told me silly jokes. Starved for laughter as I had been, I basked in its healing power.

It was good to laugh deep from within. The mood in the room was that of children playing, and I felt more carefree than I ever had as a child. My delight formed a mood halo that encircled the room, and compensated me a hundredfold for my former misery.

Next to the side table between our chairs was a crystal bowl of brightly polished, smooth stones. Because of my newfound lightness, they captured my attention that day, and I reached over and selected one that had a particular appeal for me. It was burnished red in color, small and oval in shape—which, for some reason, I identified with myself. Then I selected a second, larger stone of translucent gray and brown that was etched with delicate lines resembling a Japanese painting.

I held the two stones for a moment, charmed by their beauty and uniqueness. "This one is for me," I said, motioning with the red one. "And this one reminds me of you," I continued, holding up the other.

"May I see them?" Dr. Lustig asked as he reached out his hand for them. Then, closely regarding the gray one, he continued. "It's strange," he said, "that you would select this particular stone for me. Of all the stones in the bowl, this has always been my favorite. And my second favorite has been the red one here." As he spoke he placed the red stone close to his eye. I was struck by the gentle, almost tender way that he held it, turning it this way and that to better see all its aspects and reflections. "Yes," he said finally, after a thorough examination, "this *is* a *lovely* stone." Then he smiled at me and asked, "Would you like to keep it?"

"Yes," I replied. I watched with gratification as the small red stone was delicately placed in my palm.

I had always thought that love and concern were conveyed in grand gestures. I usually interpreted the intensity of feelings as their measure, and because I was a person of great intensity, I assumed that I knew all there was to know about loving. But I learned on that occasion, and on many others to follow, that love shows a gentler face— in the quiet smile that indicates confidence in your abilities, the offer of a tissue to wipe away your tears, the gift of a small oval stone, a cup of coffee comfortably shared.

Caught up for years in the drama of expansive gestures, I found that I had overlooked an altogether subtler art:

that of according to another person a full measure of human dignity, of conveying in small, seemingly insignificant gestures, respect and affection and human concern.

I left the office that day in the warm glow of affirmation. Although the aura of that day did not last, it lingered in my memory, giving substantial shape to the goal I was striving toward, making me mindful once again of possibility. If contentment could happen once, I thought, it could happen again. Its memory served me better than any good luck charm.

Dr. Lustig's gestures, that day, had subtly changed my feelings about myself. At some deep level I did not feel lovable, and Stan had unwittingly confirmed this when he told me he did not love me. But in the days ahead, as I regarded my red stone and remembered Dr. Lustig's words about it, I began to question my long-held assumption. Perhaps I was, after all, lovable; perhaps, like the stone, I had some worth. If Stan did not love me, then perhaps that was not my fault. Perhaps I, Carol as an adult, really deserved to be loved.

These were startling new thoughts, and I often felt uncomfortable with them. But in the end, it was precisely these beliefs that led me to end a bad marriage.

As for that spring, it saw me take many small steps forward, interspersed with an occasional turning back. The relationship between Stan and me continued much the same. We stayed together, ignoring a deeper alienation. The children thrived like healthy young growing creatures, and did not appear to wear the burdens of their elders.

Slowly and with much hesitation, I began to feel somewhat more complete. The difficulties I encountered that early spring were at least more evident to me than my earlier trials had been. For a while I was clearer-sighted, less encumbered by fog. Spring offered me a brief respite, standing as it did between my earlier flirtation with madness and my later immersion in it. For a few months, at least, I enjoyed a reprieve.

Chapter 2

Altogether, spring found me carrying a lighter burden of madness. When I put my ear to the ground, I could almost hear the rumble of the quickening bulbs. Hope, which had visited me little of late, crept out of the sheltered doorway of my house to stand tall in the back garden, halfway between the crocus and magnolia.

My teaching prospered as confusion slipped away, and I was newly confident that my mind would remain steady. Hope also brought me smiles as I watched my children, taking delight in the inconsequential details of their growing up—the cleverness of their observations about the neighbor's cat, their muddy sneakers after a walk in the rain, their tight little arms around my neck, the trusting in their faces that reflected the hope in mine.

It was strange that I should dream about the necklace just then, with madness receding and promise so close beneath the surface. It was a simple dream, but an odd one.

NIGHT OF APRIL 9, 1975

A man is trying to steal a necklace away from me. Intent

85

on getting it back, I flirt and coax and try womanly wiles
to win it. Failing, I take more direct action, wrestling the
man to the ground to take the necklace by force.

The necklace I dreamed about was a real one that I owned, although it had lain for some time undisturbed in a lesser bureau drawer. I woke and, uneasy about the dream, went to the drawer to have a closer look. The necklace was there where I had left it several years before, next to a discarded copper belt buckle and two mismatched socks. It was tarnished to be sure, but still the same silver cross of Alsace-Lorraine that my grandmother had given me on a day much like this one, when some passing thought of her own mortality, or perhaps a vaguer wish for demonstrable continuity, had prompted her to pass the necklace on.

The cross hung on a delicate silver chain made of flat filigreed ovals interspersed with oval faces. Although the necklace presented itself as a fine-crafted piece, something about the faces did not bear close scrutiny. The mouths were tunneled holes pierced straight through each head, while the eyes stared blindly at some inner scene. These faces belonged to a forgotten Roman gargoyle, and it was altogether mysterious how they had made their way into my delicate chain. But there they were, gaping at me, the faces of madness suddenly substantialized. I slammed the drawer shut and tightly closed my eyes. In a few minutes I was breathing normally.

Throughout the day, between classes and while I was tending my children, the faces would suddenly be there, compellingly present to my inner eye. Then the air would begin to press in on me, suffocating me as if I had been under water twenty seconds too long. I remembered the attempted seduction and the wrestling of the dream, and they seemed to speak distressingly about my femininity. They somehow made me feel ashamed. Who was this man that I could overpower in one manner but not in another, and what and why was he stealing from me? The thought went round and round in my head like a record stuck in a negative groove. And the worst thought of all that flitted in and out—what terrible thing did it mean about me that I wanted the necklace, those mad faces, back?

I took the necklace with me when I went to see Dr. Lustig late that afternoon. By this time an inner switch had clicked on again, and an inner chorus had preempted my power of fluent speech. I simply handed the necklace to Dr. Lustig and murmured something about a dream.

He examined the necklace closely with special attention to the faces, and slowly nodded when he was finished.

"Tell me the dream you had last night."

I gathered my strength to make a voice and haltingly told him about my dream. "A man was trying to steal this necklace from me. . . . I tried to get it back by being feminine. . . . That didn't work. . . . I wrestled with him and finally took it back."

"How did you try to be feminine?" Dr. Lustig asked.

I was weeping now without making any sound. I was ashamed. "I just tried to be . . . charming, I guess . . . and . . . well . . . seductive. . . ."

Dr. Lustig spoke in a calm voice. "A man is robbing you of your necklace. Charm and feminine wiles don't work, are not enough to distract the robber, so you wrestle him to the ground and get your necklace back?"

I mumbled a barely audible yes.

"That was smart." He paused for a moment. "He didn't put up much of a fight?"

I murmured again.

"He did? Then what did you do to subdue him, weak woman that you obviously were?"

I was shocked at his words.

"People usually use their strengths first," he explained. "You used your charm first. You obviously considered *that* your strength. When it didn't work you resorted to a lesser skill."

I was now weeping with abandon, my nose dripping along with my eyes, but I attempted a defense. "I think what happened at that point . . ."

"Why don't you wipe your nose?" he interrupted. "There's Kleenex over there."

I took a tissue, dried my nose, and continued my tearful defense. "I didn't care what happened at that point," I sobbed. "I just had to get the necklace back."

"So what did you do to him?" Dr. Lustig asked. "How

did you restrain him and get your necklace back? What did you *do*?"

I was silent.

"He couldn't have been *too* strong, if you wrestled him to the ground and prevailed. He must have been a weakling."

I was getting angry at these implications. "He wasn't *very* weak," I insisted. "I was just angry."

"An intense emotion does not increase the number of your muscles nor your skill in using them," Dr. Lustig replied. "Either he was weak or you were strong." He paused for a moment and then added, "Or at least, a better wrestler."

I was getting very angry. "Why do you keep saying he had to be weak?" I retorted. "Why can't *I* be strong?"

"Because when *you* selected your charm and femininity first," he replied evenly, "*you* indicated how powerful *you* considered them to be. And your strength was chosen second."

"Why can't he be strong, and I be stronger?" I said in a much stronger voice.

"Well, then, if he was strong and you were stronger, why didn't you use *that* first? What are you using this feminine charm and seduction stuff for? Why don't you just say, 'Give me back my necklace, you creep—you can't have it'? The man's using a physical threat against you and you say, 'Well, I'll use what works best against a physical threat. I'll charm the little fucker.' Why don't you just say, 'Hey, you can't have my necklace—it's mine'?"

I reflected on this sobering thought for several minutes. Finally he spoke again, very low and confiding.

"Most people use their strengths first, and if your strength was being feminine and charming, then that's what you used first." He paused as if a new thought had just occurred to him. "Of course, it's also possible that you're feminine, charming, *and* strong. But . . ." his voice trailed off.

"I was feminine, charming, *and* stronger than he," I finished for him, feeling that I had finally proved my point.

We sat in silence for some moments then. He seemed comfortable and confident and so was I, until I remembered the eyes in the faces of the necklace and how they were mad. A cold sweat swept over me with this thought, and I could feel the pressure of the air closing in on my skin.

"The point about the dream is that I want the necklace back, and the faces are mad," I said. My voice was low and anguished and miserable.

Dr. Lustig picked up the necklace and once again looked it over carefully. "Yes," he acknowledged matter-of-factly, "they are mad." He paused for a moment and then added, "Would you like me to fix it for you?"

I agreed, so he got up and crossed to a door on the left-hand wall of the room. When he opened it, I saw that it was a closet full of all sorts of paraphernalia, medicines, toys, odds and ends. I had always wondered what was behind that door. I had imagined a hidden staircase or a secret chamber, but never a simple storage room. He took down a tool chest from one of the upper shelves at the back of the closet, and got out a pair of pliers. When he had reseated himself, he took up the necklace and slowly began removing the faces one by one, carefully connecting the chain at each link so that any gap would be no more than momentary, and the whole would still remain whole. While he worked we continued to talk.

"I'm afraid to lose the madness," I said, "because it's the only thing about me that makes me unique."

"No," he replied firmly. "Your uniqueness is not predicated upon madness. Your uniqueness is based on all of you—your dark side and your light side. All of you together. You don't have to inhabit one side of yourself and stay stuck there to be unique. You're unique no matter where you are inside." He was speaking slowly in a soft, soothing voice.

"You're very familiar with both sides of yourself at this point, so why not have a bit of both? Balance yourself and stay that way." He thought for a moment, then continued. "It's really like being on a seesaw. If you stand right at the center of the seesaw you can have it balanced, and a little bit of motion or effort from you can get one side or the other to move down or up. But if you're away from the fulcrum, it becomes more complicated to keep that balance. Well, then, stay at the center and use your-self to balance the light and the dark."

"Or else get a partner to sit at the other end of your seesaw," I said, brightening. I liked this image; it made sense.

"Or else get a partner to sit at the other end," he said with amusement. "And that will work as long as the part-ner..."

"...sits there night and day..."

"...never taking a break." He paused for a moment as if relishing the thought. "And totally selfless," he added, spinning it out. "The partner must be someone whose main job in life is to be the other end of your seesaw." He paused in the game and suddenly grew serious. "Some people, I think, try that for a while, but they discover that it doesn't work for very long. Either they try to find that partner or to *be* that partner for someone else. But it doesn't work."

"So everybody's got to stand at the middle and balance themselves out?" I suggested.

"Yes," he replied. "You can get some help temporarily; you can find somebody to be on the other end. But at some point you're going to have to move toward your own center, and become adept at keeping it balanced."

I found the conversation very reassuring. Being alone at the center of a seesaw didn't seem like such a bad sense of being alone.

"But many people aren't at the center," I went on. "Many people are at one end or the other."

"True," he said. "But the center's there just the same. People make their own choices. But the center's always there to reach if they want. It will take some effort and it can be precarious, especially if it's done alone. How-ever," he continued, "some people prefer to just sit on the ground at one end of the seesaw. Then there's no movement in their life. Others prefer to move partway up the seesaw and stop. It may not be important to them to get the thing balanced."

He sat in silence for a few minutes, musing. "Yes, some people prefer to have very unstrained lives," he finally reiterated. "But if you're there at the center of the seesaw, you'll have all the pleasures of a dynamic balance. People who just sit on the seesaw while it rests on the ground are in a static balance, and don't have the ability to adjust to the swing of events. They probably think that they're better off, but it's only an illusion. There can't be any movement at all from that situation."

"What about the people who are at the other end of the seesaw, the ones hanging precariously in the air?" I laughed nervously and put my hand to my throat. "What about them?"

"The people up in the air in that way *think* that they don't have any control, but they do. They choose not to exert it. They're in a more stable situation than they realize. All they have to do is slide down the seesaw. Yet they prefer to sit there trying to convince other people that they have no control. They claim that nothing can be done about it, and expect everybody to excuse them for what they do." He began flailing his arms about and mimicking a person out of control.

"Or they complain about the one on the ground who's keeping them there," I said, thinking somewhat shamefacedly about myself.

"Yes," he agreed, becoming himself again. "Rather than figuring out for themselves what they can do to change the situation."

We seemed to have come to the end of our conversation. By this time the half-light filtered through the half-closed curtains, streaking the walls with the palest burnished pink. Dr. Lustig and I were silent for some uncounted minutes, until he reached over and switched on the lamp.

I jumped at the sudden intensity of light, and felt that I was waking from a partial dream. When I had somewhat gathered my wits, I saw that the footstool between our chairs now held a heap of separate silver faces. All the while that we had been talking, Dr. Lustig had been removing the mad faces, one by one. I watched as he set the last face with the others and finished reconnecting the silver chain.

"There," he said with a sigh, handing me the necklace. "How does it feel now?"

I took the necklace and carefully weighed it in my hand, searching out its new acceptability. It seemed to me better than it had been before, but it also carried a new sadness, as if it were mourning the loss of too many friends. He must have read the uncertainty in my face, because, when I looked up, he was looking at me in a puzzled way. Then all of a sudden he leaned back and laughed.

"But of course," he said, as if that explained it. "Will you give the necklace back to me?"

I watched as he carefully selected a single mad face from the pile and, with the pliers, put it back into the necklace. When his task was completed, he handed the necklace to me and asked me again how it felt.

I took it in my hand and it seemed just right. Then I smiled, understanding. Ten mad faces are too much madness, I thought, but no mad faces are just another pretty necklace.

"We have to find just the right amount of madness," he said, smiling back.

Chapter 3

JULY–AUGUST, 1975

As spring ripened into summer, I felt the efforts of earlier months gradually merge to shape the beginnings of a new self. On the eve of my daughter Elizabeth's fourth birthday, eight months after I had begun psychotherapy, I dreamed the first dream of a trilogy.

NIGHT OF JULY 14, 1975

I have just returned from a place far away. I am sitting on a low wall made of smooth round stones, swinging my legs and gazing into the garden facing me. In this "Garden of the Happy People" it is perpetually spring. Fountains burst to overflowing with pure, crystalline waters; children, with heads and arms bathed in warm sunlight, frolic and dance and play. As I look longingly into the Garden from my isolated position on the wall, I see Dr. Lustig enter from the opposite side and walk through the idyllic scene, until he arrives at a place near the wall where I am seated. He motions me to follow him.

The wall where I am sitting separates the Garden from a terrace behind me. Dr. Lustig leaps over the wall onto the terrace, and sits down on the floor. The terrace is transformed into a therapy room. I jump down from the wall into the room, and sit down on the floor near Dr. Lustig. He talks and talks to me, until I feel strong and well.

Then Dr. Lustig takes my hand and points toward the Garden of the Happy People. I see that the wall that separated me from the Garden has fallen away. I enter the Garden.

I woke from this dream with delight. I remembered a saying attributed to the philosopher Wittgenstein: "The world of the happy person is a different world from the world of the unhappy person." For me to have had even a brief glimpse of the other, happier world was utterly enchanting. I spent a splendid day with the children, celebrating Elizabeth's birthday and my renewal with a simple joy.

That night, I dreamed two further dreams.

NIGHT OF JULY 15, 1975

I am expecting a child. Dr. Lustig is both the father of the child and the obstetrician. I am standing in the room where I live, getting dressed for a therapy appointment. I happen to look into the mirror and discover that I am able to see my baby through the transparent skin of my pregnant belly. The baby is fully formed, and I realize that I am about to deliver. I am surprised, because I did not realize that it was time for me to give birth.

I give birth standing before the mirror. A baby girl is born bloodlessly and painlessly. I wrap her carefully in a blanket and cradle her in my arms. I am afraid for her safety because she seems so small and fragile. I closely regard her to be sure that she is still breathing. She sleeps peacefully on. I lay her on the bed.

Looking around, I think that I must find a present to give Dr. Lustig in gratitude for this birth. Then I realize that the birth of my child is the gift that he has labored for.

*   *   *

I woke in the night from this dream, feeling a great sense of accomplishment, as if the metaphorical birth of my new self in the dream had actually been accomplished. I rose and wrote the dream down, and then drifted back to sleep filled with contentment and overall well-being. Later that night, just before dawn, I dreamed a third dream that seemed to complete the sequence.

MORNING OF JULY 16, 1975

I am invited to a party at Dr. Lustig's house one evening. When I arrive, I am struck by the enormity of his home— it seems to go on for miles. It is beautifully decorated with both old and new furniture, and there are Japanese prints on the walls.

I wander from room to room for a while, fascinated by the harmony of all the rooms, absorbed in the interplay of color and texture and motif. Finally I sit down on a couch next to a woman. She turns to me and asks, "Who are you?"

I say, "Carol."

She asks, "Carol who?"

I reply, "Carol Allen."

She says, "No! I mean, who are you?" I don't know what to say. "I am a woman analyst," she continues importantly. "Are you an analyst too?"

"No," I reply, "I'm Dr. Lustig's patient." At that, she turns away scandalized. It is clear that she thinks a patient has no business being at a party for psychiatrists. I wander into the next room, where I see a woman crouched in a corner. She says, "Oh, why did he invite me? He knows I don't like to be seen with so many people around. What if one of my patients sees me!"

"There's a woman analyst in the next room whom you might enjoy talking with," I tell her.

I continue my journey through the house. I finally come to a large room where a buffet banquet is being served. I notice that there aren't any clean plates left, so I walk all the way back to the kitchen to get some more. The kitchen is a large square room, with a square butcher-block table set directly in the middle. I go over to the cupboards on the far wall to look for the plates, when I notice Dr. Lustig's fantastic garbage-disposal system. The walls of the kitchen sink are curved like a slide, so that garbage placed anywhere on them simply slides right down into the disposal and disappears.

I take clean plates back to the banquet room. Most of the people have gone by this time, but there is still food left. I fill my plate and begin to eat. Dr. Lustig is in the room too, talking and joking with some of the guests. He comes over to me when he sees me, and begins laughingly and playfully teasing me. I smile, knowing that we are friends.

Again I woke and, sitting on the edge of my bed in the first light of dawn, wrote out the last dream in the trilogy. I liked the progression of the dreams: from a happy garden, to a rebirth, to a friendship with Dr. Lustig. I instinctively knew that the child in my second dream was my new self, a fragile being whose growth into a strong woman would require all my care and nurturing. Only then, it seemed to me, would I be able to meet Dr. Lustig as a friend and equal.

I walked through the next month in the halo created by these images. My dream metaphors became more real to me than my real life, casting a warm, rosy glow over all that I touched. I took these dreams very seriously. I also took them literally. I am happy, I thought. I am reborn, I thought. Herb and I are friends, I thought. I forgot an essential fact about dream timework—that to enter the world of dreams is to enter a timewarp, or, to put it another way, that dreams are timeless. They can reenact and point to the past. They can prophesy and point to the future. Rarely are they solely about the present. But I took my dreams at face value. I was enchanted with the view of myself that they portrayed.

All through late July and early August, I daydreamed about my dreams constantly. Caught up in the solipsism of my inner reality, I cast out of my mind the truth of my domestic situation. Although my marriage was steadily declining, I steadfastly ignored the signs of strain beneath the surface. I pretended that my marriage had only minor flaws, that the course of marriage counseling that Stan and I had entered on in January was providing the panacea that I desired.

But the truth kept seeping in at the edges of consciousness, destroying the purity of my daydreaming escapes. Suddenly, at odd moments, I would see the image of Stan's vacant face turning away from me during our conversational attempts. I would remember the lack of essential connection, the great void of our eggshell marriage, the aimless drifting of two partners apart. Finally, the illusion of a married state could no longer be maintained. Divorce, like an uninvited actor, made a stage entrance into our marriage play.

Chapter 4

Divorce. On an ordinary day in mid-August I finally thought the unthinkable. There it was in stark relief, the word that reverberated with brutal associations—fragmentation, division, failure, defeat. Divorce. It was something that happened to other people, to other families. It had no place in my tradition or in my conception of myself.

I had grown up in a small town in Idaho, a modest town at the center of a farming valley. My parents had the values I always associated with the West. They were straightforward, honest, and hardworking. They prized independence above all else and yet, ironically, clung to the extended family like barnacles to a ship's bottom. My paternal grandparents, my uncle and his wife, my father's cousins all lived nearby. There were always holidays and picnics with the larger family. My uncle and grandfather would stop over most mornings, to chat and have coffee, before starting the day's work. The family was my primary means of identification. "Oh, you're Dick's girl," or "This is Nina's granddaughter," they would say, and in this way I would find my place.

Marriages, my family believed, required effort. "It's your responsibility to make a marriage work," they always told me. "The things that are worth having are worth

98

working for." The family was the source and guardian of all values, providing protection like some great sentinel beast at the gate, providing refuge against the inconstancy of the larger world.

Divorce was anathema within the society of my childhood. When it was spoken about at all, it was in hushed tones, like the time the neighbors' daughter came home without her husband. "She's getting a divorce," the adults murmured as they shook their heads in disbelief. "Her husband left her," they said, as if she were tarnished like a worn brass plate.

I was only a child then, about ten or eleven, but I remember the next time I saw the subject of these conversations. I regarded her closely, trying to detect in her person some sign of the stigma that so surely had attached itself to her. I saw nothing exceptional about her on that occasion, except that she looked tired and a little drawn. But I secretly thanked my lucky stars that I would never stand in her place.

Now, twenty years later, this was precisely where I stood. The thought of divorce had finally intruded, pushing itself relentlessly and painfully into my consciousness. The word bespoke failure of the worst sort, an offense for which the individual is always held accountable. And worse, a betrayal of the entire tribe.

On that particular day in mid-August, with the word "divorce" resounding in my mind's ear, I took off my wedding ring and held it in my hand. It had been my maternal grandmother's wedding ring, and her grandmother's before her. I turned it around in my hand several times, rereading the dates that were inscribed inside: "December 14, 1864," and "August 11, 1911," and next to the dates the single word "Ours."

I remembered the day my grandmother had given it to me. I was a girl of about twelve or thirteen then. The ring hung on a black velvet ribbon, which she placed around my neck. As my grandmother slipped the ribbon over my head, she told me the history of the ring: how it had always passed through the women of the family; how her grandmother, as she lay dying, had placed it around her neck in a similar manner; how it was made of twenty-karat gold that came from the California Gold Rush of '49. Because

I was the oldest daughter of her only daughter, my grandmother had passed the ring on to me. "You will be married
someday in this ring," she told me, "just as I was, and
my grandmother before me." And as she said it, I knew
that this ring wed me to my tradition.

And so in due course, I had been married in it. Regarding my ring now in the late August afternoon, I wondered
how I could even consider spoiling it with a divorce. I
was also superstitious. Would I bring bad luck to my children and the generations to follow? What harm would
come if I so dishonored the symbol of my familial bond?
I put my wedding ring decisively back on my finger. It's
out of the question; I'll never get divorced.

A week later, wedged between the drowsiness of summer
and the headier tempo of fall, came that particular week
in August when we made our annual pilgrimage to the
ocean. We piled the children into the car and drove the
seventy miles to the New Jersey shore. This year we had
added the babysitter to our entourage, hoping for some
hours of solitude and marital companionship. We had
rented an apartment situated several houses from the
beach, so that we could move easily back and forth from
house to ocean with the children.

A week at the ocean in August had become our annual
family ritual. We sought revitalization and sanctuary at
summer's end. That particular year, I think, Stan and I
had also hoped that the ocean might prove to have the
curative powers that would bind our wounds and restore
our marriage.

The greater part of each morning and early afternoon,
the beach. The late afternoon hours were given over to
solitary walks up the coast. In the evening, Stan and I
generally went out to dinner by ourselves, leaving the
babysitter in charge of the children.

These dinners became the focal point of our marital
isolation. Stan and I would sit across the table from each
other, generally no more than three feet apart, yet the
space between us might have been interstellar, for it was
just as lacking in oxygen. We sat in silence, sad and indig-
nant.

It was during my solitary walks along the ocean, in the

mellow light of the late August sun, that slowly there began to form in my mind a resolve, which gradually took the shape of a decision. Perhaps, after all, we would be better off alone. Perhaps a divorce is the only answer. The steadiness and constancy of the ocean became the rhythmic backdrop for these reflections. Its very vastness gave me perspective. It reminded me of the limited place that I and my problems occupied in the larger order of things. I found the thought of my insignificance vastly reassuring. The world would survive, I grasped with relief, even if Stan and I got a divorce.

During that week Stan must have come to a similar conclusion, although no word of divorce was spoken between us. But as the week drew to a close, he began to acquire the look of weary calm that often accompanies a secret resolve. The earlier tension between us had evaporated, leaving in its place an exhausted truce.

Chapter 5

Marriages are created and so are divorces. There comes a time when both parties know that it is only a matter of time before they part. It becomes, then, a matter of enacting a final drama, saying things that can never be unsaid, words that haunt at later points of hesitation, fortifying the will against the hours of loneliness, steeling the resolve to sever the bond.

Stan and I were walking to a marriage-counseling session at Dr. Lustig's when we made our divorce.

"I think we should get a divorce." I spoke the words for the first time, thinking about the months of silences. Our lying together at night painfully alone. Our children's faces puzzling over our faces, asking unspoken questions about what had gone wrong. Scattered conversations that became minor irritants, minor skirmishes that grated on the nerves. I remembered how the words had died one by one. How the power of speech had died with the words. How the feelings had died with the power of speech. To be sure, there had been brief firecrackers of anger, but even these sparks had trailed quickly into smoke, leaving both of us knowing as the wisps faded that it was our last Fourth of July.

"We can't go on," I said.

"I know," he said with pain cracking his voice. "I know," he repeated, "but we cannot get divorced. What about the children? Have you thought about what it would do to them?"

"Yes, I've thought about it, but it's no good for them now. It's no good for any of us now." We walked on for a few minutes.

"It's out of the question," he said suddenly and emphatically. "Just think about what our friends would say, what our families would say. It would be so humiliating, a divorce. I have to work with these people, you know. How could I face them?" I didn't say anything.

"And also," he continued, "what about our parents? What about your family, your brothers and sisters? What do you think this would do to them?" I was silent because I knew it was the truth. We just kept walking.

Finally, I marshaled my will to fight a fight I wanted no part of, to argue for a course that could only bring pain, in the belief, however foolish, that some good might come.

"Those aren't good enough reasons, Stan," I finally said. "They're all about other people. But what about us? You haven't said anything about us. Is there any reason between us why we should stay? Is there anything about me that you admire or value or want to keep?"

He didn't answer immediately. We had stopped walking by this time and were just standing there.

Slowly and deliberately he looked at me and answered my question.

"No," he said. "No, there isn't."

Chapter 6

On October 11, Stan left the house and the marriage. For
me, our separation had the finality of divorce. Weeks
before, we had decided that Stan would move to an apartment and that I would stay in our rented home with the
children. The brilliance of the autumn plumage on that
particular moving day belied the colorlessness of the occasion. I felt empty and blank.

I took the children away from the house. I did not want
them to see the movers carrying out Stan's belongings. I
was afraid that the image of clothes and rugs and chests
being carted out might linger in their minds and haunt
them. I supposed that it was better for children to have
no clear visual impression of divorce's domestic displace-
ment.

We had told the children about our decision two weeks
before. Stan and I had decided that it would be better if
we told the children together, so that in the act of dis-
uniting as husband and wife, we could confirm our parental unity.

We had all gathered together in the living room after
dinner. We sat in a circle on the floor—four-year-old Elizabeth sitting next to her two-year-old brother, and Stan
and myself facing them. Neither Stan nor I knew how to

104

tell young children about adult anguish. So, we talked about the divorce as if it were a matter of houses.

"You will live here in this house with Mommy. Daddy will live in another house just down the street."

"Why?" Elizabeth asked.

Stan looked at me and I looked at him. This was going to be harder than we thought.

"Daddy and I aren't happy living together anymore," I tried to explain. "Even though it makes us all sad now, we think it will be better for all of us later." I tried to say it in a positive tone.

"Why?" Elizabeth asked again, this time with more alarm, as if she was beginning to grasp the implications of what had been said.

At a loss for words, I sat her on my lap. If I could only have pointed to something specific—arguments or fights or abuse—something that would translate into a child's language. I was silent and so was Stan. But I could tell by his posture, as he sat leaning toward me with his hand supporting his weight in back of me, that he was silently willing me to find the proper explanation.

"Daddy and I don't want to be married anymore," I finally said. "We don't love each other anymore." I looked at her face and quickly added, "But, of course, we still love both *you and Daniel* just as much as ever, and we always will."

She looked perplexed, as if our logic escaped her. If the love for a spouse can change, why can't the love for a child? I watched her as she lowered her eyes, under the realization that love has its seasons, and that it can fade away. Her face closed up around an inexpressible sorrow. Love could no longer be taken for granted. Against all reason, her father must go.

Slowly, she raised her index finger to her mouth and made the sign for silence.

"Shhhhh..." she whispered. "It's a secret."

Her response was more terrible to me than the most piercing scream.

Daniel had not said anything throughout. He simply read our faces. In a gesture at once compassionate and matter-of-fact, he put his arms around my neck and kissed my cheek.

"Don't worry, Mommy," he said.

Then, turning to Stan, he repeated his action, as if he had looked into our sorrow and wanted to put the pain in its place.

Stan's eyes moistened and he audibly drew in his breath. I too struggled to hold back the tears.

"I love you kids," I said.

Then the four of us put our arms around each other and formed a circle of affection, knowing that it would never be the same again.

A year or so later, when Daniel was three and a half, a neighborhood girl asked him how many people he had in his family.

"Four," he answered without hesitation.

"But your dad doesn't live with you," she countered. "You only have three."

"No," Daniel insisted. "We have four. You can wear different clothes and be the same person," he explained, "so you can live in different houses and be the same family."

But that was later, and represented an understanding of the subtle force that continues to link a family, even after a divorce. For the moment we confronted a different reality, one where two houses represented fracture and defeat, two houses each of which felt like less than half a house, as if they had been created by wrenching one viable edifice apart, so that what was left was two rickety structures with sides torn out and roofs tottering. How could we, or the children, call either place home?

Stan and I did try to ease the transition for the children, by walking with them hand in hand from my house to Stan's new apartment down the road, thinking that if they could see for themselves the proximity, they would know that Stan, though gone, was still accessible.

When we arrived at Stan's new apartment that day, Elizabeth and Daniel looked it over very carefully, but quietly. They maintained the silence throughout their inspection, and during the beginning of our return walk home.

When we were about halfway back, Elizabeth finally spoke.

"Daddy, carry me," she implored.

Stan reached down and took her up into his arms, and carried her that way for several minutes.

Then she turned to me and said, "Mommy, carry me."

After I had held her for several more minutes' walking, she reached out her arms once again for her father. We continued to ceremoniously pass her between us as our procession made its way home. When we neared our front door, Elizabeth summed up the situation.

"I guess we'll just have to take turns now."

But in spite of the philosophical attitudes of our children, the details of a divorced life weighed heavily on them. The predinner hour, in particular, became for the children and me a painful confrontation with Stan's absence, tangible evidence of a family torn apart that no magical adhesive could mend or bind.

At that late-afternoon hour of the day, when the shadows had always signaled to the children that Stan would be coming home, a quiet listening crept over the house. I watched as anticipation interrupted the children's play and lighted their faces, when they heard adult male footsteps in the outer hallway. I watched the blank disappointment that followed, when the footsteps passed by our door and ascended the stairs to our neighbor's second-floor flat. Our daddy will not be coming home, their faces said. Their bodies wilted and their heads bowed a little. Then, sadly, they resumed their play.

I watched and at night, when they were asleep, I wept. Have Stan and I really done everything we can for the children? Perhaps there's a better way to navigate divorce. What about earlier in the day when I was angry with the children and hit out and yelled at them? Sometimes what I am is terrible. Why can't I be more sure myself of this separation, so that the hurt and confusion I feel will not also stalk my children's footsteps as I saw it doing today, the children both crying, bursting out with small explosions, smaller but no less angry than mine now that Stan has left? All of us angry, angry with each other, angry with Stan, or alternately subdued, retreating into private places to lick our wounds.

Do the children feel abandoned, even as I feel abandoned? How can they possibly understand what is happening to us, if I cannot? What more can I tell them, what more can I tell myself? The truth is that explanations do no good. It's the absence of Stan and a firm structure that we're all mourning.

And what about Stan and myself? Now at the end of my marriage to Stan, I thought about its beginning, how we had walked together when we first met, droplets of autumn rain clinging to the remaining orange-brown tapestry of leaves, sun occasionally peeking out from behind gray clouds that bore no thunder. As we walked, Stan had suddenly turned to me and pulled me into his arms. "I think I'm beginning to love you," he had said softly, as if he surprised even himself with his words. Why had that love on his part been possible under an open sky, but not within the confines of our marriage? Why did that early memory wash over me now like so many tears, suggesting as it did the promise that had marked our beginning, the confidence that our love would never end?

And now, Stan was gone. At first, it had been a relief, I admitted, but now I felt as if someone had jerked the carpet from under my feet and sent me sprawling. Along with Stan had gone the structure and steadiness that I had counted upon, taken for granted, that had gone unnoticed even, but was now apparent in its absence.

Why had Stan and I not prepared ourselves for this? Or was it a minor self-deception to think that any preparation was possible? What little we had done was directed toward the children. But what about ourselves? In jumping our own emotional hurdles, we had avoided the practical prerequisites of breaking apart. Who would care for the children, for example. We had never sat down and talked about sharing child care duties. We had simply assumed that we would continue the pattern set in our marriage, that responsibility for the children would be mine. Why did that seem so unfair to me now, when my greatest fear was that my children would be taken from me?

And the subject of money, that was sure to fuel the flames. But how was I to live, to survive financially? Why could Stan and I never seem to talk about that? Finding no answers to my musings, I finally slept.

The answers came later, as they are likely to do, and seemed apparent, after the fact. One aspect was shame, our paramount feeling at the time, which so distorted our good judgment, which stood between us and potential solutions. Caught up in the felt shame of our situation, and in the utter pain of dissolution, Stan and I did not confront the factors that would slowly undermine us. Rather we bore our divorce as a disgrace, a fiery brand that had to be hidden from the outside world. We covered our sorrow as best we could, as if the final indignity would be to have the truth known. Like children we pretended that it was not quite real, that if we avoided the words, it would not utterly fragment our lives.

As a result, Stan and I made no arrangements for him to visit or care for the children on a regular basis. On most evenings, he would just drop over at the house a few minutes before the children's bedtime, after they had been bathed and were ready for the night. He would talk to them for a while, then kiss them good night and silently leave.

I had had no experience facing economic realities, so I simply ignored the economic quicksand in which I stood. Throwing off the mantle of the fifties, I had embraced the philosophy of the new woman. I would do everything— have a career, have a husband, have children. The fact that I was working made me think that I was independent. Work outside the home was, to me, the symbol of the newfound equality. It was my entrée into the larger world. "Self-realization" was the slogan of our times and I, like the other middle-class women whom I knew, expected to work for self-fulfillment. I had a husband to provide the primary support for the family. I had little experience in facing financial facts or in living with economic urgency.

"I'm going for my master's degree," my friends would say. "I'm taking a few courses, and then I'll decide what I'll do." These were the litanies we recited. Work, we all believed, was a gift to the self. Work was the path out of feminine bondage. We renounced the "volunteerism" of our mothers' generation, and yet often took up work with a similar lack of economic motive.

Separation, I found, undid many of these assumptions. Work became a serious economic fact. It was a brutal awakening. I could barely support the children and myself with the income from my part-time job. The eighty dollars a week that I was earning had to pay for almost everything but the rent.

Still, I was not willing to forfeit my responsibilities to my children. Trapped between the conflicting expectations of two generations, I simply closed my eyes. The burden of reality was too sudden and too great. It was easier to dream than to address the facts.

When Stan left, he had agreed to pay the rent and give me a small amount of money for the children. But he did so as a "favor" rather than a responsibility. We had no formal financial arrangement and, blind to reality, I failed to insist that we should have one. I did not demand that the burdens of our separation be more equitably distributed. I wanted to get out of the marriage and I wanted custody of the children: These were my overriding concerns.

Also I wanted to cope, and I did not appreciate until much later how this commendable instinct undid me. Perhaps it was because I defined "coping" in the best Stoic fashion. It meant surviving no matter how unreasonable the circumstances. It did not mean asking for help, seeking support, redefining responsibilities, redistributing wealth, reducing daily pressures—in short, changing the situation.

I must cope, I must cope, was my constant litany, by which I meant hanging on in any way I could, with any sacrifice of clear-sightedness, with any forfeiture of the truth. I am a failure because I could not stay married. If I fail to cope now, I am a failure two times over. People always say that women cannot cope, but I will prove them wrong. I will not let divorce defeat me. I will care for my children, I will work, I will be even more perfect; because one humiliation can go unnoticed, but two will surely strip me of all pride.

I will not let the weary, lonely hours of the day defeat me, nor little money, nor the children, for then I might lose them. I must prove that I am a success at divorce, to diminish the string of so many other failures. Being Superwoman before was nothing compared to this.

It became paramount to show Dr. Lustig, above all others, how well I was doing, just how well I could survive. When I told him weekly that I was doing fine, I

believed my words, saw nothing of the dangers in them.
My therapy sessions had become an escape for me from
the humiliation attending the dissolution of my marriage,
a chance to make up for my felt defeat. I failed to find
the words that would have described my situation, that
would have provided a clue to further intervention, that
would have initiated a change. Wrapped in the indulgence
of failed hopes and false pride, I failed to look for the
solutions I needed.

Stan had broken off all contact with Dr. Lustig several
months before, and I talked at my appointments only in
the metaphors of my private world, forgetting in his presence the actual backdrop of my life. To have admitted my
practical plight, even to Dr. Lustig, would have been, in
my mind, the final defeat. I was disappointing everyone
by ending my marriage. Failure to cope would have magnified the problem. I did not want to let them all down.
I wanted to cope for the women's movement, for Dr.
Lustig, for my family. To have looked closely at my real
situation would have presented too clear an image of failure. So I pretended to myself that I was doing just fine,
that there were no insurmountable obstacles facing me.
I talked to Dr. Lustig about dreams and fantasies. I did
not talk about diapers or money or my terrors in the night.
I lived, more each day, on a diet of daydreams. I faced
neither the day nor the night.

Chapter 7

NOVEMBER, 1975

Slowly and insidiously my separation separated me not
just from a man, but from myself. As the days of November grew colder and darker, I retreated further and further
into myself. Some remnant of animal instinct made me
want to withdraw—to spin a cocoon, to burrow into the
ground, to hibernate in a cave, to protest the night. My
fears hummed drowsily in the gray of day but awakened
to full chorus with the encroaching darkness. Once the
children were asleep, I would huddle in my bed, hearing
the violence of the branches as they beat against the house,
listening to the misery in the sounds of the wind.

During the days I began to daydream seriously. I needed
fantasy. What else could make my situation tolerable,
suggest hope, offer encouragement, give meaning to my
present absurdity, give me the courage to face another
day? Where else but in fantasy could I seek a center to
hold on to? Please, God, I prayed even as I retreated from
the world, give me a steady point against which I can
orient myself, something to grasp and hold on to that will
prevent my disintegration, that will hold the pieces
together.

Because fantasy had not provided that center, had
become increasingly a vortex within which my ego swirled,

I had looked to three people in search of that steady point, that anchor. One was Marion, my best friend, the friend who had stood next to me at the dark door of my first dream; Marion, who had shared my therapy from its beginnings, who had over the past year become a closer and closer friend, gradually displacing most of my other women friends, so that by the time Stan left she was almost the only one. Marion and Robert, my former lover, who had quietly reentered my life when Stan left, and of course Dr. Lustig—my three moorings in an otherwise ungovernable sea.

Well, with Stan gone, at least I have Marion and Robert, I reflected one late November afternoon, as I sat sipping tea in the tomblike silence of my house. Dr. Lustig had told me that with the breakup of my marriage I could no longer expect to find everything in just one person, but would have to build a network of friends, and get a little bit from each of them. But in reality, there were so few of my friends I could talk to, not because they would not have listened, but because some hesitancy in me prevented it, as if my contact would tarnish them, rob them of their common sense.

With Marion, though, I could share the details of my therapy. Was that why she had assumed such a large place in my life lately, because my therapy was the center of my world, and she knew what that meant, because her therapy was also the center of her world? The two of us were like sisters in search of wholeness, or perhaps closer than sisters even, because we were spiritually attached, seeking refuge from a world whose men—our husbands, but not our therapists—had let us down, alike in concentrating our energy on our therapy, sharing its magic with each other.

She delighted in fantasy as much as I did, especially about our therapists' love for us, and as we talked for hours each day, we played out this theme in all its variations—Dr. Wainwright loved her and would marry her; Dr. Lustig loved me and, though I did not dare to say it out loud, would soon recognize the inevitability and correctness of our attachment. Our inferior husbands would be replaced by our superior mentors, who would provide us with true guidance in our lives, who with sensitivity and understanding would lead us to the land of milk and honey, where we would settle into a comfortable domesticity, where we would be forever loved, and never alone.

I broke off my reverie abruptly, remembering that I was due to meet Robert in an hour. I thought about Robert—how we had begun and how we now stood. Robert, who had come back into my life after Stan had left; Robert, who was so like me that it was almost painful, who dreamed the same dreams as I did, who lately had taken on a haggard look around the eyes, frequently meeting me unshaven, showing the wear of his own excruciating divorce battles in the shabby and torn clothes he wore.

I had met Robert at a party eight years earlier, a faculty party given by a professor at the college where I taught. It was the first party of that scholastic season, a party typical of the times and the intellectual life. I found myself standing to one side of the room, gazing at the dance floor that had been cleared in the center, rugs rolled up and plants pushed aside, as if readying the room for its focus on the dance. The lights were muted, the liquor and grass plentiful. The conversation was idle and intellectual, with a trace of the times in the earnestness of its tone. Beards were plentiful, as was longish hair, those outward and visible signs of an inward and spiritual purity, untainted by establishment values, Vietnam, crass commercialism, or gray flannel suits—people caught up in a time that allowed for righteousness, that provided a cause.

Several colleagues and I had been chatting idly about Bergman—the Kierkegaardian and Heideggerian themes of *The Seventh Seal*, the brilliance of the time imagery in *Wild Strawberries*. Just as I was tiring of the talk, and ready to depart, a feeling that I was being observed crept over me. I felt a tingle go down my spine, and suddenly and unaccountably I was alert.

Unobtrusively, for I did not like to be obvious, I glanced in the direction from which I felt the presence come. I was confronted by the unshuttered gaze of Robert Anderson, an English professor whom I knew of, but had not met. We looked at each other a fraction of a second longer than is common, and in that glance the room emptied and we found ourselves alone.

I watched him make his way toward me. With inevitability I saw his lips move as he asked me to dance. The stereo was playing "Ruby Tuesday." I heard the words through a filter as if cotton stuffed my ears. As we danced, Robert hopped around the makeshift dance floor as if his footsteps could not keep pace with the leap of his spirits. Then in one instant, with one further look, the dancing leaped from his feet to his eyes.

After that, we walked outside into the crisp autumn darkness partially illumined by a quarter moon and a smattering of stars. We did not hold hands, but as we walked, we brushed together, like magnets drawn to their complementary poles. Hungry for words to confirm our affinity, we talked of Plato and other realities, about growing up in the West (he was from Colorado) and how it had shaped us. I laughed for no reason and quoted Yeats. He laughed for no reason and quoted e. e. cummings.

So our love had begun, and so it had continued until our very alikeness had driven us apart. But the physical affinity between us had never entirely dissipated, could be reignited at any moment, we had found. And so it had not surprised me that now, years later, in the midst of our divorces, Robert had returned.

I silently compared Robert and Dr. Lustig in my mind. Though I loved Robert now and had loved him earlier, before my marriage, how could I find in him an anchor, adrift as he was in his own divorce? And our sexuality, which had always been a mix of lightning and velvet, why was it alarming me now? Whenever I met Robert, usually covertly because of his complicated divorce, I was left with a physical satisfaction, but also a sinking stomach, a vague nausea, a desire to flee, a tendency to wrap a layer of daydreams even tighter around me—perhaps because of the spiritual desperation and raw physicality of our union, the hope that our sexual blending would vanquish our darker demons, would drive out the daily world made up of bitterness and despair.

But the fantasy was no longer working. Real sexuality with Robert was no longer offering an escape, was itself becoming a reality that I needed to escape from. Better to daydream about Dr. Lustig, who presented a clearer illusion, whose eyes were not haggard from sleepless nights, children's tears, a vindictive spouse, or personal failures glimpsed through a magnifying glass.

My fantasies about Dr. Lustig, in contrast to the reality of Robert, offered me an appealing escape. Ensconced in it, I possessed virtues and powers beyond my expectations. I was whole; I was healthy; I was a healer. He and I would be true companions and spend our days together. I would paint watercolors and he would do therapy. These were intoxicating reveries, safer than the sexual reality I shared with Robert. Robert was a mirror that perfectly reflected my own plight. Better to drift along on dreams about Dr. Lustig, free from more tortuous truths and messier realities. I can't go on seeing Robert, I decided. I can't meet him today.

But I felt immobilized. I sat as I was for another hour, until the time of my rendezvous with Robert had passed. Finally he called me.

"I'm just too ill to see you," I said. "I'm sorry, but I just can't right now."

He seemed to understand immediately and I sensed relief in him as well. "Be good to yourself," he said as he hung up.

My thoughts drifted back to Dr. Lustig again, how he was my partner in magic, being endowed as he was with equal gifts. Together, we would read the hidden signs all around us and speak our private tongue. I had even tried it out. During each office visit lately, I would closely regard his crystal bowl full of polished stones. Sure enough, I could, upon close scrutiny, detect a shift in their arrangement—the brown one or the gray one had subtly changed its position since the last time we met. I would smile inwardly, full of satisfaction. It's as I thought, I said to myself. He's sending secret messages that only I can interpret.

Then there were the keys. Dr. Lustig had two bathroom keys in the waiting room—one saying "girls" on one side and "women" on the other, the second labeled "boys" and "men." When I entered the room, I would search out the exact angle at which the keys lay, confident that Dr. Lustig was telling me of his love by the way they were juxtaposed on the table. And sometimes I would rearrange them myself, in full confidence that he would be able to interpret my symbolic message to him.

Then there were the numbers. The dates and the times of my therapy appointments assumed special meaning. If the therapy session was particularly helpful, its date and time began to carry magical powers. Alternately, any pain associated with a date condemned that number forever. Eighteen, for example, was a good number, being a combination of 8 ("eternity") and 10 ("wisdom"). Likewise, 25 carried a positive effect, being 5 ("healing") multiplied by itself.

Twenty-nine, by contrast, filled me with dread. Nine was an upside-down 6, and 6 was the number of "sexuality." Twenty-nine compounded this omen by also carrying a 2, the number for "divided." And so it went. If I saw Dr. Lustig on 10/8/75 at 10 A.M., the auspicious numbers of that date and time could only ensure my well-being: 1 brought "unity," 10 "wisdom," 8 "eternity," 7 "comfort," and 5 "healing."

Since Dr. Lustig was my mentor in magic, the need for explaining anything to him directly was circumvented. His thoughts, it was apparent to me, were running along a course similar to mine. I had proved it with the stones and the keys. We could communicate through our mutual understanding of the signs. We had no need for words.

"How are things going at home?" he would ask me.

"Fine," I would reply, smiling. I knew we weren't talking about home, because it was ten o'clock in the morning and my red stone, which I had previously returned to Dr. Lustig's crystal bowl, was nestled close to Dr. Lustig's gray one.

"How are the children?" he continued, closely watching my face.

"They're doing well," I replied confidently, my face softening into a peaceful expression. "The children," I was thinking, obviously refers to himself and me.

"The children are happy and playful," I said aloud. "They're adjusting to the separation better than I had hoped." I waited expectantly, eager for him to grasp my secret message.

"Wonderful," he answered. Now I knew for sure that he understood. There could be no doubt, for we were both wearing brown that day—the color of earthiness or being down to earth. He loves me and is glad that I'm getting a divorce, I was thinking. Perhaps he's even thinking about marriage.

"How are the children getting along at nursery school?" Dr. Lustig continued.

"They like school," I replied. School must mean therapy, I was thinking. He's asking me how I like psychotherapy with him.

"How are they sleeping and eating?" his questions continued.

"Fine," I smilingly replied. Perhaps he's telling me he wants to sleep with me, I thought rapturously. He must care about me more than I thought.

And so I continued, placing magical meanings on the most ordinary of Dr. Lustig's words, construing them to the satisfaction of my needy imagination.

My need for this fantasy following my separation from Stan might yet have been diminished, however, had not circumstances intervened that turned reality and fantasy upside down, so that what was increasingly a tenuous connection with the world and with Dr. Lustig as its spokesman was finally and forcibly severed.

Chapter 8

NOVEMBER–DECEMBER, 1975

As I drifted on daydreams of my spiritual union with Dr. Lustig that late autumn, Marion's fantasies were taking on a new and unexpected reality. Gradually, it seemed, or so she confided in me, Dr. Wainwright, her therapist, had begun to fall in love with her. He was like a father to her, she told me, so it had begun by her sitting on his lap for comfort. Then one day he began stroking her breasts, all the while telling her what a lovely woman she was. He began to share confidences with her. He was writing a diary about her, he explained, using a secret code, for he wanted to write of his love for her, and still hide his growing feelings from his wife of twenty-five years.

Somehow, at the time, her confidences seemed only right. There was an inevitability about the direction of her therapy that fueled my own ideas of perfect love. Perhaps someday Dr. Lustig will feel the same way about me, I thought, alight with new passion. Love with a therapist had become a possibility.

Finally, the day came when she told me they had made love.

"In his office?" I asked, wondering about the mechanics of the situation. "On the floor, with his wife in the house nearby?" I elaborated, suddenly feeling shaken and alarmed that fantasies should come true. The good of them, I was thinking, is that they are the mind's solace, but their actual translation into physical reality seemed perilous to me.

"He wants to have a baby with me," she said, her face aglow with her recent lovemaking. "A boy," she continued. "It's our private dream."

"You shouldn't be telling me about this," I pleaded. "Please don't tell me any more."

"But it's the most important thing that's ever happened to me in my life," she persisted. "Would you deny me the pleasure of telling my best friend about it?" Her tone was coaxing and she was smiling happily. "I need to tell someone," she said.

I nodded, feeling panic slipping over me like a familiar gray fog.

"Please keep this secret for me," she asked earnestly. "Do you know what *they*, the establishment, would say if they knew about this? They just would never understand about our love."

So I carried her secret for many days, sworn by my loyalty to her to a silence that was deafening. My conscience warred with my need to confide what I knew to Dr. Lustig, for I wanted him to tell me that such things were not possible, that in spite of my fantasies about him, he would never betray me by succumbing to them. But my friendship held me back.

After each meeting with Dr. Wainwright, Marion would hurry to my house to give me a detailed account of their lovemaking. "Please don't say any more," I told her finally, when I could stand it no longer. "This is something between the two of you. Leave me out of it."

But she insisted that sharing it with me was the only way she could contain the joy of his presence and the loneliness she felt when they were apart.

My silence had another reason. I felt I owed a debt to Dr. Wainwright, because he was the psychotherapist who had sent me to Dr. Lustig.

I thought about Harding Wainwright on the one and only occasion when I had seen him. I remembered vividly how he, an older, established, and highly respected member of the Philadelphia psychiatric community, had been standing on his front lawn waiting for me, because I was late for my consultation, having lost my way to his house. As I drew up to his house, I had seen a white-haired gentleman, tall and distinguished looking, wearing a tweed suit and a very substantial pair of shoes, giving the overall impression of an Oxford don who specialized perhaps in Near Eastern studies. He had walked over to meet me, concern obviously registering on his face.

My meeting with him confirmed in my mind his kindness. He led me inside and offered me coffee, and when I had composed myself somewhat, we talked about my first dream. "What did you know that no one else knew?" he asked me, and with that question he gained my confidence. Now, more than a year later, I remembered how supportive he had been to me, how he had been intent on finding me just the right therapist, how I owed finding Dr. Lustig to him.

The weight of these loyalties, however, finally became unbearable. Unable to carry Marion's secret any longer, I finally spoke of it to Dr. Lustig, telling him the facts in the form of a story, as if this transparent ploy could somehow salve my conscience, make me less disloyal to my friend and her lover. But my simple story-telling expedient, employed to soothe my scruples, did not for a moment disguise Marion's identity or that of her therapist.

Shortly after I left that day, Dr. Lustig phoned Dr. Wainwright to tell him what had been said, he told me later, supposing as he did that one of Dr. Wainwright's sicker patients was slandering his reputation. Dr. Wainwright denied the affair, implying that it was Dr. Lustig's patient, and not his, who was out of touch with reality.

Marion was waiting for me when I returned home that day. Dr. Wainwright had phoned her and instructed her to disavow the affair to me. When I realized that she knew I had betrayed her confidence, I shrank back, ready for her anger or censure. But she seemed strangely calm, pleased even, as if now, finally, the truth was out.

"I'm supposed to deny that we are having an affair," she said to me grinning. "So let's just say that I've denied it and leave it at that.

"You know what you'll have to do now," she continued. "You'll have to go and deny it to Dr. Lustig. He would never have believed your word, anyway," she concluded. "You know these therapists all stick together. They never believe a patient if it's her word against one of their own."

Feeling guilty about my betrayal of her confidence, and swayed by Marion's words, I dutifully went back to Dr. Lustig's office that afternoon, and told him that what I had said was not true.

"Are you sure?" he probed, sounding as if he was beginning to wonder about it after all. "Are you sure that this was something Marion was making up?"

"Yes," I replied, my voice dying in my throat. "Yes," I said again, repeating my lie. Finally, Dr. Lustig appeared to be convinced. "I never doubted that what *you* were telling me was what you believed to be true," he assured me. "I'm glad that Marion has now told you the truth." I said nothing, grimacing inwardly at the irony of his words.

I had never felt so tired or so sad, for with my lie I had broken my trust with Dr. Lustig. If I could not tell him the truth, if he could not believe the truth when I told it, then how could he ever again distinguish dreams and reality for me? With that one lie, the therapy room ceased to be a refuge, and Dr. Lustig ceased to be truth's arbiter.

I wondered often afterward why telling a lie is so much worse than being told one, why my lie to Dr. Lustig had finally severed an already fragile trust that had been partially rent by his betrayal of my confidence in the first place. Was it because with my lie I could no longer trust myself? Was it because I had chosen between my mentor and my friend, had been thrown irrevocably into Marion and Dr. Wainwright's camp, where truth and sanity could be sacrificed for the sake of a reputation? Was it because Marion had issued a command that in my guilt and in the absence of a countercommand I had obeyed, because it had at least clarified a clouded situation, dissolved the confusion of conflicting loyalties that ran in too many directions? Was it because my lie had been successful, had fooled even Dr. Lustig, who, by some omniscience, should have known the difference?

It wasn't until the following spring, when Marion married Dr. Wainwright, that Dr. Lustig finally knew the truth. "I'm very sorry. I just didn't know," he told me. He apologized for the way his not knowing had contributed to my blurring of illusion and truth. But by then it did not matter, for I had survived the ordeal that was to be its outcome.

For the moment, however, as I plodded home, I knew only that I was irrevocably alone. Stan was gone. Robert was gone. Marion was acting more and more strangely as her affair went on, wearing boys' clothing, talking to me about how bisexuality was really better, frightening me with her implicit hints and gestures, introducing a possible sexuality into our friendship. And Dr. Lustig, whom I had counted on most to tell me what was real, ignoring the very reality about Marion and her therapist that I knew to be true; my ultimate denial of it myself, my unforgivable lie to him that had broken the bond between us. How could I find in him an anchor anymore, when he did not believe what I knew to be true?

There was nowhere in the world left for me to stand. Even fantasies about Dr. Lustig, *most of all* fantasies about Dr. Lustig, had to be replaced. Magic was all that was left.

My growing immersion in magical thinking brought me relief in the beginning, sheltering my mind against the harshness of my felt isolation. But gradually I became trapped there, in a magical kingdom that seemed totally beyond my control, where occult powers reigned unchecked, and where the best defense was a sorcerer's crystal ball. The magical signs began to gain supremacy, and the task of interpreting them correctly became an obsession that took more and more of my time.

When the numbers were bad, waves of pain would sweep over me. I felt like an octopus whose eight arms were shot through with burning fire. Terrified, I would try to get a grip on my mind, to lessen my anguish by an act of will. But my will was ineffective in the fight against the forces of chaos and caprice. My only chance for survival lay in anticipating their ravages, in order to steel myself for their onslaught. The outside forces impinging on me followed magical and mysterious laws that could not be calculated with reason alone. I continually tried to decipher the magical signs, and desperately sought to discern their rules of grammar, so that I might defend myself by harnessing an equally powerful counterforce.

Numbers, the seat of quantification, had lost their objectivity and no longer quantified. What had begun as innocent numerical play became a compulsion to record each and every number in my life. Ordinary time had collapsed. The present acquired vectors reaching into the past and into the future. What was happening *now* suddenly had magical import in all three time frames. Numbers came to represent the most potentially powerful weapon in my arsenal, because they could predict what might happen.

The grocery list presented the ultimate challenge. I taught my philosophy classes on Tuesday and Thursday. On the alternate days, I would shop for groceries during the part of the morning when my children were in their preschool classes. I would drop the children off at 9:30 and pick them up at 11:30. In between, I would mindlessly race to the grocery store, intent on my larger purpose: to remember the name of the food item that was the referent for every price on the cash register slip, so that later I could connect the symbolic meaning of the foodstuff to the numbers in its price. I would speed home with my store-bought goods and frantically begin recording the food names on the grocery receipt, in the belief that the numbers would allow me to predict future happenings on the parallel dates and times, or at least anticipate those forces which might impinge upon me with violence at any moment.

If bread was eighty-nine cents, then I knew I could expect some sign of beauty or flowers (because bread is made with "flour") on the eighth of the month at nine o'clock. Lettuce ("let us") implied some permission at the hour and day of its price. Meat meant that I would "meet" someone, and so my associations raged. The exact time when I recorded the grocery numbers (usually 11 A.M.) also went into the magical calculation, along with the time and date of their purchase. Eleven o'clock became a terrible hour for me, made worse by the fact that 11 is two 1's that are standing apart, divided. If I worked very quickly, I had just enough time to complete the recording process before picking up the children at 11:30. By that time I was spent, exhausted by the staggering enormity of the surplus magical significance.

As the days of December deepened, the distinction between me and the magic of the outer world collapsed. I became one with it. I could not distinguish a separate self apart from it. I became disorder and the absence of reason. No ordinary laws of causality operated within me. I was pushed and shoved indiscriminately—a leaf torn from its tree, adrift at the mercy of an alien wind. I did not make events happen; they happened to me. The more I struggled against the magical forces, the more powerful they became. The less I struggled against those currents, the less fragmented my fantasy became.

But sometimes I would fight to assert my separate identity. I would record messages to myself—reminders that there still existed within me some remnant of control. "I am a professional," I would write down. "I am a woman," I would remind myself. Then, caught up in the magic once again, I would quickly forget that personhood involves *acting on* the world, rather than being acted upon by it.

Sometimes when I was most flooded by magic, I would sit down and do logic problems, to insist on some order, to defeat the magical numbers with ordinary quantification. I would feel soothed by these intellectual exercises, if only momentarily.

Sometimes I simply begged the forces to let me go. On occasion they consented, and I would have an hour's rest. But then they would reassert themselves and gather me up again into their chaos and confusion, robbing me of my place in the ordinary and ordered world.

What had begun as a simple divorce from a man ended as a profound divorce from reality. Madness, with its charms and the stuff of dreams, had lured me away. But its enchantment soon turned to nightmare, and I could not wake up. Like Orpheus, I had glanced back over my shoulder, and had lost both Eurydice and the world.

PART III

Blinded by the Sun

Madness

I stared into the light and knew what madness was.
Caught in a terrible vision, neither great nor common,
Still without movement in a time unredeemably present,
In a place without the solace of a touch, a human moment,
Wounded without the grace of the artist's dance.

Chapter 1

They came on silent feet out of nowhere, visitors from another dimension. I knew them immediately when I saw them, and from the intent way that they stared back into my eyes, I knew that they also recognized me. At once alien and familiar, like a stranger on the street who is mistaken for a friend, they marched out of my imagination and assumed a visible shape. They were not surrounded by shadow or mist. They had the dimensions, colors, and sharp outlines by which we distinguish the real from the illusory. Only their eyes, and their sometimes bizarre dress, indicated that they belonged to a different reality, were manifestations of the surreal. They came as friends of my solipsism. They were terrible only because they made me mad.

The first time I saw one of them, I was sitting on the deacon's bench in Dr. Lustig's waiting room. It was nine o'clock in the morning on a rather dreary early December day, and I was waiting for my appointment, in a daze devoid of thought. All of a sudden, my attention was inexorably drawn toward the hallway door. I watched, fascinated, as the door slowly opened. A woman stood in the doorway dressed in a short flared red costume, such as those worn by cigarette girls in old movies. Her white blouse was ruffled at the neck, suggesting the collar of a clown. A tray of candies and other confections hung around her neck. She did not speak, but stared intently at my face. As she stood there regarding me, large tears slowly began to pour out of her eyes. Then, turning away sorrowfully, she stepped back into the hallway and gently closed the door on the larger world.

I was not frightened. Instead, I felt a curious kinship with her. She too belonged to the secret society of lonely magicians. She too understood the messages that were not of this world. It seemed only natural to me that she should appear as messenger and ministrant to my isolation.

I said nothing to Dr. Lustig about my strange encounter in his waiting room. But some of my confusion must have been apparent during the appointment, because he mentioned, for the first time, the possibility of hospitalization. The thought was so terrible to me that I promptly put it out of my mind. The next day, when "sunglasses people" began appearing, I did not tell Dr. Lustig about them, either.

I was sitting in a local eatery having lunch with my friend Mimi, when I saw the first one. I was seated facing the entrance to the restaurant, talking with Mimi, when I happened to glance up from the table. There he was, waiting in line to be seated. He wore the costume of a rhinestone cowboy, an elaborate exaggeration of the dress worn by real cowboys I had known in the West. He was suited in a mass of purple satin. Sequins on the costume caught traces of the bright December sunlight streaming in at the windows. Beige-colored buckskin fringe ran up and down his arms, contrasting strangely with the shiny surface of his attire.

But the strangest thing about him was his large sunglasses. They stood like two black voids aligned in his face. They were absolutely opaque. No glimmer of light passed through them; no reflected light bounced off them. Like black holes in space, they seemed to capture the light from every direction. The black eyes attracted my gaze like magnets. My eyes felt pulled inexorably toward them. I stared fixedly at the two black orbs, as if my eyes had been lassoed and were being roped in. Deeper and deeper my gaze was drawn in, until I had no will to free it. Seconds passed like hours. I forgot to breathe. I became terrified by my paralysis.

Finally, gathering together the remnant of energy left within me, I willed my eyes away from his face and back to the table where my friend sat. "I'm so excited about teaching there," she chatted on unconcernedly. "I hope the job comes through." I tried to concentrate on what she was saying, realizing that I had not heard most of what had gone before.

I had, during the preceding month, become increasingly isolated from my friends who, to that point, had always formed a ready support system. It had become painful and straining to be with them, for I could not tell them about my mental anguish, or about the magic that was enveloping me. With everyone except Marion and Dr. Lustig, I sought at all times to appear ordinary, so that no glimmer of my madness would shine through my armor, no clue of my desperation could show itself. I had to protect them from insanity's curse. I was afraid of my friends' instinctive recoil if they were to find out.

Sitting that day in the restaurant, I wanted to ask Mimi to turn around and look toward the door, to confirm whether a sunglassed cowboy was standing there or not. But fortunately my vocal cords did not respond, for if I had asked her to look and she had not seen him, then I knew she would know that I was mad.

I stared intently at her for some minutes, summoning my attention back to the conversation. "Maybe we can get the kids together this afternoon to play," she was saying. I nodded, consciously avoiding looking at the spot where the cowboy had stood, knowing even as I did so that I would eventually have to look again, if only to know for myself where my sanity stood.

I steadied myself, took a deep breath, and quickly glanced toward the spot where I had seen him. He was no longer there. Cautiously, I looked around the restaurant, afraid that he would be there, more afraid that he would not. But he had vanished as neatly as he had arrived.

The waitress brought our sandwiches. "It looks good," my friend said, as she began to eat. I picked up my hamburger automatically and took a bite. But I tasted only the bitterness of defeat. I am mad, I finally acknowledged to myself.

After that first encounter, I began seeing people in sunglasses wherever I looked. This was not odd in itself, since we were having a streak of brilliant December days, with the sun almost painfully reflecting off sidewalks and off mounds of leftover snow. It is beneficial and common for people to protect their eyes against the glare on this kind of day. So sunglasses, in themselves, were not odd. What was odd was my perception, my instinctive certainty, that some of the sunglasses people were not real, even though their visual image was as sharp and as clear as any normal sight.

Several days after seeing the cowboy, I was walking over to the neighborhood bank before its usual closing at three o'clock in the afternoon. On the way, I passed five people wearing sunglasses. Two of them, I suspected, were real and ordinary people. Two, I suspected, were not. The terrible thing was that I could never be sure who was coming toward me: which ones were ordinary people wearing sunglasses, and which were alien folk disguising themselves as ordinary people wearing sunglasses.

With the clear memory of the rhinestone cowboy fresh in my mind, I trembled as each figure in sunglasses passed. The first one I encountered had the suggestion of eyes behind his sunglasses. He did not seem to notice me. He is real, I thought with some relief, reading his lack of interest as a sign of ordinary existence. My body, however, remained tense as I continued along the path to the bank. By now, any appearance of sunglasses provoked in me a serious alarm.

Farther down the street, about half a block from the bank, stood a second person in sunglasses. She appeared to be an elderly woman with white hair and stooped shoulders. She stood at the window of the neighborhood travel agency, as if she was looking at the vacation displays. I stepped up my pace to walk rapidly past her, but I could not prevent one brief glance in her direction.

As I did so, my terror exploded. Like the cowboy, she caught me with the dense black voids that were her eyes, and began to draw me into them. My feet kept walking, but my eyes became trapped in her gaze. As I passed directly by her, my head swung around unwillingly in her direction, as if my eyes were being pulled by a puppeteer's string. At the same time, her head pivoted toward me, so that she continued to track my movements as I walked past. For an instant we were fixed in an encounter of absolute recognition. The glare of the sun was blinding. We stood motionless, she wearing sunglasses to protect her eyes from too much light, while I was being helplessly exposed to its overpowering intensity. I knew that she knew—that her eyes sought mine in recognition of our common dilemma. She too knew the suffering of too much significance. She too knew what it was like to be isolated in the middle of an alien light.

Finally, after several seconds of extreme scrutiny, her eyes shifted away and let me go. I scurried past her down the street. I walked on a few hundred yards, and then glanced back over my shoulder. She was nowhere to be seen. She had looked completely real. Was she, in fact, an idle passerby who sought information about possible journeys, who had simply stepped into the travel agency? Or was she a product of my imagination? Was she—I finally said the word to myself—was she, dear God, a hallucination?

I stumbled into the bank and made my deposit. Then, still shaking, I walked toward the outside through the revolving glass door. Just as I exited, a man in sunglasses was entering through the door. My gaze went to his eyes. His head swung around as he looked toward me. Oh, my God, I thought. I cannot take any more of this. My feet stumbled forward, toward home. Two more people in sunglasses were crossing the street directly in front of me. They looked like an ordinary middle-aged couple. I glanced at them briefly and then quickly looked away. I was afraid to know whether they were real or not.

When I arrived home, the babysitter was there with the children. They came toward me, eager to tell about what they had been doing. But I couldn't focus on what they said. I heard their excited little voices, but the content of their words did not come through. I patted their heads absently, and then asked the babysitter if she could stay with them for an extra hour. "I don't feel well," I told her. "I need to lie down for a little while." She said that it would be no problem to stay. I walked to the bedroom, turned down the covers, and got into bed completely clothed. I lay on my side, curled my body into a ball, and pulled the covers up around my head. I quaked there for the next hour, until the babysitter came in and told me that she had to go home. Then I dragged my body out of bed and, summoning my last ounce of strength, went into the living room to watch the children. I simply sat down in a chair and let them come to me. I answered their questions automatically, and expressed interest in the pictures that they had drawn.

"Mommy, please come and play blocks with us," Elizabeth pleaded, pulling at my arm.

"All right, honey," I said dully and rose to my feet. I spent the next hour on the floor of the study, building houses and structures that were far steadier than I. The rest of the afternoon and evening passed with me, as often happened, on automatic pilot. Twice the image of the sunglasses people came into my mind, and I felt that I was on fire. Then the images faded, and my limbs turned to ice.

When darkness fell that night, it no longer had the power to frighten me. I had discovered, that day, the even more elemental terror of too much illumination. Somehow or other, the metaphor had reversed itself. I had started out being frightened by the black room of my dream. Now, I had discovered an even worse terror, a second realm of light—a double intensity of seeing that illuminated things that were not real, a clarity more terrible than the darkest dark.

The darkness, when I closed my eyes that night, was a comfort. I was glad to exchange the realm of seeing for the more concrete realm of touch. I was glad that my distorted sight had been taken away, if only momentarily; glad to touch the familiar bedroom objects around me in the dark.

My hand clung to the edge of the mattress as I fell asleep.

Chapter 2

To know oneself to be mad is the worst of all possible predicaments. Complete insanity offers sanctuary. It allows one to slip behind a limitless veil of illusion, without any self-conscious monitoring to acknowledge the extent of mental wastage. But to be mad and to simultaneously possess some fragment of consciousness, whereby one glimpses with horror one's true situation, is to slice the protective shield of illusion with a knife and turn up the center raw.

My days in December were filled with endless drownings; endless struggles to surface for air, before once again slipping beneath the sea of unreality. The sunglasses people continued to be my frequent visitors. They beckoned me from the driver's seats of passing cars, from crowded sidewalks, from any public place. Only at home was I safe from their scrutiny. The more I saw them, the more powerful they became. Turn away from your pain, their presence seemed to say. Follow us to a place that is safe and free. I longed to comply and definitively renounce the world. But something in me still resisted and clung to the earth.

Christmas came again. Elizabeth and Daniel had gone to the Midwest with Stan to visit his parents for the hol-

136

idays. I was left with few obligations to the real world. One of them was to grade a handful of papers from the academic semester that had just ended. During the morning and afternoon, I sat before the study window with the blue books piled up before me, reading essay questions on Plato's cave and Descartes's *cogito ergo sum*, routinely using that disciplined part of my mind that could function virtually on its own. Another part of my mind, however, kept slipping out through the window into a nonrational dimension.

After grading some exams each day, I would go shopping. I shopped with compulsion, moving determinedly from store to store in search of the perfect gifts for those I loved. They had to be presents surrounded with all the proper magical symbols of completeness, to compensate for its lack in my life now. Nothing less than perfection would do. As I looked and bought, I scrupulously recorded the time of each purchase and its price, hoping to find in their numbers a reassurance of the fitness and propriety of my gifts. Because the stores were open late, I often shopped in the night.

One evening several days before Christmas, I drove to the nearby shopping center. I had seen a pair of Lalique swans in the window of one of the small jewelry stores there, and I felt compelled to return to look at them again. They were exactly like the crystal swan that I had given Dr. Lustig in November, on the anniversary of my first year in therapy. In one of my early therapy sessions, we had talked about fairy tales. I had told him that my story was *The Snow Queen* by Hans Christian Andersen. He had told me that his story was *The Ugly Duckling* by the same writer. So I had brought him a crystal swan at the first opportunity, to remind him of his beauty. The piece I stared at so intently now was the same, only doubled— two swans intertwined. I knew that I did not deserve such beauty, but I derived some comfort from standing in front of the window, and looking at the swans anyway.

As I drove near the thoroughfare of shops that was my destination, I noticed a group of grade-school-age children assembled in the middle of the street. There had been a snowfall the night before, and freshly fallen snow still covered the ground. The children formed a circle, as they crouched down on the deserted, lamplit street. From my car I could not see what was in the center of the circle, but from the children's rapt attention, I knew that it must be something at once fascinating and important. My attention was transfixed by the circle as my car neared the place where they were playing. Just as I drove slowly by them, I caught a glimpse of the children lighting matches, just like the little match girl of the fairy tale, in order to warm their hands and have some light. Matches were strewn all over the street. I drove on, profoundly moved. I lifted my hand to my cheek and felt the tears there, unsurprised but saddened by what I had seen.

I parked the car near the jewelry store where I had seen the swans. Reverentially walking to the window where they were displayed, I stood silently before them, as before a shrine. Maybe someday I can be one of the swans, I thought. It saddened me that I could not be one of them now.

I had been standing there for several minutes, completely unaware of the time, when I glanced around and saw a man in sunglasses about five feet away. He too stood silently on the sidewalk, staring into a neighboring store's window display. I quickly looked away, before my eyes could be drawn into his gaze, feeling the familiar terror rise in my gut. Is he real? I wondered, afraid to know the answer. But why would anyone be wearing sunglasses in the dark? I asked myself.

I ducked into the jewelry store and approached a store clerk, a nice-looking young woman with an open, friendly, freckled face. "How much are the Lalique swans in the window?" I asked her. She went to look at the piece and returned with the price. "It's fifty-nine ninety-five," she told me. Too much, I thought, as I carefully recorded the price and the time next to it on my shopping list. "Swan— $59.95—6:49 P.M.—Monday, 12/22/75." Somehow the numbers will tell me what will happen, I thought, although I did not define to myself just exactly what it was that I expected.

I left the jewelry store and, worried about the reappearance of the man in sunglasses, glanced around me. Seeing no one, I walked automatically back to my car. I drove home to a darkened house. Dully switching on the lights inside, I realized how weary I was, as if my body had stolen some of the tiredness away from my mind.

I went directly to my bedroom, switched on the television, then got undressed and plopped into bed. My watch said it was only 7:32. Drowsily, I began to watch the flickering screen. An episode of *Star Trek* was playing. Then something happened that, in its simplicity, seemed stranger and more terrible than all the demons that had been gathering. I entered a timewarp. I was a teenager again, and my mind was perfectly normal. No madness, no Dr. Lustig, no dreams had ever happened. No therapy, no struggle, no pain, no twisted thoughts. An earlier, completely normal perspective had been restored. I had no recent history; the slate was wiped clean. Nothing that has happened to me during these last years has been real, I thought. The clarity of this perspective was frightening, abolishing as it did my recent past and, in so doing, annihilating *me*. It seemed the final irony, the final trick— that to be clear-eyed about reality, I must deny myself.

I turned off the TV and curled myself into a protective ball in my bed. I lay there for some time, feeling myself drowning. It felt as if I had been underwater for a very long time and my breath was almost spent. I wanted to struggle to the surface, but something unknown and unperceived seemed to hold me beneath the water against my will. I clawed my way about frantically, losing all sense of orientation and direction. Even if I had wanted to surface, I did not know which direction to follow. Where is up? I asked myself. Finally, I let a partial breath out, and watched carefully as the bubbles moved away from me. They shot out to my right. That must be the way to the surface, I thought, and started swimming furiously in that direction. Just as the blackness of asphyxia began to creep over my consciousness, I felt myself emerge from the water and break free. I took a deep breath, feeling an enormous gratitude for the air. I will survive, I thought, as I drifted into sleep.

Chapter 3

On January 2, Stan's thirty-sixth birthday, the children returned home from their Midwest Christmas vacation with their father. When I saw them get off the plane, my heart lightened. I grabbed them and hugged them to me, grasping after their physical solidity and presence, as if they were two small planets of sanity in the midst of a chaotic solar system where the sun was falling apart. I held on to them and begged God to let me become a whole sphere myself, that they could depend on me, as children ought.

But my plea was not immediately granted. I found, in the days ahead, that even the children's presence at home, calling me back to the world of practical affairs, was not enough to defeat the army of illusion and unreality that had me fast in its grip. The sunglasses people continued ﹖ my frequent and silent visitors, now on occasion even appearing when I was with my children. Those times were the worst, for then my visions posed a direct threat to my functioning as a mother. At those times, I would turn my eyes away from the alien beings, assiduously ignoring their intrusion. Since the children did not see them, we could continue as if nothing had happened. But inside I would know the nature of my peril, the power of

140

that alien call. Each time I resisted them and turned my attention back to the children, I wondered whether the next time I would have the strength.

The turning point came in mid January, when I attempted to resume my teaching responsibilities in addition to caring for the children. It was then that my functioning ultimately faltered and failed.

It was the first day of the new teaching semester, and I was scheduled to meet with two new classes. I was confused and nauseated and filled with dread. How could I stand up in front of a classroom of youthful, eager students and outline a rational program of philosophy for the semester? How could I tell my students about Plato, caught as I was in the blinding sunlight outside the cave?

Years of self-discipline came to the fore. I will go to my classes and get through them at whatever price, I told myself. So I dressed, made breakfast, and readied the children for the babysitter, all the while trying to steady myself. After what seemed an eternity, although it must have been only an hour, the babysitter arrived and I was free to leave the house. By 10:30 I was on the campus and walking toward my assigned classroom building. I had never taught in this building before, and everything about its modern appearance seemed sterile and strange. Bracing myself, I ordered my feet to march forward and up the three flights of stairs. They obeyed, and soon I had arrived at Room 303, where I was scheduled to teach an introductory course at 11:00 A.M.

I walked to the desk at the front of the room, and registered the look of surprise on the students' faces that I had come to expect. "She's younger and prettier than we thought," I could almost hear them murmur to themselves. I smiled automatically at the students, and then began shuffling through my papers and notes for the class.

Suddenly, the terror surfaced. Nausea swept over me. Fiery hands ran up and down my arms. It was time to begin, but I could not move. I glanced at the students. They looked at me expectantly. I looked away. I must go home, I thought. I am not well. I looked back at the students, who were beginning to rustle in their seats. I stood up and walked to the first row of chairs facing me. Making my voice as composed as possible, I spoke.

"I'm sorry," I told them, "but I'm feeling quite ill. I'm afraid I'll have to cancel class today." So saying, I hurried from the room.

Overwhelmed by a sense of failure, of having let everyone down, I stumbled down the hallway, through the doorway, and across campus to my car. With terror now compounded by guilt, I started the engine and shifted the transmission into drive.

Missing one class won't matter, I tried to persuade myself. I *will* be able to keep going. I *will* teach my classes. And so resolving, I drove directly to Dr. Lustig's office. As I drove I was aware of gliding through red traffic signals—three in all. I must stop, I told myself. The red lights are telling me to stop.

Arriving unscathed and unarrested at Dr. Lustig's office, I sat down in the waiting room and tried to compose myself. An ebb tide seemed to have caught me up, pushing me farther and farther out to sea. Dr. Lustig seemed to be the only person who noticed my fate. I saw him standing at the water's edge with a life preserver in his hands, alertly ready to throw me a line. Once or twice, I could almost hear him shout, "Carol, don't go too far out. I must be able to pull you back to shore."

I looked at my watch. It was 2:35. The door to his inner room was closed, indicating that he was seeing another patient. Five minutes, then ten minutes passed. I began to feel frightened at the thought of seeing him. He'll think badly of me, I worried. If he finds me here in the middle of the day, he'll know that I'm not doing what I'm supposed to. He'll be disappointed in me; he'll know that I'm a failure.

But he's here to help you, another side of me argued. Just tell him what happened, and he'll help you.

He'll be angry, something in me countered. He told me that he would try to keep me functioning and out of the hospital. I failed him this morning. If I go to the hospital, I make him a failure too.

Then my mind went blank. I must go, I thought. I fled Dr. Lustig's waiting room.

I got back into my car and drove the block and a half

home. The babysitter was still out for a walk with the children. I went through the quiet house to the storage closet where we kept our suitcases, and grabbed one automatically. Carrying it, I walked directly to my bedroom. I began pulling out clothes and methodically placing them into the suitcase.

I must go to the hospital was my only thought. Once the suitcase was packed, I walked to the study, picked up the phone, and dialed Dr. Lustig's number.

"Dr. Lustig," I heard him say.

I was silent.

"Hello, Dr. Lustig speaking," he said. Still I could not speak. Dazed, and with infinite sorrow, I hung up the phone.

To ease my panic I reached for my medicine bottle. I had found myself taking more and more medicine lately, often at irregular intervals, when the numbers were auspicious or when they foreshadowed doom. But even these measures were not enough. The medicine itself had begun playing tricks on me. I couldn't be sure if I was taking the proper amount. Was I taking too little, or was I taking too much? Too little, and the terror and pain prevailed; too much, and the fog and confusion rolled in. So I played games with the medicine, worrying and guessing over each dose, but taking steadily more until I was so surrounded by fog that I could not remember how much I had taken. My confusion had become so great that I lost track of the number of pills that I was swallowing, although I knew I was taking several each time. But the fact remained that I could no longer trust even my medicine.

The babysitter soon returned with the children. I felt myself moving in slow motion as I prepared their supper, settled them in front of the television, and later got them ready for the night. At eight o'clock when Stan arrived to see the children, I asked him if he would put Elizabeth and Daniel to bed that evening. I gave him no explanation, just walked apathetically toward the bedroom and got into bed without undressing. Stan followed me into the bedroom, concern on his face.

"Is everything all right?" he asked worriedly.

"No, it's not," I answered wearily. "But I'm too tired to talk about it, okay?"

"Okay," Stan replied, and then, turning, uncertainly left the room. "I'll lock the door as I leave, after the children are asleep," he called to me as he left.

I simply buried my head in the pillow and slept.

The next day, Friday, I did not have to teach. I had an appointment with Dr. Lustig. I stumbled toward his office, my feet mechanically following one another across the shopping center and up the stairs. After I sat down in his waiting room, an indescribable tiredness crept over me. My head could not be held upright. Of its own accord, it fell down toward my chest. Gravity folded my body into a ball and my arms clutched one another in sympathy and support. I silently remained in this position until Dr. Lustig came to the door of his inner office and told me to come in. Slowly rising to my feet, I dully followed him into the inner office and sat down in my chair. My head still hung low; my hands still clutched my arms. I could not look at him.

Registering the extent of my distress, he did not begin the session in his usual manner.

"We're going to do something different today," he said. "Do you see that plant over there?" He paused, gesturing toward the large rubber plant that stood in the corner, behind my chair. I looked up at him with a dazed and confused expression, and nodded. What is he doing? I wondered. Still I did not speak.

"Will you help me care for that plant?" he asked gently.

I didn't move, so he continued, "I'd like you to help me clean and polish the leaves."

He got up, took some cloths from his closet, and approached the plant. Slowly and gently he began to wipe its leaves, one by one.

Still I did not move. I had turned my head just enough to observe out of the corner of my left eye what he was doing. I watched him as if he were a person from another planet whom I was observing on a television screen.

When I still did not move of my own accord, he gave me more explicit instructions.

"Come over here and stand by the plant," he said calmly.

I obediently got up from the chair and haltingly moved

toward him, until I was standing just a few inches from him and the plant.

He extended the cloth toward me. "Now take this cloth," he said gently and firmly. "Take the cloth and wipe each leaf clean like this." As he spoke, he ever so carefully grasped one of the broad leaves with his left hand, while his right hand wiped the dust from its surface.

I followed his lead and began methodically wiping the leaves, one by one. I felt my movements to be jerky, as if my nerves and muscles were disconnected. Since it was a large plant that reached almost to my height, our cleaning continued silently for the next half hour.

Finally, we were finished. I had found our task very soothing. I felt that I, like the plant, had been dusted and cared for and wiped clean.

We returned to our seats and I found that I could talk quietly.

"I'm so tired," I sighed lifelessly.

"Of what?" he asked softly.

"Of fighting to stay together," I replied.

Then I remembered the dream I had had last night, a voice that had urged me to go to the hospital to get away from Marion. I pushed the thought aside, wanting so much to prove that I could cope.

"How much medicine are you taking?" he asked.

I told him that I couldn't remember.

He took one of his cards and scribbled briefly on it. "Take the medicine only as I've written it," he instructed, handing me the card.

I nodded dumbly.

After seeing Dr. Lustig, I went home and unpacked my bag. I'll make it without going to the hospital, I said to myself. Once again, I resolved to keep performing my duties. Once again I resolved to go the next Tuesday and teach my classes.

By Tuesday morning, January 20, however, the mental fog of confusion and unreality had again moved in. Struggling against the terror that the prospect of standing in front of a class now produced within me, I dressed and set out for the college.

Again, I made my way to the appointed classroom. A few students were already at their places; others were ambling in. I sat down at the desk in the front of the classroom, bracing myself for the ordeal.

Today I'll be able to do it, I told myself. To be certain of that fact, I had brought the red stone that Dr. Lustig had given me on my last birthday, which I had reclaimed from his crystal bowl. It was a symbol that I had imbued with magical powers, a talisman that would not allow any other occult forces to take hold of me. So long as I can hold on to this stone, I told myself, no harm can come to me.

I took the stone out of my purse and, clutching it tightly in my right hand, stood up to begin the class. I began telling the students about philosophy—how it was a rigorous discipline with its own language, questions, issues, and fields of investigation. How, as a discipline, it little resembled "philosophy" in the common sense meaning of the term. I continued lecturing, outlining some of the philosophers and issues that we would be discussing.

For the first five minutes of my talk, all was well. My stone is protecting me, I thought as I proceeded. Then suddenly, the stone turned on me. It became hot, scorching the flesh of my right hand. I clutched it more tightly, and it became a piece of burning coal. The pain that had begun in my hand now began to travel up my arm. I was on fire.

I stopped speaking abruptly in midsentence, gulped, and tried to continue. But no more sounds came out of my mouth. I was paralyzed. I'm going crazy, I thought. The stone continued to eat into my flesh.

"I'm sorry," I found myself saying to the students. "I'm afraid that I am still feeling rather ill. If you'll excuse me, I must go."

I fled the room, still clutching the burning stone. The good magic has finally betrayed me, I thought. Once outside the door of the classroom, I opened my right hand and, prying it away with my left, threw the stone into my purse. The burning stopped abruptly.

I must go to the hospital, I said to myself as I drove home. There's no other choice. Suddenly I knew I must trust my dream. I would only escape the madness and

Marion by going there. A calm came over me. I knew that my decision was correct and final. Finally, I would rest.

I may die there, I thought, but I was too tired to care. The thought of death was not an unpleasant one. Perhaps, after all, it's as Plato said in the *Phaedo*—death is but a sleep undisturbed by bad dreams. Arriving home, I walked resolutely to my bedroom and, one final time, packed my bag for the hospital. Then I called Dr. Lustig on the phone. I waited till the hour, so that I would not disturb him if he was with another patient.

"I must go to the hospital," I said calmly, with resolve in my voice. "I'm sorry, but I must go," I repeated.

"Yes," he said quietly. "I'll make the arrangements. Will Stan or someone else be able to drive you there, once everything is arranged?"

"Yes," I said flatly.

"I'll call you back, after everything is in order," he said.

"Thanks," I said, and carefully replaced the phone on the hook.

Next I called Stan. "I have to go to the hospital," I told him over the phone. "Will you come over and take me there?"

"I'll be right home," he said, as if he had momentarily forgotten that he no longer lived there.

I went into the living room and sat down on the couch to wait. The children were still outside with the babysitter. I knew that Stan would take care of them while I was gone. I pushed the thought of the children out of my mind. Leaving them was too painful to think about.

The phone rang jarringly. I moved tiredly toward it.

"Hello," I said in a tired semblance of my ordinary voice.

"It's Elaine," I heard my friend say. "Is everything all right? You don't sound like yourself."

"Elaine, I have to go to the hospital," I said flatly.

"I didn't realize you were sick," Elaine replied sympathetically. "Is it for tests, or what?"

I realized that she didn't understand the kind of hospital I meant.

"A psychiatric hospital," I muttered. "My doctor agrees that I have to go."

"Those damned psychiatrists," Elaine began angrily, and then stopped herself. I knew what she was thinking. I understood her total incredulity, since I had so assiduously kept the truth from her. But I was too tired now to dissemble. I wanted her to know the worst.

"I have to go, Elaine," I said quietly and calmly. "I was driving back from the college Thursday, and I ran three red lights. I know it's time for me to stop."

There was a considerable pause at the other end of the line, as if Elaine was suddenly realizing the extent and nature of the problem. "Were the kids in the car?" she asked quietly. I told her they were not.

"Well, maybe it *would* be a good idea for you to go into the hospital *for a rest*," she finally said.

"What will you do with the children?" she continued. "Can I help take care of them?"

"Thanks, Elaine, but no," I said. "Stan will take them."

"He certainly ought to take some responsibility at this point," Elaine retorted, and then, collecting herself, continued more mildly. "Please let me know if there's *anything* I can do," she told me. "I'll be in touch with Stan, and if you'd like, I'll visit you. Don't worry. Remember, we all love you."

"Thanks, Elaine," I said. "Goodbye." I set the receiver gently back on the hook, and reseated myself on the couch.

The phone rang again. It was Dr. Lustig. "I've arranged for you to go to the sanitarium," he said. "It's a private hospital, the best in the area. Dr. William Otto, a colleague that I know and trust, will treat you while you're there."

"Can't *you* take care of me there?" I asked.

"Only psychiatrists who are members of the staff can treat patients there," he replied. "And I'm not one of them. But I *will* visit you."

"But you're my doctor," I protested feebly, suddenly feeling abandoned.

"Carol, I've done everything I could to prevent your downward spiral, but nothing has worked recently. It would benefit both of us if a different doctor were to assess you *and* your treatment. Please allow it. I'll be in close contact with Dr. Otto, and will reserve your regular appointment times here, for when you return. Please understand."

"Okay," I assented sorrowfully.

"Thanks," he replied.

"Who will be taking you to the hospital?" he resumed after a moment's silence.

"Stan."

"Well, have him call me when he gets to the house," he said.

"I will," I answered with finality. "Goodbye."

"You'll be all right," he told me firmly.

"Yes," I replied, not really caring one way or the other. "Goodbye," I said again and hung up the phone.

A few minutes later, Stan arrived. He looked very distressed. He was also angry. Anger was the way he sometimes expressed his concern. Almost immediately after walking into the room, he began speaking in an irate tone.

"Have you thought about the insurance! You know, this could be very expensive. Have you made sure that our insurance policy covers this kind of thing?" He spoke as if I were an irresponsible child. When I did not immediately reply, he continued challengingly. "Well, have you thought about it?"

Stan and I were standing on opposite sides of the living room. As he was speaking, I looked into the large square mirror that hung over our fireplace mantel behind him. I saw a face in agony. Strain had furrowed its forehead; the cheeks were sunken; the eyes were glazed. It had the pallor of the walking dead.

Suddenly I could not endure it anymore. I looked again at the face in the mirror, then I looked at Stan. I became hysterical. I began screaming.

"I have to go to the hospital," I shrieked at him. "I have to leave my babies...I may die there...and you are talking to me about *insurance*?" I began to cry in great gasping sobs.

My outburst startled Stan. "Okay, okay," he said, trying to calm me down. "I'll take you to the hospital." He reached out to touch my arm, but I recoiled.

Stan and I both lapsed into silence, while we each composed ourselves. Finally, I felt my hysteria pass.

"What about the children?" I asked.

"I'll take care of everything," he replied sincerely. "You just take care of yourself."

Then he told me that he wanted to speak to Dr. Lustig. He walked into the study to place the call. I remained seated where I was, letting my mind go blank. I didn't even remember Dr. Lustig's instruction to have Stan call him.

About half an hour later we were ready to leave. Stan picked up my suitcase and led me out the front door. By 6 P.M., we were driving through the darkness to the sanitarium. Neither of us spoke on the way.

Chapter 4

Entering the lobby of the sanitarium was like stepping back a half century in time. Ornate chandeliers hung from the high ceiling; a grand curving staircase swept upward to the left. Finely crafted period furniture was placed elegantly and comfortably in discrete conversation areas throughout the large room. Potted plants brought a touch of green and life to the softly modulated color scheme, while elaborately carved moldings graced the walls and ceilings. All together, the impression was one of a grand hotel rather than a mental hospital.

Stan and I approached the receptionist. We were told to take a seat nearby, and wait for someone to come and receive us.

I looked around dazedly. The room was reassuring. No barred windows or other signs of imprisonment marred its beauty.

"You'll take care of the children?" I again asked Stan searchingly.

"Of course."

"Will you bring them to visit me?"

"Certainly. You're their mother."

We sat in silence until a brisk-looking young man, dressed in a business suit, approached us.

"Allen?" he asked.

"Yes," Stan and I both said at once.

"I'm Dr. Phillips," he said, shaking our hands. "Follow me, please."

He led us across the large lobby and down a corridor to the left. Soon we were seated in an office, he behind a desk, and we on a sofa to the side. Several comfortable chairs remained empty in front of his desk.

He shuffled through some papers and then addressed me. "Let's see," he said. "You are Dr. Otto's patient?"

"Yes," I mumbled.

"All right," he continued. "Now, can you tell me why you're here?"

I found it difficult to frame the words. Words had become slippery and would not stay still. A thought would flicker across my mind, but before my tongue could form its sound, the word's meaning would melt into another meaning, and from there to yet another thought. I tried to speak, but I knew I was rambling.

"I can't go on. . . . I said in the barest whisper. "The children . . ." Guilt swept over me, and I began to cry. "I had to come to the hospital. . . ." I said pleadingly through my tears, trying to justify my action in leaving Elizabeth and Daniel. "I'm so tired and afraid. I had no choice." I fell silent. I could hear the doctor's pen scratching on his pad.

"Do you know where you are?" Dr. Phillips asked me, when I did not continue.

"Of course," I replied, affronted. "I'm at the sanitarium."

"Do you know what day it is?" he continued.

"Yes, it's Tuesday, January twentieth," I replied, collecting my thoughts.

"Then could you explain to me again the events that led up to your hospitalization?" the young doctor asked.

I remembered the eyes of the sunglasses people and how they stared. I remembered how I had run through three red lights, to tell myself that this madness must stop. There was so much to explain. "My mind is betraying me," I finally answered. "I can no longer trust it, and I am afraid I will die."

"Are you afraid you're going to kill yourself?" Dr.

Phillips spoke impassively, as if bored with yet another admission.

"Of course not." I answered stiffly, wondering why this fact was not readily apparent to him.

After a few moments, a few more scratches on his note pad, Dr. Phillips shifted his line of inquiry.

"I'm going to tell you several sayings," he explained. "There isn't any one right meaning for them. Just tell me what they mean to you."

I nodded.

"Ready?" he asked. I nodded again.

"A rolling stone gathers no moss."

I tried to think. "I guess it means that everything changes," I said.

He nodded approvingly. "Okay, what about this one: People in glass houses shouldn't throw stones."

I looked at him intently. That one seemed so obvious. "Everything is so fragile," I said softly. "Everything is so likely to be broken."

"Fine," Dr. Phillips said, busily recording what I had said. "Now," he continued after a pause, "do you ever see things that you aren't sure are there, or perhaps hear voices near you, but when you look around nobody is there?"

"Yes," I confessed. "About seeing things, that is." I felt I had to clarify. "I never heard voices or anything like that."

"What did you see?" he continued matter-of-factly.

I froze. I couldn't tell him about the sunglasses people. My mind went blank. When I didn't reply, he didn't insist. He jotted down some more notes, and then, sifting through some papers, took one out and handed it to Stan.

"Will you sign her in?" he asked, addressing Stan.

"No!" I said emphatically. "I'll sign myself in." It was a matter of principle and pride. If I have to go to a hospital, I thought, then at least I'll do so voluntarily. I will have final control over what happens to me.

"I'll sign the papers," I repeated more calmly.

"All right," the young doctor said, and he handed me a form. "This will be for thirty days," he explained and pointed to the line where I was to sign my name.

The formalities completed, he called in an aide who took my suitcase.

"Why are you taking my suitcase?" I anxiously asked him.

"It's just part of our admission procedure," he answered imperturbably. "They'll check its contents and label your clothing, so that it doesn't get mixed up with anybody else's while you're here."

"But the swan," I said, "I must have my swan."

Over the Christmas holidays, I had found a glass swan, larger and less delicate than the crystal swan that I had given Dr. Lustig. It had cost three dollars. The swan had brought me comfort during these last weeks. I had carefully packed it in my suitcase, along with a picture of my children, when I readied myself for the hospital. These symbols were my only links to Dr. Lustig, my children, and the outside world.

"Please," I said to the young doctor, "I know it's glass, but please can I keep my swan?"

"All of your things that aren't dangerous to you will be brought to your room," he answered noncommittally.

I nodded and didn't say anything more.

Dr. Phillips rose from his chair. "You'll be staying on the third floor," he said. "Follow me and I'll take you there."

Stan and I followed him down the corridor to an elevator at the end of the hall. We entered and he pushed the button for the third floor. The elevator hummed as it rose.

We stepped off the elevator into a small lobby. Directly in front of us, protruding into the lobby area, was a small sitting room with glass panels on the two adjacent sides facing us. "That's what we call the Fishbowl," the young doctor explained. "It's where we have group therapy sessions."

I nodded, wondering why group sessions should be held in glass rooms. To the right of the Fishbowl was a closed door with a glass peephole at eye level. Dr. Phillips pressed the buzzer to the left of the door, and an attendant unlocked it from the inside.

We walked through, into a large common room. Aside from the one locked door, there were no signs of security.

Comfortable couches and chairs were placed in the sitting area. A few patients, of all ages and both sexes, were sitting and talking or walking around, mostly in groups of three or four. The room had bright modern furniture and a cheerful look, with light yellow walls and a number of windows looking out onto the night.

A pleasant-looking black woman, dressed in street clothing, approached us smiling.

"I'm Mrs. Jones," she said. "I'm the administrator for this floor." She smiled at me reassuringly, and then, putting her arm loosely around my shoulders, she added, "but you can call me Edith. Everyone does."

"I'll see to Carol now," she said turning to Stan. Stan looked like he didn't know quite what to do or say.

"I hope you feel better," he said hesitantly, as if he recognized the inadequacy of his words. Then, he leaned over and gave me a kiss on the cheek. He followed the young doctor out.

Mrs. Jones, Edith, led me across the large communal room and down a hall. I looked into the rooms on each side of the corridor as we passed them. They looked pretty much like sparsely furnished hospital rooms, although ordinary beds took the place of high-railed hospital ones.

We came to a room near the end of the hallway, and Edith told me it was my room. It had a single bed, and a dresser with a mirror above it, although I had noticed that in some rooms we had passed, the mirrors had been removed. On the far side of my room, a door stood open leading to a small bathroom.

Edith sat down on the chair in front of the dresser and motioned me to sit on the bed.

"Now," she said brightly, "I have just a few questions to ask you. It's just part of our procedure," she explained somewhat apologetically. "It won't take long, and then you can get to sleep."

It was clear to me from the first question that she was administering some kind of psychological test.

"Which do you like best, cats or dogs?" she asked.

That's a question about male and female, I thought. "I like them both a lot," I answered carefully.

"What do you do when you're happy?" she asked.

"I laugh," I answered.

"What do you do when you're sad?" she continued.

"I cry."

Although the questions struck me as very transparent, I continued answering them patiently until she was through.

"I guess some of these questions are kind of silly," she said, as she finished the last question. I smiled reassuringly at her. I liked her.

"Your clothes probably won't be up until sometime tomorrow," she explained. "I'll get you a gown to wear for tonight."

"Thanks," I said. "I *am* very tired."

Just then, there was a commotion in the hall outside my door. I glanced toward the door to see what was happening, but Edith took my arm and pulled me back gently.

"That's just Debbie," she said. "She has to be restrained sometimes. Unfortunately," she continued, "the seclusion room is the next one over. Ordinarily we don't put anyone back here in this room, but we're full. We'll move you to a room up front as soon as we can. For now," she said, "if you hear anything, just ignore it. Nobody will harm Debbie, but she may scream a bit. I hope it doesn't disturb your sleep."

I nodded dumbly, trying to ignore the muffled shrieks from the adjoining room. Through the uproar, I heard several voices talking patiently. Surprisingly, the ruckus did not particularly alarm me. Terror lay in the world outside; pain within, I could comprehend.

A few minutes after Edith left, another young doctor came by. He introduced himself as Dr. Sutton, the resident on the floor, and seated himself on the lone chair. He had a very friendly, open face, and seemed to take his job of reassuring me very seriously. We chatted pleasantly for quite a while, he asking me questions about how I felt, and nodding sympathetically to all that I said. Some of the sadness that I was feeling must have come through my somewhat rambling conversation, because he said at one point, "You're very sad, aren't you? I can really *feel* your sadness."

"Yes," I replied, warming to the calm concern and understanding in his voice.

After about half an hour, Edith reappeared with a hospital gown for me to wear, and Dr. Sutton said goodbye and left. Somewhere in my mind, I again registered the sounds of distress coming from the seclusion room. I hadn't heard them while I was talking with Dr. Sutton.

I put on the hospital gown and got into bed. I lay quietly, all feeling spent. I knew that I was finally alone. Alone and locked inside my mind. No place for people here. No place for fears or human tears. Locked away. Locked away, alone.

"Sleep, my child, and peace attend thee, all through the night." The melody of the lullaby ran through my mind.

My neighbor was still screaming as I fell into an exhausted sleep.

Chapter 5

I woke early the next day. I lay still with my eyes closed for a few minutes, letting the memory of where I was seep slowly into my consciousness. The sanitarium. The place where I would go and die. I had always thought of it as the end of a story, the place where one went after final defeat. But, I reflected after my night's sleep, perhaps, after all, it's a place of rest and not death, a place of order and not defeat.

I opened my eyes and looked around the sparsely furnished room. No sounds were coming from the hall or the seclusion room next door. Either the woman there last night had been removed or she was asleep, I concluded. Either way, she was safe.

I rose slowly, feeling the familiar dull ache in my limbs. With careful attention, I got dressed in the same clothes I had worn the night before. I wondered when breakfast would be served, and whether the patients ate alone in their rooms as in a regular hospital, or whether there were communal meals.

I wandered out of my room in search of information. As I passed the adjoining room, I glanced through the glass peephole of the closed door. I saw a girl of about fifteen wrapped up tightly and bound to the bed. Her face was turned toward me, so I could see that she slept. I remembered the screams of the night before, but I still felt no particular alarm.

I continued past the room into the long corridor. Nobody was about and the hallway was darkened, so I guessed that it was still very early. As I approached the large common room, a male attendant whom I had not seen before approached me. I asked him about breakfast and he pointed to the adjoining dining room, where, he said, all meals were served. Breakfast was at seven o'clock, he explained. By his watch it was now a quarter to six.

I sat down on one of the couches to wait. He sat down comfortably near me and started chatting with me about the weather and himself. He was on the night staff, he explained, and was due to be relieved soon. Then he planned to go home and get some sleep, and do a little shopping later in the day. His ordinary prattle put me quite at ease, although I said little, still feeling too dazed to talk.

Soon, other patients drifted out of their rooms, many shuffling sleepily, and assembled in the common room to await breakfast. Then a bell sounded and everyone went into the dining room to be served.

The dining room was filled with small square tables, each seating four people. I was placed at one of the tables near the door, with two other women. My first cursory glance at the woman on my right startled me somewhat, so I turned my full attention to the woman seated on my left. She seemed to be about my age and was casually dressed. She smiled pleasantly at me, and I returned her smile, wondering, as I looked at her perfectly ordinary demeanor, why she was here.

Then I glanced again at the woman on my right. She was disheveled in her loose-fitting white hospital gown, which barely concealed her sagging shape. Her hair was a tangled mass of gray. She had a look of total confusion and alarm, like that of some wild animal cornered in an unexpected trap, uncomprehending of the nature of its constraint.

From my glimpse, it was clear to me that she had lost the world—her tongue flickered in and out of her mouth; saliva dribbled down her chin; the power of ordinary

speech escaped her. From time to time throughout the
meal, she would ramble in her own invented language—
punctuated with words like "doggy" and "wolf." She wore
long, baggy, red wool socks that she would continuously
roll down, take off, and then put on again, as if she was
performing some ancient and private ceremony.

Oddly enough, I was little disturbed by this sight of
madness *in extremis*. The sober reality of life here, with
even such as this, was altogether less terrible than my
own self-imposed tyranny. I had lived with invented, staring, black-eyed strangers. I had been governed by the
magic of numbers and occult noncausal laws. This disheveled woman's countenance had no power to alarm me.
January in this modern, humane mental hospital was benign
compared to most of my December days.

In fact, it was a relief to see insanity surface so openly.
When madness intrudes into a normal setting, it has the
power to provoke panic in all but the stoutest heart. In
the broad daylight of a well-governed midtown street, one
instinctively recoils at raving street people, as if turning
away from some minor, if private, embarrassment. But
within the world of the asylum, where it was legitimate
to be insane, I found it somehow also fitting that madness
be displayed. Here its public appearance resembled a mirror held up to the darkness, bridging the division between
what was outside myself and what was within. At last,
madness, that most private of all experiences, had a public
and easily discernible face.

Slowly, I turned my attention back to the ordinary-
appearing woman on my left, who introduced herself as
Ellen. Martha, she explained, indicating our dining companion, had been in the sanitarium for the last twenty
years. Ellen spoke about Martha as if Martha weren't
there, a custom that, I discovered, was commonplace at
the sanitarium, where ordinary rules of politeness gave
way to more direct statements of fact.

Just then Martha howled angrily, and in a single force-
ful gesture swept her cereal bowl off the table onto the
floor. An attendant hurried over and cleared away the
mess, all the while speaking calmingly to Martha. Then
Martha was led away.

I watched and listened as these events took place, and

found that my assessment of my own mental condition was rapidly gaining some perspective. I could see myself as located somewhere in the center of a continuum—as far away from Martha as I was from normal. I found that meeting Martha made me feel less mad.

Ellen and I chatted about hospital procedures as we continued to eat our meal. The patients, she told me, filled out menus for each day on the evening of the preceding day. There was a daily morning meeting after breakfast for all the patients and staff, at which attendance was required.

As we talked, I noticed the medications nurse making her rounds of all the dining room tables, stopping to chat with each person as she administered the medicine. Although her manner was casual, I noticed that she watched carefully to see that each patient swallowed the pills.

She approached our table and handed me three tablets, one of which I did not recognize. Stories of hospital patients being drugged or overmedicated flooded through my mind. I looked again at the three pills lying in her outstretched hand.

"I'm sorry," I told her, politely but firmly, "but I won't take any medicine that I don't recognize." She explained in a patient voice that the pill I did not recognize was just a side effect medication that my attending physician had ordered for me.

I wasn't convinced, and she did not insist. I obediently took the two recognizable tablets. She said that she would speak to my doctor about it, and suggested that I do the same. Then she moved calmly on to the next table.

After breakfast, I followed the other patients out of the dining room into the common room, where everyone was assembling for the daily meeting that Ellen had told me about. I saw patients and staff members alike pulling sofas and chairs together to form a large circle. Ellen and I sat down on one of the couches. Other people filed in and seated themselves. I recognized Edith, the floor supervisor who had gotten me settled the night before, and also the young resident, Dr. Sutton, who nodded and smiled at me from across the room.

Doctors, nurses, attendants, as well as patients, it

appeared, all participated in the daily meeting. Feeling foggy and deadened inside, I simply sat passively and observed what was taking place.

As the meeting progressed, it became clear that various privileges were proffered to the patients within the hospital context—freedom to walk to the snack bar downstairs, freedom to walk outside on the grounds without an attendant. And, it became evident, it was the group as a whole—doctors, nurses, staff, and patients—who granted these privileges.

The first person to speak at the meeting was a youngish man—in his twenties, I guessed.

"I would like to ask for grounds privileges," he said, addressing the group. "I feel that I am now able to be responsible for myself. I've been doing real well all this last week. And Sue," he said, pointing to the woman sitting next to him, "Sue will tell you so too."

Sue spoke. "I have taken Bill around with me for the whole week," she said. "He didn't try to run away or anything. I think he should have grounds privileges." Several doctors, nurses, and patients nodded in affirmation.

"Shall we vote?" Dr. Sutton asked. He appeared to be leading the meeting. "All in favor of granting Bill grounds privileges raise their hands."

Almost all the hands went up, with the exception of several patients who seemed too dazed to comprehend.

"Bill is granted grounds privileges," Dr. Sutton said, smiling his approval. "Congratulations, Bill."

Several people shook Bill's hand. He beamed proudly.

The meeting progressed. There was some dispute among the patients over the hours for viewing television. Another patient claimed loudly and angrily that one of the nurses had given her the wrong medication.

I could see from their faces that the staff took this particular charge very seriously. An investigation would be conducted, it was agreed. A woman in her mid-thirties, short, dark-haired, and gaminlike in appearance, suddenly stood up on one of the coffee tables and began shouting obscenities. A nurse and a male attendant rose and, taking her by the arms, drew her down from the coffee table and back to her seat, all the while speaking quietly and soothingly to her. But she was not appeased. So the same two attendants led her out of the meeting and back to her room.

Another woman stood up and spent five minutes commending the sanitarium. "I've been to many hospitals," she said, "but this is definitely the best of them all." Everyone nodded and appeared gratified at her endorsement.

The meeting was dismissed shortly thereafter. Edith, the floor administrator, approached me and explained that there were various activities, such as art therapy, crafts, and sports, that I might sign up for. I thanked her and told her that, for the moment, I preferred to rest.

Edith nodded sympathetically. "Some of the staff physicians would like to talk with you for a while in the Fishbowl," she told me. "Let's say at about ten-thirty."

I nodded, wondering somewhat uneasily what they wanted to know.

My eyes were bothering me, and I found that I could not read the hands on my watch. I asked Edith to tell me when it was time for the interview. She cheerfully agreed, and then left.

I spent the remaining time in the common room, seated on the L-shaped couch, a spot that seemed to be a popular sitting place for many of the patients. On the coffee table placed at the center of the L was a radio tuned to station WMGK, popularly known as "Magic."

How appropriate, I thought to myself as I listened to the broadcast. A radio station called Magic at the center of a madhouse.

The couches were the focal points of much of the social activity in the large common room. People came and sat for a while and then wandered off, often within the course of several hours making a journey from one seating area to the next, until the entire room had been traversed. The L-shaped couch, however, was the hub of the room. A steady procession of patients vied for the seats there and, if successful, sat for a time, so that it was almost never empty.

As I sat at my station, I appraised my fellow patients. I noticed that there were both men and women on the floor, of all ages and degrees of distress. There was even a young boy, I noted, who appeared to be about nine or ten but who was actually thirteen. The patients leafed through magazines, watched television, or talked quietly for the most part. Many of the women were crocheting, under the supervision of Edith.

I noticed that the patients' conversations were often punctuated by giggles or outright laughter. What can be so funny here? I wondered to myself, feeling too tired for any sort of humor.

At 10:30 Edith came over to me and led me through the locked ward door into the adjoining room called the Fishbowl, and departed with a brief goodbye. Somewhat apprehensively, I sat down. Five or six staff physicians, who appeared to be older and part of the establishment, were assembled to interview me. I looked for a familiar face among them, but found none.

After I had seated myself, one of the gentlemen, as distinguished looking as the others, spoke.

"Carol, we're here to find out some information about you, so that this hospital will be able to help you better."

He waited, and I nodded.

"What events led up to your being here in the hospital, Carol?" he continued in an evenly modulated voice.

I tried to think and be very honest, but somehow the question did not make much sense to me.

"I don't quite understand," I said earnestly. Another doctor to his left tried to explain.

"Why are you here, Carol?"

I thought again for a moment. "Because it is so terrible and I have been so afraid."

A psychiatrist on the opposite side of the room spoke up eagerly. "What was so terrible—why were you afraid?"

"I think I'm losing my mind," I answered, bowing my head.

"What makes you think so?" somebody else asked.

"My mind plays tricks on me," I responded.

"When did you notice that your mind was playing tricks on you?" came from somewhere.

"I'm not really sure. Around Christmastime, I guess."

"What sort of tricks were they?" Again I heard the slight edge of eagerness in the voice across the room.

"Hallucinations," I said.

"What kind of hallucinations and what were they like?" I heard from the right.

I felt panicked. Although they were speaking calmly, I felt that I was surrounded by questions being fired at me from all sides. I couldn't tell these strangers about the sunglasses people, either. What to do?

"I can't tell that to anyone but my own doctor," I said anxiously. "Please," I added, meaning, "Please understand."

They immediately dropped that line of questioning and shifted to questions about my history.

"We'd like to find out something about your background," the most senior-looking doctor said. "Where did you grow up, Carol?"

"Idaho. In a small town," I answered.

"What was your father like?" another doctor inquired.

"He's a good man," I replied. "A rational man, who's very kindly, although somewhat authoritarian. He's somebody who I always felt safe with," I continued musingly.

"What about your mother?"

"She's a dietician who gave up her career to raise her children," I answered. "She's very intelligent, like my dad, and they both encouraged all the children to further their educations and learn all they could about the world."

"What about your brothers or sisters, then?" the doctor on the left asked. "Can you tell us about them?"

I was slowly growing more and more upset. What's wrong with my family and my past? I wondered. I had always thought that they were decent enough, before. Perhaps these doctors can look into my past and know something that I don't know about myself. My answers will only confirm my insanity to them, I thought, feeling even more panicked. If it's all a matter of the past, then there's no hope for me in the future.

"What about your brothers or sisters?" the doctor repeated. I could not speak. Slowly, tears rolled down my face.

"Why are you asking me all these questions?" I implored, crying fully now.

"We're just interested in finding out more about you, Carol," one of the more distinguished-looking doctors said.

"Thank you for telling us. Perhaps you'd like to go and rest now?"

I nodded and slowly rose to go. I left, feeling assaulted and stripped of any protecton. My foundation, which I had always taken for granted, had been impugned. If I could not count on the beneficence of the past, what was there left to trust? The doctors' questions only raised more questions in my mind. Perhaps, I thought, as I walked toward my room, perhaps I've always been crazy. And all these years I've only thought that I was sane. Am I doomed by my past to remain forever mad?

The perspective about myself that I had gained earlier that morning, by seeing the spectrum of madness around me, was quickly evaporating. I could no longer locate myself and my madness on a continuum in the present. The staff physicians had introduced a backward-looking measuring tape, and all its numbers pointed to the past. The immediate, the now, was eclipsed by their careful backward scrutiny. But like Lot's wife, when I looked back, I turned to stone. I was nothing now, because there was nothing *now* that I could do.

I arrived at my room and my mind went blank.

Chapter 6

JANUARY 21, 1976

I didn't remember anything else until Edith, the floor supervisor, arrived at my room to announce lunch. My psychiatrist, Dr. William Otto, whom I had not yet seen, would visit me shortly after the meal, Edith informed me.

I ate my meal in a daze, feeling myself suspended on a wind current somewhere outside my body. I was not connected to anything, neither the activities nor the physical objects in my surroundings. I stared at my knife and fork. They seemed to be alien objects belonging to someone else. I noted absently that Ellen was again seated on my right, but it was as if a glass panel now separated her from me. Martha, the madwoman, was nowhere to be seen. I felt completely alone, having no sense that my isolation was self-imposed.

Following a silent lunch, I quietly seated myself on the central couch, from whose vantage I caught my first glimpse of Dr. Otto about a half hour later. I watched as a tall, attractive-looking man stopped at the front desk and then made his way toward me. He looked as though he was in his mid-forties and was casually dressed in slacks and a bulky turtleneck sweater. He had sharp, pointed features that gave him a slightly raffish look. He wore his hair long and swept to the right, covering his bald spot. However, what most caught my attention was his voice—deep, rich, and resonant. It was like a reverberant call back to the present. His was a voice that I instinctively trusted, although I was prepared to trust him anyway, because Dr. Lustig had told me that I could.

I looked around, wondering where we could hold my therapy session with any privacy. But Dr. Otto answered my question before it had been articulated. "We'll meet in your room," he informed me, motioning me to follow him. I walked a step or two behind him down the corridor, but halfway down he paused so that I could catch up. We walked in step the rest of the way.

Arriving at my room, Dr. Otto closed the door and seated himself on the lone chair, while I sat down yoga fashion on the bed. I looked at him again, and saw that he returned my direct gaze. Scattered thoughts raced through my mind until they coalesced around the Fishbowl interview. I began telling Dr. Otto about my experience with the staff physicians. My alarm poured out of me in a staccato of speech, punctuated by rapid breaths.

Dr. Otto listened attentively and shook his head several times during my narrative. "We'll have no more doctors interviewing you," he said emphatically in his deep bass voice. "I'll see to it. If anyone here starts probing and asking too many questions," he continued, "don't talk to them. Just tell me about it at once."

I took heart from his determination, feeling the strength of the protection he was offering me. I sat still for several minutes after that, just letting the newfound feeling of safety wash over me. Dr. Otto was silent himself, as if he was waiting for me to compose myself. Then, in a rush of words, I began to tell him what was happening to me. I just started in the middle, where I had left off with Dr. Lustig. As I talked, I was vaguely aware that I wasn't making much sense, because my speech was disjointed and I was talking in symbols. I stopped talking abruptly.

"Well, I see that you're eager to do therapy," he said with a slightly raised eyebrow, registering just a hint of irony. Then he told me the first of many stories I was to hear from him during my stay at the sanitarium. That day his story was about a Sufi leader, a wise man, who suddenly one day left his followers without explanation. The

Sufi master walked to the top of a mountain and entered a cave, where he stayed for some days. His followers, puzzled by this behavior, and taking it to be an omen, finally approached him and asked, "Master, what does it mean that you have come to this cave?"

The wise man regarded them in silence for some minutes. Then he spoke. "A Sufi must know when it is time to rest," he said.

I nodded and smiled to myself, glad that Dr. Otto understood so well my need for rest and my right to it. "Yes, I need to rest," I affirmed.

"We'll have plenty of time to do therapy," Dr. Otto continued. "But for now, there are a few practical matters we need to discuss. I understand that you have two children. Who's taking care of them?"

I explained that Stan had taken them.

"What about your job?" Dr. Otto continued. "What have you told them?"

"Nothing," I whispered, shrinking inside, feeling the burden of the outside world pressing in on me again. "I don't know what to do or say about being here."

"Well, you'll have to let them know you're in a hospital, so that they can get a substitute to teach your classes," he said matter-of-factly.

"What if I call and the head of my department wants to visit me?" I said, panicking. "I can't let him see me here."

"Just call him and tell him you're in the hospital, and that you can't have visitors right now," Dr. Otto advised. "You needn't mention which hospital it is. Tell him you'll let him know as soon as possible when you'll be returning to work. You can estimate that it will be probably from two to four weeks. If he wants further information, tell him he can call me."

So Dr. Otto thinks I'll be all right in that amount of time, I thought. He's talking as if this stay is only temporary, not permanent. It was a new thought and the beginning of a different perspective on my hospital experience: a rest within a defined time frame. Suddenly, it did not seem so bad.

Dr. Otto and I talked some more about being in the hospital, and how to use the experience in order to get well. He talked to me as if signing myself in was a very sensible and appropriate thing for me to have done, and that my being here, and working hard with him, would lead me out of the morass and back to even better functioning in the world. He also told me that Dr. Lustig would be visiting me at least once a week. I remembered Dr. Lustig's promise to visit me, and the gladness I felt made me realize the importance of this essential connection with sanity in the outside world.

Before leaving that day, Dr. Otto told me that he would see me as often as possible, and that he thought I could profit from daily therapy sessions.

"This is your chance to get yourself together, without having to cope with all your other responsibilities as well. We'll work together to get you back in shape."

I thanked him, feeling profoundly grateful. His visit left me feeling tired but relieved, reinforcing as it had the fragment of sanity that I possessed.

After Dr. Otto left, I went in search of a telephone to call my department chairman, as Dr. Otto had instructed. One of the male aides agreed to accompany me downstairs, since I was not yet allowed to go alone. As I dialed the number of my department chairman, I was filled with dread. I struggled to compose myself as I heard Father Michaels answer the phone. I told him I was ill and in a hospital, without mentioning which one. He was concerned and eager to help.

"I'll take your classes for you," he offered. "So don't worry about that. And, of course, I'll come and visit you."

"No!" I almost shouted, and then somewhat more calmly repeated. "It's very nice of you, but I'm not allowed any visitors."

"But I'm a priest," he persisted. "They always allow a doctor or priest to visit a hospital patient."

I panicked, wondering what to say. "I really think it would be best if I didn't have any visitors right now," I said. "But thanks anyway. It's very kind of you."

"Well, okay," he said as if he was puzzled and just beginning to feel alarmed.

"Which hospital did you say it was?" he asked.

I took a deep breath, deciding I could not lie to him, hoping he wouldn't have heard of it as I spoke its name.

"Okay," he said noncommittally, and I could not be sure whether he knew now or not. Suddenly, I didn't care.

"You can contact my doctor, if you have any further questions," I said dully. Then I assured him that I expected to be back to work in two to four weeks.

He asked me to call again when I knew more definitely when I would be back.

I hung up relieved. It had been one of the most difficult telephone calls I ever made.

I returned to the ward, accompanied by the aide, went directly to my room, and fell asleep. I must have slept for several hours, because when I woke the winter sky was darkening. I got up, washed my face in the small bathroom, and walked back to the lounge area to inquire about dinner. I was told it would be served at 5:30. I took my watch out, but my eyes were still too foggy to read the time. I asked a nearby patient what time it was. He looked at me blankly. Then I found an aide who told me that it was five to five. Just a half hour till dinner, I thought. I seated myself, once again, on the central couch near the radio. A man and two women were already seated there. I found myself listening to their conversation.

"There's a dance tonight on the second floor," the young man said. "Are you guys going?" As he spoke, he clutched his hands nervously together until his knuckles were white. Then he began wringing them.

"I don't know," said the small middle-aged woman seated to his right. Then she giggled like a schoolgirl.

"Stop doing that with your hands!" the second woman said, addressing the man who had spoken. "You're driving me crazy."

"Sorry," the young man replied sheepishly. He sat on his hands to prevent them from wringing.

Just then, a hulking teenaged boy walked by. He was dressed in shabby jeans and his eyes were opaque, as if he had been heavily medicated. "That's Don," the outspoken woman next to me said loudly, as if she were speaking about someone who wasn't there. "He has no family. His parents deserted him when he was a child. He's been in and out of mental hospitals ever since. Or correctional institutes," she added ominously.

Don started moaning like a dumb, hurting animal. He began flailing his arms around, as if fending off an attack.

"Settle down, Don," the outspoken woman said. "Or you know what will happen."

"What will happen?" I asked her softly.

"They'll give him more medicine," she replied matter-of-factly. "Or if that doesn't work, they'll put him in restraints."

I remembered the crying woman in the room next to mine the night before. I'd better be careful, I admonished myself, without articulating exactly what I had to be careful about.

The dinner bell sounded. We all got up and took our places in the dining room. I sat down at the table that I had been assigned to earlier. Ellen was there. Martha, the woman who spoke her own private language, was still absent.

Ellen and I chatted quietly throughout dinner. After we had established some rapport, I asked her directly why she was there. She smiled somewhat enigmatically. "I tried to kill myself," she said. "They have to send you here if you do that. But I expect to be out in a week or so."

I wanted to ask her why she wanted to kill herself, but I was reluctant to broach what might be a sensitive subject. She continued, however, without further prompting.

"You know that man that visited me today," she said. I nodded. "Well, he's married. I've been seeing him for seven years. He kept promising me that he'd leave his wife and we'd get married. But something always came up to prevent it. I just couldn't stand it anymore. What are you to do?" she concluded philosophically.

"I'm sorry," I said.

"What about you?" she asked me.

"Oh, I was seeing things," I said somewhat vaguely, wondering how much to say. "I'm so tired," I added.

She nodded sympathetically. We didn't talk much for the remainder of the meal, but the silence between us was not unpleasant.

The evening passed much like the rest of the day. My head was foggy, so I didn't do much. I just sat on the couch and let the waves of conversation and interaction sweep over me.

I noticed the nice resident, Dr. Sutton, standing in one corner of the common room talking to several patients. I decided to go over to say hello.

"Hi," I said approaching him, suddenly feeling like an embarrassed schoolgirl.

He looked around nervously, and then spoke to me quickly. "I can't talk to you," he said in a lowered voice. "All the staff physicians have been given strict orders to leave you alone. I'm sorry," he continued, looking genuinely regretful, "but I'm not supposed to speak to you, at least not about anything of substance."

"That's okay," I said reassuringly, glad that Dr. Otto had kept his word so promptly about forbidding any hospital physicians from probing my psyche.

"I just wanted to say hello," I continued. "Maybe we can talk about the weather." It was a feeble sort of joke, but we both laughed anyway. So we stood there and chatted in a friendly manner, for five minutes or so, until Dr. Sutton was called away. Then I returned to the couch.

At around eight o'clock, trays of sandwiches, fruit, cakes, and buttered toast were brought out of the kitchen and placed on one of the dining room tables. "Our nightly snack," one of the patients explained.

I was too tired to eat anything more. I approached one of the staff members, a six-foot-tall black woman named Sally. "Is it all right if I go to bed now?" I asked her.

"Sure, honey," she said. "I'll get somebody to give you your nightly medication early. You go and get changed into your pajamas."

I did as she suggested and then returned to the common room. The medication nurse came over to me and handed me my pills. "I spoke to your doctor," she said. "He agreed to give you just what you're used to."

I looked at the pills in her hand, and sure enough, they were all the familiar ones. "Thanks," I said.

Then I retired to my room, where, curiously enough, I sat down at the dressing table and meticulously set my hair in curlers. I saw nothing absurd about this simple social act, even though I was in an environment that was totally estranged from society at large. It was part of my nightly routine and, without a thought, I continued it throughout my stay at the sanitarium.

In its own way, maintaining my appearance proved to be a means of asserting self-respect. Whereas before, in the outside world, maintaining the appearance of normalcy had been an enormous burden, a mask covering over a darker reality, here it was simply one option among many. Deviations in appearance and behavior were accepted, so that finally I could choose how to look and what to show.

That fact did not change what I did, for I continued to dress and behave within the norm. But it considerably changed how I felt about it. I could choose to present a normal countenance, but I was not *required* to do so. The choice made all the difference.

That night I slept soundly, lulled to sleep by the realization that, at last, I was free to rest.

Chapter 7

JANUARY 23, 1976

The morning of the third day dawned cold and clear. As I opened my eyes, I could see a sunny blur of whiteness through the screened grating of my bedroom window. I sat up in bed, stretched, and looked intently through the window, trying to detect the almost invisible line where the opaque white of the snow-covered ground merged with the slightly more translucent white of the sky. I swung my legs off the bed and felt my stomach rumbling. It was a simple, pleasant feeling of bodily attachment. Once again, my stomach belonged to me.

I carefully got out some jeans and a blouse to put on. My clothes had arrived the day before, in the late afternoon. I had returned to my room to find them all there, neatly labeled with tags bearing my last name. The glass swan was missing, I noted, as I sorted through the clothing, but the glass in the framed picture of my children had been left in its place. Delighted with the picture, but puzzled by the seeming irrationality of the acceptability of one form of glass over another, I had set the photograph up on my dressing table. Now, the smiling faces of my children greeted me.

The children's picture reminded me that today would be an eventful day. Stan was bringing the children to see me shortly after lunch. Later in the afternoon, I was to have a therapy session with Dr. Otto. In addition, Edith had told me that the night before, Dr. Lustig had phoned and said that he would visit me at 6 P.M.

The thought of seeing Elizabeth and Daniel produced mixed feelings in me. Excitement at the prospect of seeing them and holding them near competed with twinges of failure and guilt at having left them behind. My feelings about Dr. Otto were simpler. I looked forward to talking with him. As for Dr. Lustig, he still represented my strongest tie with reality and the hope of health outside these hospital walls.

At breakfast, I found out that another activity also awaited me that day. Edith told me that Dr. Otto had arranged for me to visit the art room following the morning meeting. I explained to her that I still felt too tired to do much of anything, but she assured me that I could just sit there if I liked, that it would be good for me to get off the ward.

At the appointed time, an accompanying staff member unlocked the front door to our ward and escorted me and several others to the building's first floor. We walked through several passages to the room at the end of the corridor.

Entering the art room was like entering a cathedral of light. One entire wall was composed of windows that were two stories high. Sunlight flooded the room. Workbenches were scattered about and the wall was lined with cubbyholes, where bits of handiwork peeked out. There were looms for weaving and, from behind a tall partition, the sound of hammers pounding could be heard. All together, the room was immense, cheerful, and reassuring.

We crossed the room and approached a young, pleasant-looking woman, who was introduced to me as Suzanne, the art therapist. She smiled at me, and suggested that I get a cup of coffee at the table to my left, and then come and sit by her and relax. I did as I was instructed, and found that just being in the room lifted my spirits. I seated myself on a tall stool next to Suzanne. She chatted with me quietly, asking me about my children and interests. I wondered if I was supposed to be doing something, but I didn't raise the subject, being so content just sitting there sipping coffee. We were interrupted from time to time by patients asking for Suzanne's assistance. But it was all very low key and calming.

After about a half hour, when I was feeling very relaxed and a bit better oriented, Suzanne asked me if I wanted to do something that would not be too straining. She suggested making moccasins. I had noticed other patients wearing them, and it seemed like a nice idea to me. Better than basket weaving, I thought with pleasurable irony. She handed me the precut leather pieces, a top and a bottom for each foot. The holes had already been punched out. All I had to do, it appeared, was to lace them up, joining the bottom leather to the top.

I began working intently. At first, I laced slowly, then faster and faster, as if some accelerating inner tempo was driving me onward. I pulled the leather laces tighter and tighter, intent on doing a perfect job.

"Stop being so compulsive—they're all right just as you have them," Suzanne's voice intruded. I looked up astonished, and then I blushed. Ashamed, I abruptly stopped tugging at the strings.

"They're all right as they are," Suzanne repeated in a softer voice. "You're doing just fine." She patted my arm reassuringly. "Don't try so hard," she added. I nodded and went back to work on the remaining moccasin, more slowly and surely, but still feeling embarrassed.

Presently, one of the aides from my floor appeared at the door to take us back. Our time in the art room was over for the day. I had not yet finished my second moccasin, but Suzanne said I could complete it the next time I visited her. Our group returned with the aide to our ward. Back in my room, I flopped down on the bed and rested until lunchtime.

At 1 P.M., just after lunch, another aide came to fetch me. She led me downstairs once again, but in a different direction—to the coffee shop. There I met Stan, Elizabeth, and Daniel. I greeted Stan with a nod and embraced the children excitedly. I took in their appearance at one glance. They looked fit and healthy, if a bit subdued. Elizabeth, particularly, showed uncertainty on her face. Guilt swept over me when I saw that look, but I quickly pushed the feeling aside.

Stan, the children, and I sat down at the Formica-topped table in the snack bar and ordered liquid refreshments for ourselves. I concentrated on talking normally, for I wanted the children to feel that I was all right. I frequently reached out to touch them during the conversation, to reassure myself that they were really there.

As we sat and made small talk, I wondered what Stan had told them about my hospitalization. I wondered if I should say something to them now. But since they asked me no questions and I did not know what to say, I took the easiest course and left the subject alone.

After we had finished our drinks, we got up and walked, hand in hand, toward the central lobby of the building. It appeared that as long as Stan was there with me, I was free to move about the grounds. We walked and chatted idly. As we returned toward the snack bar, I suddenly began to feel overwhelmed. And guilty. I left my babies, I thought. How could I do it? I'm a bad mother. A tear fell onto my cheek. I began to panic. What if I'm still harming them? I looked at them again, trying to compose myself. I stopped walking, and stooping down to their eye level I hugged them to me, as if for the last time.

"I have to go now," I said to Stan without explanation. Kissing the children one last time, I turned and fled back to the ward. The last thing I saw was Stan's startled face watching my retreat.

I went straight to my room and, flopping onto the bed, sobbed and sobbed. I reached out for the children's picture and clutched it to my breast, crying even harder.

The tears had finally dried when Dr. Otto arrived for my therapy session, but my eyes were still swollen and red, and my cheeks sunken. Hollow-eyed, I sat up and regarded him, as he seated himself on the single chair in the room.

"You saw Stan and the kids?" he inquired.

I nodded yes, and began weeping all over again. "My babies..." I cried.

"Your children are not being taken from you, nor you from them," Dr. Otto said. "You're just on vacation here for a while. You're here for the rest cure."

I nodded again, and sobbed out my fears. "I'm a bad mother. I'm harming my children."

Dr. Otto did not seem upset by this revelation. "How did they look?" he asked me. "Did they look well and all right?"

I murmured yes and stopped crying.

"Were *they* distressed at seeing you or at leaving you," he continued, "or was it *you* who was distressed?"

"It was me," I acknowledged. "They looked fine."

"Well, they *are* fine," he said firmly.

Suddenly I was very tired and sad.

"I miss them," I said softly, "but I also know that I must be here. I must rest and get myself together so that I can go back home."

"Yes," Dr. Otto confirmed. "That's right." He smiled at me and I smiled back. "Now rest some more, and take it easy. I'll be back tomorrow," he said.

After Dr. Otto left, I lay down again and slept for the rest of the afternoon. I woke as it was getting dark outside. My eyes were still so blurred that I couldn't read the face of my watch. I felt the urge to record all the day's events and their numbers, in the way that I had throughout the last two months, but almost protectively my eyes prevented me. I went to the dresser drawer anyway and took out a sheet of paper. I picked up the pencil and tried to write, even though I could not read my words. Then, just as abruptly, I stopped. Yes, I thought, I must stop this recording. It really doesn't matter. I pushed the paper and pencil back into the drawer and shut it.

I changed to a nicer pair of slacks and put on new makeup. I was going to see Dr. Lustig soon.

I was still sitting at the dinner table when Dr. Lustig arrived. I saw him enter out of the corner of my eye. Hurriedly pushing my food aside, I got up and went to meet him.

He stood there in his winter coat, all bundled up, looking slightly uncomfortable and unsure of what to do. Then he leaned over and kissed me on the cheek, just as if he were greeting a friend. I was surprised and pleased. Then we went over to the lounge area and sat down on one of the sofas to talk.

He asked me how I was doing. "I feel *so* much better," I said. He regarded me carefully.

"Yes," he said, "I can see that this was the right thing

for you." There was relief in his voice as he spoke. Hearing that relief, I believed as I never had before that he did care and that he had been worried about me. It was such a simple revelation of his humanity, but it touched me more deeply than any other thing he had done.

Just then, Martha, the crazy woman who spoke the unknown language, approached us. After two or three interactions we had become "friends," in the hospital sense of being at ease with each other. She didn't alarm me and, with some animal instinct, she knew it. When she indicated that she wanted them, I would give her cigarettes. I had even become familiar enough with her language and gestures to know a little about what she meant.

She came up to us and stood right in front of me, with her hand outstretched. I didn't have any cigarettes with me. "Go over to Ellen," I told her firmly. "She'll give you a cigarette."

Martha nodded and shuffled over to Ellen.

I turned back to Dr. Lustig. "I'm getting along just fine with the people here," I told him.

"Yes, I can see," he said, and he seemed impressed.

Dr. Lustig stayed and talked with me for about an hour. Then he said he had to go, but that he would return next week. I thanked him for his visit. He still stood at the center of my universe, along with the children. Together, they represented my most essential connection with the outside world.

After Dr. Lustig left, I seated myself on the central couch again and visited with the other patients. One of the aides, Sally, the strapping tall black woman, joined our conversation. Earlier she had told me proudly that she counted as one of the "men" who had to be on the floor at all times, due to her physical strength.

I had liked Sally from the beginning. She was direct and kind and also a believer in astrology. She would guess the patients' signs, and more often than not, she would be right. She read a detailed horoscope each day, and when we confided in her the events or feelings of our day, she would nod knowingly and tell us, "Yes, it was bound to happen that way. It's in the stars." There was something vastly reassuring about Sally and her interpretations. The world, for all its strangeness, she seemed to say, did after all have some rhyme and reason.

That evening, she regarded me with clear observant eyes as she seated herself on the couch.

"Well, Carol," she said, "I've been watching you and I'll bet you're a Pisces."

"Yes," I replied, surprised at the accuracy of her perception.

"Well," Sally continued in a soft southern drawl, "Pisces are very sensitive and intuitive. But occasionally," she added, "occasionally, there's a Pisces that's a strong one too. You're one of those."

I didn't know what to say, but I was very pleased by her remarks.

Shortly after, she invited me to help her make the evening snacks in the kitchen. As a rule, the kitchen was off limits to patients. But I noticed that Sally often enlisted assistants, and that the patients regarded it as an honor to be invited by her to help with the preparations.

"Thanks," I said sincerely, in response to Sally's invitation. So, together, we went into the kitchen, and soon I was making toast and buttering it, and making sandwiches. The routine of this simple domestic duty was very soothing. So was Sally's calm, solid presence.

That evening, I stayed up and had some snacks. When I finally did retire at about ten o'clock, I felt more at peace than I had for a long time. The routine of the hospital—the regularity of the meals, medication, and sleep—had begun to nourish me. The sanitarium had organized my external world for me, so that I could contend better with my internal chaos. Freed from all responsibilities to my children and my job, I could focus all my energies on myself—and have the luxury and time to introduce order there, as well.

I drifted off into a restful sleep.

Chapter 8

The next several days passed uneventfully. I continued to observe the ebb and flow of life at the sanitarium, too divorced from myself to be an active participant, but reassured nonetheless by the activity and camaraderie around me. I began to make friends with some of the patients. Like survivors on a lifeboat, we naturally clung to each other for support, finding the bond of our common situation a considerable adhesive. Although the patients were often blunt about deviations in behavior, they were remarkably reserved, respectful, and discrete about the psyches of their companions. I found that they accepted me, as they did most every newcomer, matter-of-factly and without intrusive questioning. Their manner conveyed that I was there and they were there. That was all there was to it.

And in their own way, many of the patients, except those who had totally lost the world, conveyed a certain human dignity, despite their inner turmoil and failures in functioning on the outside. A prime example was Geraldine. She was a tall, regal personage in her late fifties or early sixties. She had white-tinged gray hair, tied back severely in the fashion of an earlier time.

Geraldine was always meticulously and elegantly

dressed, usually in tailored clothing, with a cameo brooch at her neck. But her uniqueness lay in her self-appointed task. Each day, for the entire length of the day, she would walk up and down the longest corridor, up and down, up and down. When she reached the end of the passageway, she didn't hesitate for a moment, but pivoted gracefully and began her return journey.

Geraldine walked like a queen surveying her troops, with a regal tilt to her head and direct proud eyes. She would nod and smile at the people whom she passed and, often as not, greet them by name. How she learned our names I never knew, but by the third day of my stay she was calling me Carol. Beyond her initial greeting, she never stopped or paused long enough to converse, and it was only if you joined her in her walk that you could hold a conversation with her.

Geraldine's husband was an elderly, solemn gentleman. On his frequent visits to the sanitarium, he would accompany his wife in her endless walk. They rarely spoke to one another as they traversed the length of the hall, but the very manner in which they fell into step suggested an understanding that had no need for words. They would walk in all solemnity for an hour or so, and then her husband would take his leave. When his visits were over, Geraldine would resume her walk alone.

One day, he came to the sanitarium and took Geraldine away. Probably the insurance money had run out, we speculated, and she had been taken to a state hospital. In any case, I never learned what happened to her after that, nor did I ever learn what inner force guided her steps. All I could see was the seeming endlessness of her journey. Like Sisyphus, the mythical hero whose fate for all eternity was to roll a rock up a mountain only to have it continually fall back down, Geraldine's pointless repetition seemed to speak of the absurdity of life. But how, I later wondered, must she have felt at the corridor's end, just before she began her journey back? Did she, like Sisyphus, scorn her fate, and thereby triumph over it with every smile?

Don, the unruly teenager who wore ragged jeans and the blank overmedicated look, perhaps the most unlikely candidate for dignity that I saw, had, I discovered, his own brand of courage. Wounded and frightened, with little left but animal instinct, he nonetheless illustrated the remnant of humanity hidden inside even the most troubled of us there. Don had received little education from any of the institutions that made up his life, but he would sit for hours over his third-grade text, trying to do his homework, trying to learn.

When he found out that I was a professor, he asked me humbly if I would help him with his schoolwork. His assignment that day was to transpose a simple statement of fact into a question, but in spite of my hour's worth of tutoring and counsel, he could not do it. Although he was often frustrated, I never saw him toss the book away in disdain. "I gotta do my work," he would say, as he continued to stare at the text.

I thought, at first, that Don was retarded and had somehow been misdiagnosed as mentally ill. But I soon discovered that Don was very smart in his own way, especially at poker. Seated at a table with cards before him, his whole being would brighten. "Come on," he would call to whatever group was assembled in the common room. "How about a game?" Usually he beat us all soundly.

But what most remained in my mind was the day that the social worker came to talk to Don. As I walked by, I saw the two of them seated on one of the couches, huddled over some papers.

"The State is your parent," I heard the social worker explaining. She was apparently trying to persuade Don to voluntarily transfer to some othe institution.

"I don't have no parents," Don was insisting, as if at least on that one matter, he knew his facts. "My parents are dead."

"Yes, I know, I know," the social worker said. "That's why the State is your legal guardian—like a parent."

"I don't have no parents," Don insisted, again. The social worker was becoming exasperated.

"You just have to sign these papers," she was saying, "and then everything will be taken care of for you."

"I don't want to sign no more papers," Don insisted stubbornly.

"We're just trying to help you, Don," she said cajolingly. "Really, Don, there's nothing to be afraid of."

But Don stuck to his point, and finally she left in obvious chagrin.

"They want to send me back to Bradyville," Don said to me after she left. "The kids have knives there. I got beat up lots of times. Don't want to go back there. This is better," he added.

I wondered what kind of nightmare Don must have lived in for his fifteen years, that this was the best he had ever had. "Wanna play poker?" he asked me then, and no more was said that day about his possible transfer.

Clara was another patient I particularly liked. She was a short, somewhat round woman in her fifties who was diabetic. She had short, unruly blond-gray hair and a cherubic smile and giggle. Her favorite task was crocheting an afghan throughout most of the day. All I discovered about Clara's situation was that her husband and five sons regularly beat her up when she was on the outside. But you would never have known it from her demeanor or constant smiles.

Clara was a devout Catholic, and each day at 6 A.M. she would meet her Catholic doctor. They would spend half of the hour praying together, Clara told me, and the rest talking. Clara derived considerable comfort from both. I respected her doctor for his commitment to her and for his willingness to utilize their common set of beliefs as the framework for a treatment that Clara could most understand.

Clara was also absentminded, and frequently dropped stitches while crocheting. She would laugh good-naturedly when she did, and then rip out the row and start over again.

"I can just see you standing at Saint Peter's gate," I joked with Clara one day. "You'll be dropping stitches in front of the angels too."

Clara giggled and smiled, pleased with the reference. The rest of us roared with laughter.

Clara was good-hearted—she prayed for all of us each day—and, as a sign of special liking, gave me a religious medal of the patron saint of mental illness.

Another patient was Ginny, a girl of about sixteen, slim and lithe, who had undone much of nature's bounty by bleaching her hair into straw pre-punk blond and masking

her face with the greasepaint of clowns. I saw little of
her, actually, except for the afternoon she approached the
couch where I was sitting and withdrew a tiny gray toy
mouse from her pocket. She stood silently in front of me,
stroking it.

"That's a nice mouse," I said, opening the conversation.

"Do you think so?" she replied distractedly. "But I
don't know whether it's a boy mouse or a girl mouse."

I asked her if I might hold it and she handed it over.
I stroked it thoughtfully as she had done.

"I'm sure it's a girl mouse," I said, because it seemed
so obvious to me.

"Oh," she whispered, as if she no longer cared. She
drifted away.

A week later, I noticed her again, or rather we all
noticed her with her new doctor. He was tall and slim, a
handsome man, meticulously suited, almost too studied
in his dress, with a penchant for silky ruffled shirts, in
short a dandy—Dr. Dandy, we called him—not gay, but
touched by a feminine sheen.

We regularly giggled as we saw Ginny and her doctor
pass by, because they seemed such a comic pair; he positively strutting in his finery, one hand on her shoulder,
lightly guiding; she shuffling along, disheveled, with her
painted scarlet face.

Two weeks later, Ginny took off her clown's mask for
good, revealing a strikingly beautiful adolescent woman's
face underneath. We recognized it as a breakthrough, the
first, after three years of institutionalization.

"You look wonderful, Ginny," we all chorused and she
grinned, which she did more of lately.

I decided that dandy doctors are best for little gray
mice who don't know whether to be a girl or boy mouse.

Then there was Ken, a quiet handsome man in his
twenties, who usually sat in a corner chair, staring blankly
into space, his mind, along with his demons, blown away
by electroshock. That was about the only thing that really
scared me at the sanitarium, the thought that electrical or
surgical intrusion could reduce me to an idiot. That and
two people I considered dangerous—one was a young
male staff member with crazy eyes who seemed to relish

putting patients in restraints, especially Debbie, the severely deranged patient whom he was assigned to most of the time and whom he enjoyed bathing behind closed doors. The only other dangerous person, I felt, was a fellow patient, a well-educated, articulate man who for some reason made me uneasy. I learned later that he had killed a number of his own men while an officer in the Israeli army, thinking them to be Syrians. I stayed out of the way of both these people.

Toward the end of my first week at the sanitarium, Marion came to visit me, bringing flowers. She stayed for about an hour, talking the whole time about her mother and the problems she was having with her.

My mind kept blanking out as we talked, and by the time she left I was engulfed in fog. Then the sobs began. Throwing myself on my bed, I cried and cried. Finally, I called one of the staff members and insisted on talking to Dr. Otto. Although it was a Sunday and he was not scheduled for a visit, the staff member, seeing my agitation, reached him by phone.

Near hysteria, I mumbled to him about Marion's visit. I couldn't explain to him the real story, knowing how my first attempt at telling it to Dr. Lustig had turned out. I nevertheless communicated the extent of my distress.

"Stay away from her," Dr. Otto told me firmly, and then continued with an irony that he could not appreciate, "It takes a trained therapist to deal with someone like that."

"You must break off your relationship with Marion," he repeated the next day during our therapy session.

"But how?" I asked. "What can I say to her? What reason can I give?"

"Don't give any explanation," Dr. Otto recommended. "Just don't see her anymore."

Sorrowfully and reluctantly I followed his advice. The next time she called, I told her I could not see her anymore.

"I was afraid this would happen" was her comment. "I wasn't sure you could keep your friends."

Heavy and at the same time light, I hung up the phone.

I continued to meet with Dr. Otto every weekday. Because the sunglasses people had not invaded the safety of the sanitarium, I was willing to tell Dr. Otto about them. I spoke about them in a small frightened voice, but he did not appear to share my alarm.

"Have you seen any of them since you've been here at the sanitarium?" he asked me.

"No," I admitted, although I still felt somewhat apprehensive that they might reappear.

"Well, then..." Dr. Otto said, letting his words drift off into the air. It was clear that he was shrugging them off, as if they were not the real issue.

Then Dr. Otto resumed the line of questioning that he had adopted since the second day.

"How do you feel this morning?" he would ask.

"Kind of foggy and confused," I would reply. "And the pain still runs down my arms and legs."

"Exactly what happened this morning?" he would continue. I couldn't understand why he was introducing such irrelevancies, but I would dutifully recite the events and feelings of the day.

"What happened after that?" he would ask. When I finished replying, he would continue in the same vein.

I was puzzled by this questioning, because I had lost all sense of myself as an active force in the world—myself as an agent *causing* events. My inner world worked by association, and was always subject to magic and myth.

Then on the seventh day, under Dr. Otto's sequential questioning, I finally made the connection.

"You mean that how I feel is related to things that are actually happening around me now?" I nearly shouted the question, delighted to find a rational explanation for my distress. How I feel and what I do are the result of *everyday* occurrences, I realized with astonishment. Magic is not ruling me or the universe. I am an actor and participant in the world. I am tied to other people and other events. I affect them and they affect me.

Dr. Otto nodded and smiled. "Yes," he said, "you're tied to people and events in the world."

It was a simple enough revelation—one that most people take for granted daily. But for me, it was like a lifeline. For the first time in months, I was again able to see myself as part of, not apart from, the world. I was once again placed in the mainstream of events—I had joined society again.

As if to note the essential nature of the connection that I had just made, I found that within hours my eyes had cleared up. They had become blurry during my first day at the sanitarium, conveniently preventing me from endlessly scribbling the events, dates, and numbers with which I meant to capture the future. This blurred vision, which appeared to be a physical impairment, was indeed, I realized now, a gift from my body to myself. By being prevented from compulsively recording, I was taken one step further from madness and one step closer to the real world. And by the time my eyes had cleared up, the dysfunctional habit of recording had been broken.

Superstitious as always, I took my improved vision to be a good omen, as well as a practical advantage. I could read the hands on my watch, which, for me, had always been the symbol of reality. I couldn't wait to tell Dr. Otto, and Dr. Lustig when I saw him, about the improvement in my eyes.

At my therapy session with Dr. Otto the next day, I eagerly told him the news.

Dr. Otto responded approvingly. "Yes," he said in a pleased tone, "your 'I' is indeed better."

"My *eyes* are better," I repeated, thinking he had misunderstood me.

"Your 'I' is better," he said again, this time writing the letter *I* in the air. "Your 'I,' your *self*," he explained.

"Oh, I see," I said, surprised and happy. "Yes, it's true, my 'I' is much better now."

Dr. Lustig was equally pleased that evening when I told him. "Having a self, an 'I,'" he said, "means that you are in charge of you—that you make things happen, even inside yourself. And," he continued, "being in charge of yourself, of your inner and outer worlds, means that you deny the power of magic."

I was reassured that the power of magic was gradually diminishing, that a sturdier "I" was being formed, that the veil of illusion had lifted at one edge.

"I *am* getting better, aren't I?" I asked Dr. Lustig with hopeful uncertainty.

"Yes," he said. "Yes, you are."

Chapter 9

Of all the aspects of the sanitarium, perhaps the most wonderful was the matter-of-factness of its inner life. Madmen babbled and mirrors broke but somehow the voice of sanity also spoke. Whatever was bizarre was openly displayed, and whatever needed containing was openly contained.

At the sanitarium, there was little need for hiding the inner demons at work. Society at large disavows demons, but mental hospitals exist to provide them with a place. When I had been on the outside, in that larger society, the chaos within me had had to hide from my fellows, until at last, yearning to be acknowledged, it had demanded an outward, if illusory, face. But inside the hospital all this was reversed. Madness was everywhere apparent: in the eccentric behaviors, in the distorted postures, in the babbling of voices—speaking untold terrors, in unknown tongues. What need was there, in this place, of hallucinations? Here, my private demons had many a public address.

By the second week of my stay at the sanitarium, I was making substantial progress. The mental connectedness I was beginning to experience was continually reinforced by my newfound social bonds. I became an active participant in the events and social life of the hospital, and in doing so moved one step closer to connection with the outside world.

The world inside those walls was almost a microcosm of the larger society. Like a somewhat grimy mirror held up to the world's face, the hospital did not reflect perfectly, but still bore a resemblance to the society that was its model. We held poetry readings, and at one session I wrote a haiku. We made artificial flowers at the craft workshops, laughing good-naturedly at our ineptness and many false starts and stops. There were yoga classes where I experienced another way to enter an altered state of consciousness that was calm and restful, and that, the instructor noted at the end of the session, completely transformed my face. We assembled in the gymnasium for sports and played lively games of volleyball. We even danced one evening at a communal square dance.

These activities and social encounters acted like a further adhesive—tying me not only to others but to myself. Being in the society of real people who, in the midst of their pain and struggle, could laugh at the foolishness of it all eclipsed my need for imaginary companions. This society, combined with the new causal thinking that I was learning in my therapy, at last had the power to drive my visions away. The sunglasses people disappeared, and as the days went on and they did not resurface, I realized that they were gone for good. My world of myth and magic was gradually being replaced by a reality that, inchoate and halting as it was, was nevertheless of this world.

Paradoxically, I became profoundly sad when my hallucinations left. Mournfully, I watched my world of magic go. It was as if I had suffered a great loss, a death of that part of myself which had given them birth. A place in me was empty, and would remain so for some time, until the outer world could again step forward and assume its proper place. I wondered at my sadness and my sense of loss. Why, when they had been so terrible, was I so sad to see them go?

My question went unanswered, but I was left knowing that the loss of illusion is a real loss, that we are bonded to what we create, even when what we create is not real, that the death of illusion is akin to the death of hope, even when that hope is worn and walks the street.

We love what we labor for, be it a child or our mind's own invention, and as we sit at the deathbed of our smallest creation, we mourn its loss more than the imagined loss of our own life. So when the sunglasses people died in my mind, as I watched my invented world of magical connections go, I wept long and bitterly at their demise, knowing the special sorrow of a world without their blinded sight.

The sadness, in its way, may have filled the place that terror had occupied, as if the space that had been stretched within me to accommodate the demons would remain to be filled by other feelings, and would finally be the seat of an enlarged perspective. For the moment, however, the sadness prevailed.

But there were compensations. I discovered, in the art room, a new outlet for my need to create. From lacing moccasins two weeks earlier, I now found myself painting watercolors. One picture in particular I considered an achievement—a lavender and blue butterfly with touches of purple and rose, perched ready for flight on a purple-pink-blue hedge. To me, the butterfly was a symbol of my newfound metamorphosis, and I eagerly presented it to Dr. Lustig as a gift when he next visited me. I also showed him the haiku that I had written:

> A butterfly pauses on a leaf
> A moment of silence
> Before the beat of the wings

He nodded several times, as if in wonder at my transformation. He beamed as he accepted my gift. I'm going to frame this and hang it in my home." He turned the picture this and that way in the light. "It's really very lovely." He continued studying the painting, then stopped abruptly and asked, "Would you please write your haiku at the bottom of the painting, and sign your name under it?" I proudly complied.

When I had finished, he considered the picture again. "It's sure a gigantic leap from moccasins!" he joked. We laughed together.

It is one of the subtleties of giving that it rekindles the giver's self-esteem. Perhaps I'm a healing, not a harmful, person, I reflected. Perhaps there's something in me of value.

The other patients must have instinctively sensed my changed perspective, for many of them began to seek me out for company. It started with my daily morning walk within the sanitarium courtyard before breakfast, after I had gained grounds privileges. I began inviting other patients to walk with me, and soon it became a social event. Within three days, fifteen or twenty patients were assembling at 6 A.M. to troop around the courtyard to enjoy the crisp winter air.

This daily parade of inmates may have seemed comical—a strangely costumed procession of unworldly clowns. Some participants marched stiffly with near-military bearing; others straggled, barely keeping to the path. Some were outspoken, joking or shouting encouragement to those around them; others were silent and mechanical as they stepped along. But to all who marched, there was a belonging in our queer assemblage and self-appointed task, a common purpose and companionship that soothed many an individual isolation. For the first time, many felt, I now belong.

I gained credibility when it became known that I was a professor.

"Are you really a professor?" they would ask hesitantly, sometimes puzzled, sometimes amused that a "professor" shared their fate.

"Yes," I admitted, "I teach philosophy."

Most of them did not know precisely what philosophy was, but, as it was presumed to be learned and intellectual, I was sought out as an adviser on many practical matters.

"When I'm home, my husband does nothing but work on his cars. He completely ignores me, as if I don't exist. I don't know what to do," a young married woman confided.

"It sounds like he should have married a car, not a wife," I said jokingly, and we both laughed.

"I think that nurse on the morning shift is giving me too much medicine, because I feel terrible after I take it," another woman who was subject to constant headaches told me. "Would you talk to her for me?"

"I'll talk to her with you," I said. "But it's something you should really do for yourself."

"I want to ask for grounds privileges, but I'm too scared to talk in the group meeting," the youngest patient, a boy of twelve or thirteen, said to me shyly. "Will you ask for me?"

I told him he'd have to ask for himself, but that I would sit next to him.

"I'm afraid to go back home—it just seems so hopeless," Ellen, my dining companion, told me.

"When I feel powerless and hopeless, it makes me angry—very angry," I said.

"Yes, I guess I *am* angry," she agreed.

"Well, maybe you can use that anger to hold yourself together and change the situation," I suggested. "It helped me."

Talking to the other patients was, in many ways, like talking to myself. I told them what I was trying to learn—to be in control of my own fate, to stop being a victim of real or imaginary forces. Saying these things to others strengthened my resolve to learn better survival skills for myself. It also made me realize that, in many ways, I already *knew* what to do—it was putting it into practice that was the hard part.

Toward the end of my first two weeks at the sanitarium, Dr. Lustig and Dr. Otto both encouraged me to return to my teaching. They wanted to reinforce my rational thinking processes. They also wanted to facilitate my reentry into the world with the gradual resumption of a portion of my former responsibilities.

It was agreed that beginning on Thursday, I would leave the sanitarium on my regular teaching day, go to the nearby college where I taught, teach my two classes, and then return to the sanitarium for the night. In that way, I could step into the world's waters one foot at a time, without experiencing the shock of total immersion. Even though the situation with the children and Stan had substantially changed during the two weeks of my hospital stay, I was not yet ready to take full responsibility for the children.

Not only had Stan been caring for the children on a daily basis, but he had begun to take pride in doing so. I could see the change in him when he brought the children to visit me that evening. He spoke about his care of them with an air of confidence that I had never seen before. "At first I wasn't sure exactly what to do," he confided, "but I'm learning. And I think you can see that the kids are doing as well as can be expected. They miss you, though." A twinge went through me.

Stan hesitated for a moment as if he was unsure whether to continue. Then he took a deep breath and went on. "Elizabeth painted a completely black picture at nursery school the other day," he said worriedly.

The image of that darkness swept over me, followed by waves of bodily pain. "I'm so sorry I'm causing this to happen to her," I said, feeling overwhelmed with defeat and guilt. "But at least you're there for them, Stan. That must mean something."

I wanted to weep and run away from the thought of Elizabeth's pain. Black upon black, that was all that I could see. Everything around me took on the heightened clarity of unreality.

"I must go now," I told Stan and the children abruptly, wanting to run from the image of Elizabeth's picture and what it might mean. I'm harming my children, I thought again, wanting only to hide from that black thought. But the image followed me back up the corridor and into the ward. There's no escape from the sight of so much pain, I cried inside, as I returned to my room and pulled the covers over my head, trying to blot out the conviction that I was a bad mother. Then another side of me spoke up. You must put all your effort now into getting well, so that you can return to your children, it said. I clung to that notion tenaciously, in order to drive the darkness back. But its forces submerged me again. My child's black picture, black upon black. A wellspring of pity poured forth. I was not sure whether it was for my daughter or for me.

It would take me some time to resolve my maternal conflict about guilt and inadequacy. But during it all, I could count on the love of my children, and the love of my extended family.

My mother, on first hearing from Stan that I was in the hospital, had immediately taken a plane from Idaho to be there to help me. She visited me in the hospital with words of love and encouragement, and homemade brownies, but most importantly she set about putting my home in order, and helping Stan with the children. "I cleaned out all the closets, and I'm getting the house in good order for when you come home," she told me. I felt the burdens attached to the outside world lighten considerably.

My father, sister, and brothers also called me with words of reassurance, and my sister sent flowers to the sanitarium, as if it were a regular hospital and I had a regular sickness.

A day before I was scheduled to begin teaching, I spread out my class notes on the hospital bed and went over them. I found my mind clear and precise, and felt no doubt that I could teach the material. I was anxious about standing in front of a class once again, but, as much as possible, I put that unease aside. I was determined that I would return to the classroom. I needed to make it up to my students. I needed to know for myself that I was a competent and functioning person.

On the day that I was scheduled to teach, my mother picked me up at the hospital in my car, and set out to drive me to the nearby college. Our route lay through the middle of the urban slum that surrounded the sanitarium. As we slowly traveled past gutted, decaying buildings, with the smell of poverty and hopelessness in the air and sullen hostility on the faces of the residents, I began to panic. It was like stepping back into a nightmare, only this bad dream was the real world—peeling paint on crumbling walls, boarded windows, lifeless interiors, broken lives. The magnitude of ugliness and despair overwhelmed me. In a frightened voice, I begged my mother to hurry.

She picked up my alarm and agitation. But, unfamiliar with the city, she promptly got lost.

My panic was assuming gargantuan proportions.

"I've got to get to the college. Please," I begged my mother. I began to cry.

My mother, in panic, brought the car to an abrupt halt and, leaping out of the car, started running down the street to ask for directions.

"Come back," I yelled after her in terror, knowing that her interactions with her western, small-town neighbors had not schooled her for a chance encounter on an inner-city street. But she didn't hear me. I watched as she approached an idle man standing on a street corner. As if through a filter, I saw her hands gesturing and her mouth moving. Then she seemed to be thanking him, and came running back to the car.

"I got the directions," she said in a still-panicky voice. I quickly locked all the doors and we sped off toward the college. We arrived in one physical piece, but my mind was still reeling from the horror of that image of danger and defeat.

I got out of the car, patted my mother on the shoulder, and thanked her for driving me. I took several deep breaths and started up the steps from the parking lot to the classroom building where I was to teach.

I'll take a cab next time, I decided, sorry that my mother, who was trying so hard to be of help, had caught my panic from me.

The contrast between the college campus, with its green manicured lawns and its bright well-scrubbed faces, and the brick-and-concrete hell from which we had just emerged could not have been greater. I wiped the memory of our harrowing ride out of my mind and focused on the classes I was about to teach. I was still trembling, but my mind was clear. Plato, I thought, with relief. Plato, with his orderly, purposeful world—that's what I must think about now.

The chairman of my department, Father Michaels, met me at the door of my classroom. Knowing, as I suspected he did, about the nature of my recent collapse, he had obviously come to see whether I was well enough to teach.

"I'll just sit in on your class," he told me. Since he had also been my substitute for the first two weeks of the semester, I could not argue with him.

Father Michaels stood at the front of the classroom on the left; I stood on the right. He began the class with a few words of introduction, diplomatically stressing how happy he and the students were that I was back. Then he turned the class over to me and seated himself at one of the front desks.

With my heart pounding, I began. I started that day's lesson on Plato, hearing my voice talking in an even, coherent tone. I asked several simple questions about the assignment, but the blank looks on the faces of the students told me that they had not understood the material, even at an elementary level. The few who did try to answer seemed to be using abstract labels, without at all comprehending the ideas involved.

I realized that I would have to begin at the beginning of the semester. But Father Michael's presence in the classroom posed a dilemma. How could I reteach material he was supposed to have already taught?

"Perhaps it would be best if we just go back and *summarize* what you have learned about Plato to this point," I told the students. Then, beginning at the semester's beginning, with Plato's *Apology*, I began to teach.

"Why do you think this dialogue is called the *Apology*?"

"Why was Socrates being tried?"

"Is Socrates apologizing?"

"What were the charges against him?"

"What analogy does Plato use in this dialogue?"

"Who is the one true trainer of horses analogous to?"

"How does Socrates use this analogy as an argument in his defense?"

"Is it true that a person can't do evil intentionally?"

"How does Socrates use this argument to refute the charges against him?"

"Is it ever right to defend oneself against evil by doing evil?"

The questioning and answering continued.

As the class progressed and I watched the students begin to sit up in their seats, the dull look on their faces evaporating, I knew that it was going to be all right. I began to enjoy the class. Before I knew it, it was time to adjourn. Father Michaels came over to me and shook my hand. He looked relieved.

"I'm glad you're back," he told me.

"I'm glad to be back," I said. "Thanks so much for taking my classes while I was sick."

He nodded, as if it were nothing, and left.

I'm going to be all right, I thought joyously. I'm going to be all right.

Chapter 10

But my reentry into the world was also rough-edged, as I learned on the following Saturday, when I returned home for a brief visit with my children. After experiencing the euphoria from my successful teaching, I had assumed that all my other duties could be as easily resumed. I was unprepared for the torrent of emotional uncertainty that swept over me at the sight of my "abandoned" children.

As they ran toward me with outstretched arms, I began to cry uncontrollably. Joy at their presence quickly turned to guilt, and I felt the world tumbling down around me. I clutched the nearby table, and began to chant over and over, "I am a bad mother. I have failed my children."

Surprise and alarm registered on my children's faces, which only confirmed in my mind the truth of what I was saying. My mother immediately grasped that the situation was out of control. She gently but firmly led me by the hand, away from the children and into another room, all the while patting my arm and speaking soothingly to me.

"Why don't you go out with a friend for a little while?" she suggested. "Or perhaps you should go and see Dr. Lustig."

I remembered that I had scheduled an appointment with Dr. Lustig for twelve noon. Although some forty-five minutes still remained until my scheduled visit, I knew I must leave the house. I could not remain with the children if I did not calm myself, which I was not yet able to do. I decided to go to Dr. Lustig's office and wait in the waiting room.

I was still sobbing, but with more composure, when Dr. Lustig opened the inner door at noon.

I sat down in my armchair opposite him, and immediately articulated the one thought that had been going round and round in my mind.

"I am a bad mother. I have failed my children."

"What did you do that was so terrible?" Dr. Lustig asked me offhandedly, as if it could not be that bad. When I didn't reply, he continued, "In what way have your children been failed?"

"They must know, *somehow*, about it," I said with conviction, certain that my hospital stay *must* have had some detrimental effect on them. I marshaled the one concrete bit of evidence I had for believing that they had been harmed by me.

"The other day, Elizabeth . . . Stan told me . . . Elizabeth painted a completely black picture!" I waited for Dr. Lustig to acknowledge the seriousness of this incontrovertible proof.

"If she had painted a completely *white* picture, what would your reaction have been?" He was not responding as I had expected.

I sat confused, thinking. "I would have thought a white picture was a bit strange," I admitted, "but I wouldn't have been so worried." Doesn't he understand the symbolism involved with black? I wondered.

"What if she had painted a completely *purple* picture?"

"It'd be all right," I admitted.

"What about a completely *pink* picture?"

This was getting ridiculous. I sensed that he was not going to give up on this line of questioning. I was rapidly getting the point.

"How *old* is this daughter of yours?" he asked, as if a new thought had occurred to him.

"Four and a half," I answered dully.

"It's okay if she paints a completely white picture, or a completely purple picture, or a completely pink picture," he summarized good-humoredly, "but it's *not* okay if this four-and-a-half-year-old girl paints a completely *black* picture. Is that right?"

I felt foolish, but I wasn't ready to concede the point. "Don't you *see*," I said, "that if she paints a completely *black* picture, she must know there's something wrong with me! Or she must be *very unhappy*," I amended.

"Good possibility!" Dr. Lustig replied. "What does she know when she paints a completely white picture?"

His constant shifts were confusing me. It had all seemed so simple before; my failures had seemed self-evident. But now, to my discomfort, it was all being turned around.

"What's so special about *black*?" Dr. Lustig resumed. "People wear it all the time. Women look particularly attractive in it when they're going out at night, more attractive than in some of the other colors."

"It's just so obvious that it's the color of doom," I replied.

"For *you* it may be the color of doom," he responded, "but did anyone *ask her* what the picture meant?"

I said that it had not even occurred to me. "Then," he continued with some indignation, "how can you be so presumptuous as to assume that *you* know its meaning, when *she* is the final authority on it?"

By this time, I was at a complete loss for words. I kept trying to grab hold of my original thought about being a failure, but it was becoming more and more difficult to remember exactly what I had been thinking. It was as if Dr. Lustig's line of questioning had blocked the mental path of that earlier idea. I couldn't seem to remember what it was that I was trying to say.

I remained silent, straining to remember why I had been so worried. "There's something about her face.... I can see something in her face...."

"Most people can, when they look at another human being. What did you see?"

"A terrible sadness."

Dr. Lustig sat forward in his chair.

"Do you think your children miss you?"

"Yes," I softly replied.

"Right!" he affirmed. "Do you think your kids are sad because you're not with them?"

"Yes."

"Right! Do you think your kids are going to be irrevocably harmed by your absence?"

"That's what I'm afraid of."

"Wrong!" he exclaimed. "A four-and-a-half-year-old girl . . . sure she's going to miss her mommy," he continued joshingly. "But to say she's a banana, no ma'am! To say her mommy's a banana, could be."

Laughter flooded over me, bringing relief. Dr. Lustig had articulated, and then dismissed, the thought that I could barely acknowledge to myself: If I was crazy, it would make my children crazy too.

We sat in silence for a few moments. I basked in the newfound relief I was feeling.

"I guess I'm *really* worried about going back home," I finally resumed, seeing the issue for the first time in a more rational and practical light, "that I won't be able to take care of the children very well."

"Good thing to worry about!" Dr. Lustig said approvingly. "Particularly since you haven't done it in a while . . . particularly since it was so difficult for you before you went into the hospital . . . so what are you going to *do*, to make sure you have it easier, when you *are* back home for good?"

"Well, my mother's going to stay on with me after I get out of the hospital."

"For how long?"

"She says as long as I need her . . . I would guess for another couple of weeks or a month."

"After that, what are you going to do? . . . Now that Stan's trained, how are you going to use him? The guy's a pro now, right? Two weeks with the kids?"

"He'll be much more helpful than he was before," I agreed, suddenly feeling better just remembering that Stan would be there to share the responsibility.

"He says, or you say?"

"Well, I really haven't talked to him about it."

"Think you might want to?"

"Yes. That's a good idea."

"When are you going to do it?"

I realized that I should talk to Stan immediately and formalize the child care arrangements, so that I would know what to count on from him and what I had to do for myself.

"As soon as I can," I answered, but that was not immediate enough for Dr. Lustig.

"Well, today's Saturday. . . ." he stated, giving me the clue.

"I'll try to talk to him today. Maybe we could set some . . . specific hours when he takes them, and I wouldn't feel quite so alone."

"Or burdened," he added.

I sat, reflecting on what had been said. Yes, it would be better when I got home, I realized. With Stan taking an active role with the children, it would be much better.

Then my mind shifted gears and I thought again about my failures as a mother, how I was causing my children pain. "What about Elizabeth's black picture?" I repeated, again focusing all my concern on that one symbol.

"Do you think a four-and-a-half-year-old girl painting a totally black picture is rampant psychopathology?"

"It's what I worry about, I guess."

"Do you want to know what to do to make that concern disappear?"

I nodded vigorously, eager for a solution.

"Has she shown you the picture yet? No? Well, ask her to show you the picture, because her daddy had told you about it. And then tell her what a *lovely* picture of the heavens it is, but that she hasn't put the stars and the moon in it yet. And then you and she do that together."

I smiled to myself. It was another example of Dr. Lustig's ability to change a symbol, and then the meaning and feelings that went along with it. "Yes," I said, at last satisfied.

I sat contentedly, until Dr. Lustig again spoke.

"You know you can't do everything all at once," he said reflectively. "Some things you can teach your children *now*, and some things will have to wait till later. It is your obligation as a parent, at *some time*, to teach them what they need to know. What you can't do now, though, you can just do later."

I could see that he wasn't going to let me indulge in guilt and self-pity about my inadequacies as a mother, or allow me to think my children had been irrevocably harmed. It wouldn't be too late to help them later, when I was stronger, he seemed to be saying. But, in spite of madness, my responsibility to the children remained.

I returned home that day happier than I would ever have expected, calmed, knowing that it would be all right with the children. And two weeks later, when I returned home for good, Elizabeth and I took care of the completely black picture, by painting silver stars on it and a golden moon.

I don't know who felt better—Elizabeth or I—after we changed the picture. We hung it on the refrigerator, where Elizabeth proudly showed it to every friend and neighbor. The new picture represented for me a fundamental lesson about the powers of the imagination and how, by using them effectively, I could make them a healing force.

Chapter 11

My second two weeks in the sanitarium had a different texture. The mental cripple who had arrived there was gradually giving way to a somewhat unsteady, but better-functioning, person. The daily sessions with Dr. Otto still continued, centering more and more on the practical requisites of my return home.

"Who are you going to have to meet?"

"What are going to be their concerns about you?"

"What are going to be their reactions to you?"

"What will be their greatest fear about you?"

"Tell me what these people are like, so that we can figure out how you'll handle them."

"What will Stan's role be when you get back?"

"How long does your mother plan to stay?"

"What will you do for child care help when she leaves?"

Dr. Otto's questions demanded that I think realistically about the situation I would be confronting, and oriented me once more toward the larger world. In addition to Dr. Otto's practical advice, I once again had a professional identity to rely on. I was no longer just a crazy person, I was again a working professor. This simple fact further expanded my role within the social framework of the hospital.

The incident with the student psychiatric nurses was an example. It seemed that the student nurses were asking the patients a lot of probing personal questions. A number of tearful patients had talked to me about it.

"I feel like they're trying to analyze me all the time," Mary, a depressed young mother, told me. "They keep trying to talk to me about why I tried to kill myself. They ask me about my family, and about when I was a kid, and I get so upset. She burst into tears.

I heard the same story from several other people. It made me think about the healing process. Why were some of the staff so effortlessly helpful, while others sowed the seeds of further distress? I thought about it all day.

The concern of the patients became known to several of the doctors and staff members, as well as to the student nurses' instructor. Consequently, at the morning meeting the next day, all the student nurses had gathered, as well as several men whom I had not seen before, who appeared to be either doctors from other floors or hospital administrators. Everyone was upset, especially the nursing instructor. She was the first to speak about the issue at the meeting, and she spent her time capably defending her trainees. As she spoke, the patients began to sag into their chairs. The student nurses looked ashen.

After the nursing instructor had finished speaking, hot words began flying back and forth. "We want you out of here!" a patient shouted at the students. "They're just trying to do their jobs!" their protector countered.

I waited until the hubbub had subsided, so I could get the floor. Then I stood up.

"I would like to speak about what has been most helpful to me, personally, since I've been here." Half the audience quieted down and turned to listen to me.

"Most of us are here," I said, "because we have found it difficult to live and do well in the outside world. Many of us have been separated from that world by the disturbances in our minds. But we're trying, in whatever way we can, to get back to that world, to again find someplace for ourselves in it." I felt everyone listening intently now.

"This is where the staff, including the student nurses, can be such a valuable help to us. They're our link with that outside society. They can remind us of what it's like to be a normal and ordinary and competent person. They can form a bridge between the sanitarium and the places we've left behind.

"The people who have been the most helpful to me since I've been here"—I paused and mentioned a few names—"those people have been not only supportive and kind. They've been helpful to me precisely because they've treated me like an *ordinary* person, and talked to me in an *ordinary* way about *ordinary* things. It hasn't mattered whether we were talking about the weather, or about our knitting, or about what their child did in school that day. Their ordinary conversation helped me to be a little more ordinary myself.

"It may seem to you," I continued, turning to the student nurses, "if you have ordinary, seemingly insignificant conversations with us, that you're not doing anything special for us, that you're not doing your job. But just the opposite is true. Most of us have a doctor or other person whom we talk with about our personal dilemmas. They're intensely private problems and, therefore, cannot be talked about with everyone. What we patients have been trying to say to you is that this kind of probing of our psyches, by people whom we don't know well, is distressing and, in fact, makes us more upset than we already are.

"This doesn't mean that the student nurses, or the staff, don't have critically important roles in our healing process. They do. Please let us take advantage of what you have most to offer us—an antidote to the bizarre and disturbed and frightening inner worlds that we ourselves have created. Give us what we most need from you—a dose of the ordinary, so that we can remember how it is to be a person with an ordinary life." I finished and sat down.

The room was completely silent for a few seconds. Then everyone started talking at once. Patients turned to the nurses and apologized tearfully. Misty-eyed nurses apologized in return. The nursing instructor came over to me and shook my hand. Mary, who had first told me about the problem, came over and thanked me for explaining the patients' side of the situation. Edith, the floor supervisor, approached me and smiled. "We should hire you for the staff."

After that, life in the sanitarium was very different for me. I enjoyed a newfound status as an intermediary, carrying the concerns of the patients to the staff, and the concerns of the staff to the patients. My new role helped me feel that, soon, I would be able to take up my other responsibilities, and once again become a full-fledged member of the human community.

The following days melted into one another in relative comfort for me. I continued my teaching two days a week, and was otherwise engaged in the activities of the hospital and its society. Don, the semiretarded teenager whom I had befriended, was leaving in a few days to go back to the state institution that he so despised. I discussed with several other patients what we could do for him before he left. Since he had only one torn pair of jeans to his name, we decided to take up a collection, so that at least he might have a decent set of clothes. One by one, we went to the downstairs office, where our money and valuables were kept, and withdrew our contributions. When we had finished, thirty dollars had been collected. Ellen bought a card at the canteen and we all signed it. Then we presented the card, with the money inside, to Don.

Don's words of appreciation were incoherent, but his tear-streaked face showed the extent to which he was moved by our gift.

"Nobody gave me nothing before," he finally mumbled as he wiped his eyes. It was an eloquent speech.

During that time, I noticed one of the more interesting aspects of hospital life—the way the patients used humor to numb the cutting edge of their despair. We all took particular delight in "fooling" the outside world at any opportunity. On the first evening of my fourth week at the sanitarium, my chance finally came. A group of us had taken a foray into the larger world, and had walked, supervised by several staff members, to a nearby ice-skating rink for an evening's exercise. We had paid for our skates, and then spent several enjoyable hours skating and mingling with ordinary people in an ordinary setting.

Toward the end of the evening, one of the staff members, Judy, asked me if I would supervise Debbie while she took a turn on the ice. I was glad to comply. Debbie was the severely disturbed patient who had been my neighbor in the seclusion room on my first night at the sanitarium. She always had a vacant look in her eyes, and her head was perpetually bandaged from her frequent rhythmic beating of it against the walls.

While Debbie and I were sitting in the public dressing room, a man entered with his children. As they changed from their shoes and laced up their skates, I found him periodically looking from me to Debbie, and then back to me again. Apparently determining that we were together, he nodded toward Debbie and addressed me.

"What happened?" he whispered, as he gestured in Debbie's direction.

Without a moment's hesitation, I replied in an equally confidential whisper. "It was a terrible automobile accident." He nodded sympathetically. "The family likes her to get out," I further explained. Again he nodded sympathetically, and exiting the dressing room with his children, he wished us both well.

Later, when I repeated the story to some of my friends in the hospital, we all laughed uproariously. Underneath our laughter, however, there was a sadness at a world whose compassion extended to auto victims, but not to their psychiatric counterparts.

During my stay at the sanitarium, I had grown very fond of many of the patients and staff, so when it was time for me to go, I said a tearful goodbye. The sanitarium had been good to me. Like a benignly uncritical family, the sanitarium had been a safe haven, within which I could consolidate an identity. Like the child that I was when I had entered its halls, I had received a child's care. But now it was time for growing up.

The parting from my hospital friends was like telling childhood chums goodbye. We talked of writing and of meeting again, but I knew that it was a youthful illusion. They belonged to that time and to no other, like friends made at summer camp or on vacation in some foreign place. I knew I must choose between their society and that of the world, and for all its imperfection, I chose the world.

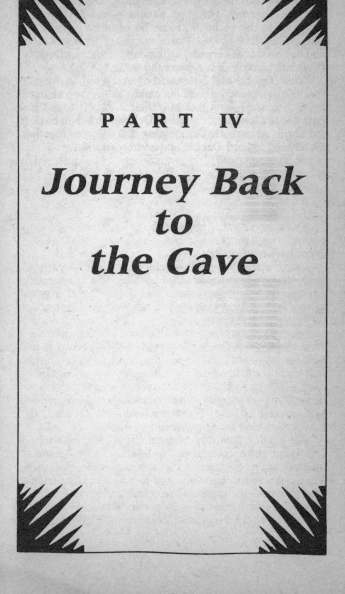

PART IV

Journey Back to the Cave

Journeys

There are many ways to travel and many places to travel to, but perhaps the most difficult and illuminating of all journeys are those that come round full circle, beginning and ending at the same place. My journey through madness had led me farther and farther away from the world, until I ended at a place where madness reigned. It was precisely there, at the sanitarium, that I turned around and once again faced the ordinary world.

My return to the world was marked by a significant shift in my perception of time. Under the influence of madness, persons, objects, and details stood out with sudden clarity, imbued with such significance and intensity that time itself seemed to slow under their burden. My return home witnessed a return to a more normal time sense. Most days flew by quickly on ordinary currents. Some days stood out with special meaning. I discovered how welcome a backdrop of insignificance can be, how necessary for perceiving the overall design of one's life. From that point on, my memory began to curl around events of importance, signposts of progress in the process of shaping a self. Against the gray and neutral background tones of the tapestry, what was vital and important began to stand out.

Chapter 1

MARCH, 1976

Curiously, the spring of my return to the world was more difficult than my month of winter in the sanitarium. At the sanitarium there had been less life to cope with. There, I wore only the stigma of the deranged. At home, I had to don responsibility's dress.

The transition from hospital to home reminded me of a ride I had taken on the commuter elevated train. Detached, I had sat back in my seat and watched the blur of life go past my window. The inside of the car had become more real than what passed outside. I gazed idly at the overhead advertising placard: DOREEN'S DISCOUNT SHOES, $12.95, SHOES ON RACKS TO SIZE 12EEE. Then in a brief instant, as I glanced out the window, my gaze focused on the reality to which the placard referred. There, on the shabby street below, stood Doreen's Discount Shoes, an unprepossessing building badly in need of repair and a coat of paint.

In just such an abrupt fashion, I viewed the reality of my situation upon returning home. I was a woman alone with two small children. I had no one to rely on but myself. I had little money. I had fewer illusions, and no invented comrades. Reality seemed shabby and bleak, like a house without laughter, like the impoverished outlet for discount shoes.

My mother's presence at home, during the first two weeks of my return from the sanitarium, softened somewhat my transition to adult society. Still, I often found myself floundering, like a child who had never been schooled in self-nurture and self-reliance. It took enormous effort for me to perform the most commonplace tasks. Driving a car again posed a serious strain; carrying keys and matches and medicine bottles again was a new demand. Above all else, I was conscious of my solemn duty to my children, at a time when I was not far from being a child myself.

Two feelings inexplicably intertwined during that time— anxiety and loneliness. My mother's care during the early weeks was like a tender cushion of love, standing between me and true aloneness. But she too had a life to return to. Many nights after my mother had gone back to Idaho, I stood over my children's beds when they were fast asleep, drinking in their physical presence, their steady warm breathing, their small bodies tousled under the covers, thinking of their innocence and trust in me. Why have I been given this gift, I wondered, when I know so little about living well myself? How can I teach my children to be strong and confident, when all I feel is a huge lump of fear that settles just under my stomach? Why do these two sleeping faces tug at my heart so, making me want to endure, as if my strength could infuse them with strength? Wanting for them, not just myself, the warmth of a man, the security of an authority for us all, someone who would feel confident about raising them, about decisions for them, as I could not. But the loneliness and anxiety I felt as I looked at them was far surpassed by the new and unreasonable apprehension I felt at work.

My anxiety that grew there daily made even the most commonplace interactions monstrous. Before one recent class, I had been so frightened I had retired to a lavatory adjacent to my classroom and huddled there in a toilet stall. Time ticked away. My class was due to start. Still, I could not pry myself from the questionable safety of my isolated perch. Steeling myself, I finally entered the classroom. Several students approached me before the class began. I was terrified by these cursory social exchanges. Inner thoughts and sensory perceptions, random pains and searing flashes pushed aside public words, crowded out common sense, made a mockery of external conversation. Sick with dread, feeling physically faint, I struggled to keep my mind on the words being spoken. I concentrated. What are they saying? Why are they laughing? Did someone make a joke? I'd better laugh too, or they'll know I can't focus.

Somehow, by some discipline, I continued teaching the class. It was as if I was conscious at two distinct levels. I could hear and follow the classroom discussion, but another deeper part of my attention was directed inward, constantly monitoring and privately commenting on my inner states. Yes, you handled that question convincingly. Is fear showing on my face? Are the students, even now, registering my alarm? Look closely at their faces. Read their reactions there. They *look* normal, so perhaps my secret is safe. If they knew that I had been in the hospital, that kind of hospital, what would they think of me? Would I be forever consigned to the ranks of the damned? Keep teaching, that's right, only fifteen minutes left. Hold your hands steady so they won't see them trembling. Almost done now, five minutes to go.

An hour's worth of living at these two levels brought me close to exhaustion. With vast relief, I would close my text at the class's end.

I looked again at my sleeping children. How can I be sure that I'm not, after all, harming them? What if my fear is making them afraid? The bad dream Elizabeth had last night—why did she dream of monsters chasing her? Are my demons contagious, invading even the sanctuary of my children's dreams?

What am I afraid of? I wondered. Is it failure? Why then, does it seem to grow worse with every successful class I teach? Is it fear of failing my children? But Dr. Lustig had reassured me about that.

It must be teaching. How can I go on teaching in the midst of this anxiety? If I pray, standing here in my children's room, perhaps I can ward off the next attack, perhaps next time it will be different. Please, God, take away my fear. I can stand the loneliness, but not the fear. Take away the confusion that lies at the center of the fear. Let me trust my mind again.

It was only reluctantly that I admitted my fears to Dr. Lustig. All I knew was that the fear was there. All I wanted was for the fear to go away.

"What are you afraid of?" he asked me when I spoke of it, as if he was surprised that, after all I had been through, I should be fearful now.

When I didn't answer, he made the question more concrete: "*When* are you afraid?"

"Usually when I have to go and teach," I answered dully. "The days I have to teach, I wake up in the morning ... terrified."

"Of what?" he asked again, as if it still did not make sense.

I sat marshaling my thoughts. "That I'll go crazy in front of the class, I guess," I said tentatively. Although it did not seem quite right, it was the only reason I could think of.

"That's certainly something worth being concerned about," he confirmed. "Have you had any of the symptoms that you had before you went into the hospital?" When I told him that I had not, his eyes opened wide in mock disbelief.

"None of them?" he asked incredulously. "Not even at home? Not even driving to work? Not even in the classroom? Not even at work? Not even in your dreams?"

"No," I repeated.

"Then you're in pretty good shape!"

I nodded, feeling some surprise and even a touch of gratification at this lack of symptomatology that had escaped my notice.

"So, what's the problem?" Dr. Lustig asked again, as if it could not be all that serious.

"Even though nothing terrible has happened, *so far*, I'm still afraid to stand in front of my classes." One can never be too careful about the future, I thought.

"Still afraid of what?" Dr. Lustig persisted.

"That's the worst part," I admitted, "not knowing. I think sometimes it's fear itself that frightens me. I get so frightened that I can't focus my attention. It's like I blank out, and then I'm even more frightened that I won't know what's going on."

"If you could have some *control* over the fear," Dr. Lustig asked, "would that make you feel better?"

"Yes," I said tentatively, wondering how this could be accomplished.

"Well, how about having some of the fear here?" he suggested. "Can you feel frightened here, now?"

I didn't answer immediately. On the one hand, I was eager for a solution, but Dr. Lustig's request warred with my conviction that my fear was ungovernable.

"I don't have any control over the fear," I answered with finality. "When I feel frightened, it seems like I'll always feel frightened. But when I'm not frightened, like being here with you now, I can't even imagine being frightened." I said all this by way of explanation, so that Dr. Lustig would know why it was impossible for me to feel the fear on demand, as he had suggested.

"Right! That's the way it usually is with this kind of feeling." Dr. Lustig spoke enthusiastically, as if he was undeterred by my skepticism. "You're reporting the facts exactly as they are. The same thing happens to people who are depressed. But could you do me a favor and *try* to feel frightened now?"

"Do you *really* want me to get frightened?" I asked, still feeling doubtful about the efficacy of such an approach. Something about it scared me a little.

"Just a *little* frightened," Dr. Lustig replied. "I'll tell you why. If you can get a little frightened now, and then let yourself return to neutral, you'll have learned how to control one of your feelings. And if you practice this skill enough, particularly if you practice it here, today, you'll be able to do the same thing on your own after you leave here. So if you practice going from frightened to neutral inside this office, you'll be able to use the same skill outside this office, when you're bothered by an uncontrollable feeling."

Something in me still rebelled against the idea. "I don't feel I have any control over it at all," I repeated insistently, shrinking from the idea that my fear was under my own control.

"I understand you don't *feel* that you have any control

over it," Dr. Lustig replied equably. "But I *know* that you *do* have control over it. You're not exercising it, that's all. And I'd like you to learn how to control it today, just like you've learned how to control lots of other things about your own functioning ... so that *you* can use it for your betterment, rather than it being used to your detriment. Now you might not be ready to learn about it *fully*, but you certainly can make a start. You don't have to get a Ph.D. in self-control right away, but you could take the introductory course, Self-control 101!"

I found myself chuckling in spite of myself. But my good humor rapidly faded. I still was not ready to accept his novel idea. I reverted, instead, to my earlier reasoning, once again trying to explain why the skill he was asking me to practice in his office was not feasible for me.

"When I'm with people and have to hide anything to do with madness, that's when I get afraid—afraid that somehow the madness is going to show. The difficulty about being frightened in this office is that, when I'm here, I don't have to be afraid of your knowing." I paused. "So," I concluded, "it's very difficult to be frightened here."

"That was well spoken, like a good professor!" he said heartily in mock approval. "But *pretend* ... just pretend that I'm some undergraduate, waiting for pearls of wisdom to come out of your mouth. And instead you talk jabberwocky!"

I smiled at this apparent absurdity, and thus encouraged, Dr. Lustig continued, "And then I'd think that you must be truly learned, because I wouldn't understand a single thing you'd be saying. That's the mark of a good professor, isn't it, being unintelligible to the students?"

I laughed again. "Are you saying that they'd never know?" I translated in relief.

"I'm saying that students *expect* their professors to be incomprehensible."

"But I *do* make philosophy understandable to my students," I objected. "That's one of the things I pride myself on. I had a student come up to me after a class recently, and she said that she was really enjoying my course. 'And I can understand what's going on,' she even added. 'Last semester I had Professor Richards for philosophy. I think he must be a *genius*, because I didn't understand a single word he said.'"

Dr. Lustig and I both laughed.

"Well, when I took philosophy," he continued conversationally, "I didn't understand a darn thing about it. I had to memorize it all, because it didn't make any sense to me. After Descartes I was lost. You mean to tell me you can make that stuff understandable?"

I nodded, granting my professional competency. Why the fear then? I wondered. Perhaps it's not really failure that I fear.

"I guess I'm not really afraid of going crazy again in front of my classes," I admitted, rethinking the whole issue. "But the amount of fear I feel there is so . . . intolerable. It's so painful that all I want to do is run away."

"Where would you like to run *to*?" Dr. Lustig replied cheerfully, reminding me that even running away has some destination.

I was confused for a moment. Where did I want to run to? To childhood, I realized. I would like to run away from my adult responsibilities. "I would just like to go home and be a child," I told him emphatically, knowing even as I said it that I was responding like a stubborn child. But I had to say it, anyway. "I would just like to have somebody take care of me."

"I don't blame you," Dr. Lustig answered heartily. "It's tough having to assume adult responsibilities when you're not sure of your own capabilities. It's a tough job to help three people to grow up, when only two of them are children!"

I laughed at this rather comic interpretation of my plight. "I *do* feel like a child," I resumed seriously. "But I feel I have to *act* like an adult."

"Well, in a way you *are* like a child," Dr. Lustig said gently. "There are lots of things about getting along in the real world that you don't know a lot about. And part of growing up is learning about those things, and becoming good at doing them. So in many ways you are like a child."

"But then I need to be *taken care of*." I felt I had finally proven my point.

"No, you just need to *learn*," he gently corrected. "You can take care of yourself, but you do need to learn. That's what children do—they learn. You don't have to live in fear. You don't have to feel like a child. You *can* be a good mother to your children, and teach them the things that they need to learn, and help them to learn the things that they want to learn. It's just a matter of learning yourself. And one of the things *you* need to learn is how to make yourself comfortable inside yourself—how you can create feelings inside of yourself and how you can control them. There's no need to live in fear. It's a terrible way to exist."

I sat and thought, still caught up in my feelings of being a vulnerable child.

"When I go home, I have two children there who need to be taken care of, and I'm like a third child," I repeated sorrowfully. "I *need* a family, and I don't have a family anymore. It's not a family without a man."

"Well, one of the things you can do is put an ad in some magazines for a mail-order husband," he replied promptly, not in the least discomfited by my imagined plight. "That way, there will at least be a man in the family." As he spoke, he pressed his fingertips together to form an arch, what we called a steeple as children. Then his fingers folded inward and intertwined, in a gesture that seemed to convey both thoughtfulness and unity. "Another way," he continued seriously, "is for *you* to acquire the skills that you think a man would have, so that you can do it for yourself."

I let my face go blank. The conversation was distressing to me. It was not going the way I liked. I was not getting the sympathy that I felt I so richly deserved.

As if he understood the turmoil behind my immobile face, Dr. Lustig, when he resumed a few minutes later, spoke cajolingly. "Now what could a man do for you that you couldn't do for yourself?" he inquired.

But I was not to be distracted from the sense of injury and anger that I was feeling. I was angry that I was alone. I was angry that I had no husband, when I so clearly deserved one. I was angry that Dr. Lustig was not more sympathetic to my situation. My face hardened. I was not going to be talked out of my plight.

Dr. Lustig, as if sensing this, or perhaps reading it from my face, said nothing further. I felt the tension in the room's silence, but my anger kept me from speaking. Five minutes turned into ten minutes. Still no word was spoken. I looked at the clock. There were only about twenty minutes of my appointment time left. Finally, unable to bear the silence and sense of estrangement from Dr. Lustig, I spoke.

"A man would take some of the responsibility," I said grudgingly, answering his earlier question about what a man could do that I couldn't do for myself. "I wouldn't have to have all of it!"

"Well, you still have a partner in raising your children," Dr. Lustig replied matter-of-factly. "Can you use Stan more?"

"Yes, but it's not the same," I said stubbornly.

"Right . . . it's not the same as having a live-in partner," he acknowledged. "But you do have a live-out partner. He can still do his part."

"How?" I asked, reluctantly.

"Tell him that he has to help more with the children. Even though you have chosen to assume the main responsibility for raising them, this is a time when it would profit all of you for Stan to do more. Tell him that you're still recovering and that you can't be expected to resume full activity immediately. It has to be gradual, otherwise you'll end up back in the hospital."

"He has been helping more," I said, defending Stan. "It's not just the care of the children that's difficult," I continued musingly. "It's the worrying about them."

"Well, let Stan worry about them. Why don't you just worry about you?

"You don't have to worry about your children," Dr. Lustig said more softly, when I remained silent. "You *do* have to do your job as a *parent*, but you *don't* have to worry about your *children*. You just worry about you."

"It's not any one thing I'm worried about," I replied, thinking again about the way that my anxiety seemed to generalize to many of the duties I was expected to perform. "I just feel like a failure at everything."

"Right!" Dr. Lustig agreed heartily. "And you can also feel that you're a success at everything, since all the emotions you have inside yourself come from you. That's the way it is in the world. Growing up means taking control of ourselves and our feelings. And we do that by learning about the mechanisms within ourselves that govern our actions and create our feelings."

"I thought being an adult was performing successfully in the world," I replied, again shying away from his insistence on personal control.

"No, it's more than that." He sat back in his chair and thought for a few moments before resuming. "Being an adult is performing competently in the world *and* being in control of oneself. People can fake performances. They cannot fake being in control of themselves. Many people are under the misconception that it's just the performance that counts. They fool other people into believing that they're self-possessed, but actually, they're scared to death inside, because they really don't know how to control their internal worlds. They'd be feeling a whole lot better about themselves if they had bothered to learn about their own inner workings, and if they had practiced the skills that would help them to take charge of themselves comfortably. It's really a very simple and straightforward process, like any other learning."

"I don't understand how you can do that," I said, finding my attention captivated in spite of myself.

"Well . . ." he said, "I asked you, before, whether you'd be willing to become a little fearful and then get back to neutral, and you adeptly sidestepped that request. You might want to go back and do it now, and practice going from fear to neutral. That's all you really have to do, be able to get back to neutral—from *any* feeling. You don't have to be totally in charge right away, but you do have to be able to get back to neutral if a feeling becomes unpleasant."

I decided to try to do as he suggested, but I found that I couldn't feel frightened in his presence. "I'm trying to get frightened, but I can't seem to do it now," I said apologetically.

"That's right—when you exercise control over your emotional functioning, you don't get frightened," he replied mildly. "But when you do not exercise that control, you get frightened. It's the absence of being in charge of yourself that causes you to feel frightened. So the more you're in charge of yourself, the more comfortable you're going to feel."

"Do you mean that, sometimes at least, I *am* in charge of myself?" At least I'm not afraid here in his office, I was thinking.

"Yes," he replied, "you're in charge of yourself when you're feeling fine. And the more you're in charge of yourself, the more often you're going to feel fine. And it *is* possible to feel fine most of the time, without medications. That's not to say you'll feel *happy* all the time, but you can feel fine!"

"Every time I don't feel fine, I assume that I'm crazy," I admitted, feeling a little foolish.

"Well, for a person who makes her living thinking, that's a lopsided thought!"

I laughed with relief. "I talked to my brother the other day," I continued reflectively. "I was telling him about the anxiety that I feel at work, how sometimes I'm so anxious that I can't tune in to what people are saying, or hear them very well, and that then I get even more frightened. He said, 'Oh, that happens to me all the time.' He's a lawyer, and he said, 'I try to avoid fading out when I'm with clients, but if it happens, I just say, "Could you please repeat that? I'm not sure that I quite understood your point." Then when they repeat it, *that time* I pay attention!'"

We both laughed. "Neat fellow, your brother," Dr. Lustig said.

"The other thing my brother said," I continued, "is that everybody has problems. They may be small problems, or they may be large problems, but everybody has some problems. Our family, though, has always assumed that we never ought to have problems or at least not show them. That's why they're denied all the time. But this assumption—that we're never supposed to show any problems—creates a very unrealistic expectation. And every time I have a problem, I think there's something wrong with *me*.

"So I don't want to expect that I'm going to be happy all the time," I concluded.

"Correct," Dr. Lustig replied. "But you can feel *fine* all the time."

When I remained silent, he added more gently, "You don't have to grow up *alone*, but you *do* have to grow up."

"I think I don't *want* to grow up," I said petulantly, feeling my anger returning.

"Well, the same thought crossed my mind too," Dr. Lustig said soothingly. "There's no need to make a decision now. But you might want to think about it, after you leave here, during the course of the next several days. Think about the price you've paid for *not* growing up, and what the rewards would be for *growing* up."

"The fear and panic that I feel lately . . ." I said reflectively, "is that the price of *not* growing up or the price of *growing* up?" I knew the answer, but I wanted to hear it anyway.

"It's the price of *not* growing up," Dr. Lustig answered without hesitation. "It's the price of *not* growing up, *not* being in charge of yourself, *not* being in control of what goes on inside of you. And it's the price you'll continue to pay. . . ." His voice trailed off into silence.

"I can tell you how to make it better," he resumed when I didn't reply, "but I can't make it better *for you*. And that's the problem in a nutshell. You've discovered the limits of Dr. Lustig's magic. It stops at your skin."

"You can't take away my fear," I said soberly, sorry that there were no magical solutions.

"Only you can do that," he affirmed. "When you did *not* get frightened and then return to neutral earlier, you tacitly indicated that you had grave doubts about learning a skill that would make you responsible for yourself. So the choice now is: *nobody* responsible for Carol, or *you* responsible for Carol. But it can no longer be: *someone else* responsible for Carol."

I was not enamored of that day's lessons. I felt the harshness of Dr. Lustig's truths. And I left without practicing the skill of self-control that Dr. Lustig had tried to teach me.

But on the next occasion when I stood before my class in a state of terror, I remembered what he had said about going from panic to neutral. Desperate, I grasped after any means of taking away the fear. I decided to try it.

I imagined "neutral" as a restful valley floor between

the jagged ridges of two mountains that seemed to represent the edges of my fear. I imagined myself settled down in this valley, beside a golden river. Warm sunlight flooded over my shoulders. Wild flowers nodded in the breeze. I stretched out my arms and imagined myself taking a deep breath of the pristine air. The edges of the mountains blurred and smoothed out. They changed from deep brick-red to gentle blue. Another gulp of fresh air. The mountains receded into the distance, still present on the horizon but no longer paramount. I felt my anxiety ease. It was such a relief that I wanted to shout with joy. Instead, I quietly continued teaching my philosophy class.

During the days ahead, I continued to use my imagination as a weapon against my fear. Calling up a neutral state took effort and discipline. I had to insist to myself that I create positive images. Some days it worked better than others. But I usually found that, with discipline, I could make my fears subside, although they rarely dissipated completely. Nonetheless I persisted with my exercises. It was not until May 27, some three months later, however, that I realized that my fear had gone. I found myself teaching that day with confidence and ease, and with a physical feeling of connectedness coursing through my body. I felt a simple pride. Even fear was no match for my imagination.

Chapter 2

As my springtime fears diminished, the loneliness that lay hiding behind them engulfed me. Stripped of a husband, I felt naked and reduced, like a wheel sliced through the middle that could not roll smoothly. Where is my other half that Plato spoke of? In the beginning, he said, people were joined at the shoulders, like so many pairs of Siamese twins. When they stretched out their limbs, they resembled the spokes of a wheel. From this position, they frolicked and played, turning cartwheels and spinning in circles. But the noise of their laughter angered the gods, who, in irritation, split all the pairs apart. Thus, we are destined to search the world over, looking for our other half.

I looked around me, but found no pairing. Only the feeling of loss, loss of a husband, which translated into loss of a family. Being married was believing that things would last. More than children, more than religion, it had given me a sense of continuity, a belief in the future, that there was a future. But now, divorce. It was as if the essence of all heartbreak had been poured into a thimble and placed before me. The fact that the portion was small and commonplace did not make it any less bitter to drink.

Saturdays, when the children went to Stan, were barely

livable, in spite of distractions such as shopping or visiting with friends. But Sundays, "family days," were days of despair. I felt as if my face had been pressed into the dirt and ground down by an unkind cosmic boot, so that I had no breath left, so that life slipped out of me. Looking toward the phone in desperation, thinking, Whom can I call that will keep me alive? Knowing that friends would be busy with their own families. Loath to disrupt such a sacrosanct time. Thinking of my own family, my parents, my sister. Calling them, eagerly hearing their voices. Assuring them that yes, I was fine, because how could I impose my lifelessness on them? Wanting to hold on to their voices. Finally hanging up the phone. The sound of my heartbeat, deafening in the silence. Pulsating on, as if it had a life of its own, independent of my anguish. I thought about people in prisons and prisoners of war. Day after day, marking notches on blank walls. Why don't they die of loneliness? Perhaps they do.

Somehow I would stay alive until the children returned at six o'clock. Then, from sheer relief, I would collapse into bed just after they did, triumphant over another Sunday.

When the children were with me, my loneliness eased, but even our togetherness couldn't make our family feel whole. So we spent our weekdays seeking out the company of families that were still intact, as if the rupture in our own family life could be healed by osmosis. I would take the children by the hand, late each afternoon, and journey down our lane to the homes of neighbors who were also friends. There, the women and I would sit and sip coffee while our children played. Putting aside for a moment the faster rhythms of our professional working lives, we working mothers would sit idly discussing the commonplace events of our day, as the afternoon shadows lengthened, until the evening brought their husbands home. Then, reluctantly, I would gather up my children and make my way home, our footsteps heavy as we marched toward an empty house.

On the day that Elizabeth asked me, upon returning home, why her daddy did not come home at night anymore, I wondered, not for the first time, how I could go on.

When I told Dr. Lustig how alone and desperate I was feeling, he reacted as if it was to be expected. The loneliness, I explained, often made me want to die.

"As a matter of fact, that is what it's all about," he said. "Facing death, knowing that we're all alone. Looking death in the eye and deciding to go on living.

"I believe that some philosophers have written about it," he added. "I don't know what the philosophers have said, because I'm not a philosopher, but I do have some knowledge about looking death in the eye . . . and choosing to live."

"I've suffered too much," I moaned. "I just feel that I can't suffer anymore." It seemed such an enormous injustice to me, that I had had more than my fair share of pain.

"Well, whenever you decide to cash in your chips, just cash them in," he told me. "Meanwhile, go on living until you change your mind. You always have the option," he continued, and then added as if it was an afterthought, "but it's such a permanent option, killing yourself, that you might as well be very sure that you want to exercise it."

Yes, it is permanent, I thought. That's precisely the appeal, a final option when things seem so bad that death seems better. Then I thought of my children, how their faces would look, the dismay they would feel if I was gone. And later, the sense of desertion they would feel, the absence of love for them that such an act would imply.

"The one thing that keeps me going is my children," I said. "I think it would matter to them whether I live or die."

"That's an antidote to the loneliness you've been feeling," Dr. Lustig agreed with conviction. "It gives meaning and purpose to your life. Actually, sometimes I think that raising children is the most important job in the world."

I thought about my children and about raising them, and an unaccountable but now familiar guilt crept over me.

"But I feel that I've failed at it," I said miserably.

"Well, what you feel is determined solely by you," he replied without sympathy, and I remembered again his emphasis on personal control. "But if you would like an objective opinion about your children, I would be glad to provide one."

After a long pause, my curiosity got the better of me. "Why do you think they're doing all right?" I could not help but ask.

"Because they're functioning adequately. And to have been through what you've been through, and to have children who are functioning adequately, is a triumph!"

I felt my face flush in spite of myself. Dr. Lustig's face showed just the trace of a smile.

"It is important to have meaning in your life . . . to have a purpose. Not only to raise your children, but to raise yourself. You have to be the best person you can be for as long as you possibly can . . . until, of course, you cash in your chips."

It's not just my duty to my children. I also owe something to myself, I reflected. However, I was not prepared to discard the option of suicide altogether, not just yet.

"But the world seems so bleak to me," I said softly, mustering what further arguments I could on the side of despair.

"On cloudy days, that's the way it appears to *everyone*," Dr. Lustig replied without hesitation, making me less alone even in my despair.

"I just seem to go from one kind of pain to another kind of pain, and there is no solace." I again let the feelings of suffering pass over me.

"When you're hopping from pain to pain, there isn't any," Dr. Lustig replied firmly. "I would suggest that you stop hopping from pain to pain . . . and maybe go from pain to pleasure."

When I didn't reply, he resumed, "Or . . . if you don't want to be so *outlandish*, how about just going from pain to neutral?"

I remembered what he had said before about going from fear to neutral, and I remembered practicing that lesson in front of my classes.

"The few times I can get to neutral," I said, "I feel so relieved—to be out of the pain—that it does seem good."

We sat together in silence as I considered life and death. I thought about a saying of Nietzsche's Zarathustra: "The thought of suicide is a great consolation: by means of it one gets successfully through many a bad night." Yes, that's it, I reflected. The appeal of suicide is simply that it gives one an option—something to *do*, some action to take if the pain and loneliness get unbearable. But perhaps there are other, less radical choices, I reflected. Perhaps a vacation, or a visit with my family in Idaho.

Then, in a rush, I remembered why it was that I felt so alone. Stan had left. I was no longer married. Anger rose up within me at the thought, anger that wanted to destroy something, even if that something was myself.

"I want to be married," I said with sudden intensity.

"I want to be a millionaire," Dr. Lustig replied with equal emphasis.

"I don't really want to go through a courtship..." I continued, as if I hadn't heard him, "I just want to be married!"

"I don't really want to work to become a millionaire either," he replied cheerfully. "I'd just sort of like it to fall into my lap!

"A man prays to God that he'll win the lottery," he continued anecdotally, when I did not deign to reply. "He prays night and day, 'Lord, I've been a good man and I've lived a good life.... Please, Lord, grant my one wish.' The man repeats his prayer every day, imploring God to let him win the lottery. Finally, one night, as he's praying, he hears the voice of God in reply: 'Give me a break—buy a ticket.'"

I giggled, feeling more than a little foolish.

Again, we sat in silence for some time, until gradually I felt the sorrow envelop me again.

"I've lost everything," I said.

"Everything?" Dr. Lustig replied in mock seriousness. "Your health? Your children? Your friends? Your family?"

A wry smile crept over my face at this reminder. "I do love my children, and they love me," I said.

"Then, I guess you haven't lost *everything*, have you?

"You love your children and they love you," he continued, "but the more important question is, do you love Carol?"

"Not very much," I admitted in a low voice.

"Well, I think love is an all-or-none phenomenon," Dr. Lustig replied, which unaccountably made me laugh.

"You might want to get to know the real Carol, rather than the person she was supposed to have been. You might want to get to know the real Carol and then find out whether, in fact, you can first like her. Then, maybe later, you could love her. That's part of growing up too," he added. "For most people it happens when they're very young. For those people for whom it has not happened, it can certainly happen later on. It's the exact same process, earlier or later."

"Why is it so painful, then, to try to love yourself?" I implored.

"It's not painful when you love yourself," Dr. Lustig corrected. "It's painful when you don't love yourself. It's like being allergic to yourself."

"It seems like it should be so easy," I said sadly, "but it isn't."

"Well, you might have to unlearn some improper attitudes about yourself—having to do with things like perfection, having to do with things like other people's expectations, having to do with things like normal human motivations and normal human limitations."

"I guess I do think I have to be perfect or I don't deserve to be loved," I admitted with a nervous laugh. "It's an impossible standard." I could recognize the ironic nature of that particular bind.

"Yes, it certainly is," Dr. Lustig confirmed. "In order to function according to that standard, you'd have to be a god. That's a tough business to be in."

"It's not a human business, anyway," I acknowledged.

I let my thoughts roam freely for a little while, until they finally fastened on my unworthiness. I remembered my standing in front of my students, fearing that they would find me out.

"About my panic at standing in front of my classes," I resumed, "I think that's what I'm really afraid of. . . . If the students find out about me, they won't love me."

"They don't love you, anyway." Dr. Lustig replied emphatically. "To love someone means that you really know them. Half of your students don't even know your first name."

I was startled by what he said, but also relieved. I was

not the center of the universe. My students were not judging me; they were merely indifferent.

"Who else besides family, then, really loves you?" I asked.

"Most importantly, when you're growing up, your mom and dad. And then they teach you to love yourself. Sometimes people don't get taught it; sometimes people don't learn it. But you have to love you most of all, and then it doesn't matter whether anyone else does. It's sort of nice if you can find somebody else who does later on, but it's no longer critical to your existence. But I can understand your desperation to have a man in your life," he continued, "if that man's love is what validates you as a person. Your validation really ought to be coming from your love, though, so that his love only supplements yours, but never displaces it."

Why is it so hard to love yourself? I wondered again. Why, when Stan left, did I feel so empty inside, so unsure of my judgment?

"It's not just that Stan is not there anymore," I said quietly. "It's that..." I paused to think. "It's just that... I believed in my marriage so much, I believed so much that it would last. Now, how can I ever believe in anything again? How can I believe in myself when my judgment was so bad?"

"Your judgment was good when you chose Stan. From the experience and knowledge that you had of the world at that time, you made a decent decision. And the two of you did your very best to make the marriage work. But the marriage didn't. That's the simple fact. It does not mean that either of you is defective or deficient. It does mean that the marriage didn't work out, and the two of you wisely decided to end it. And the next time you find somebody who interests you, and the next time you get to thinking seriously about marriage, you'll have more information and knowledge, more experience and wisdom to rely upon when you make the decision. But it will still require a great deal of effort on both of your parts. And there will still be no guarantee that it will last forever. But I do hope that both of you will have the hope that it will."

"You have to have the hope to stay alive," I muttered,

thinking about the primitive hope that had brought me so far.

"You certainly do have to have the hope to keep going," he countered. "You have to breathe to stay alive."

I didn't say anything immediately. With disappointment, I began telling him how deceived I was feeling. Society had seemed to promise me that, if I followed its rules, my marriage would last forever. "I admit I may be responding with childish anger," I said in conclusion, "but that's how I feel."

"Well, it's never nice to find out that some of our beliefs from childhood are just myths," Dr. Lustig replied. "But on the other hand, it can be an incredible relief. Knowing them to be myths puts them in their place."

As my appointment drew to a close, I realized how difficult it is to have illusions stripped away. I was in shock at such a dose of realistic thinking.

"I'm so weary," I told Dr. Lustig, as I stood up to go.

"Well, then, get some rest," he said sympathetically. "This is not a marathon. Take it in small steps, in small doses."

And that was what I did over the next few months. I often left my conversations with him feeling confused, as if everything that I thought had been turned upside down. But gradually, I came to have a more realistic grasp of my current situation, and began to have more realistic expectations. I sought ways to avoid my Sunday isolation. I would call friends in advance, and arrange to see them on the weekends when the children were not at home. I joined an art class and began painting watercolors on a regular basis. Slowly, I learned the art of surviving on my own. And sometimes, even small pleasures would present themselves—a good movie, a good dinner with friends, sitting in the lovely summer twilight sipping wine. And best of all I could occasionally laugh at myself.

Chapter 3

As my rampant anxiety faded into a more rational calm, and the loneliness of lost companions eased its hold on me, I found my thoughts turning to men. Men had found little place in the theater of the absurd that had been my playground. But in the mellow light of summer evenings, new possibilities of romance came to mind. One man, in particular, had recently caught my attention.

I had seen him several times in Dr. Lustig's waiting room. It was not his pleasing manner, or his impish grin, that first captured my notice—it was a kind of intensity in his light brown eyes, a ripple of energy that sent waves cascading over me. We found ourselves looking at each other, trying to frame words that would match the unspoken attraction. Our conversation was mundane, even as its effect was exhilarating.

"What's your sign?" he asked me.

"I'm a Pisces," I replied, amused at this stereotypical singles-scene gambit.

"I'm a Cancer," he announced. "Cancers and Pisces go well together."

The intensity of our mutual looking belied the banality of our words.

I watched for him after that, but it was not until the

following Thursday that I saw him again. By then, he had come to be a romantic figure in my imagination, and I was ready to pursue our initial brief connection more vigorously. I learned at our second meeting that his name was Ted and that he was a producer at a local radio station, an occupation that only heightened his romantic stature in my eyes. He was ready for me too on that occasion, for almost immediately he asked me for a date. We settled on the following Saturday at eight o'clock. "A party with friends," he told me.

I dressed carefully that Saturday, trying to achieve an impression of casual elegance that conveyed an understated sexuality. I finally chose a soft-pastel flowered dress, open at the neck but not too daring. My mirror told me that it draped me in a becoming manner.

Ted obviously approved of my choice, for he was barely through the front door before he reached over to kiss me. I was flattered and excited.

After a few minutes, I took him by the hand and led him into the living room. "Would you like a glass of wine?" I asked a bit breathlessly, striving for just the appropriate nonchalance.

"That would be nice," he replied. I heard the huskiness in his voice, as he cleared his throat. As I got the wineglasses out of the cupboard and poured, they clinked in my shaking hands.

"Here we are," I announced as coolly as I could, as I handed him his drink. "To you," he said as our glasses met. We each took one sip and then, in unison, set our glasses down on the coffee table. His arms slipped around my shoulders and into an embrace.

It seemed only natural that we should melt into one another as we did. It was just like a story. Heroes and heroines have no need for sophisticated speech. He held my face between his hands as if I were an idol. I stroked his hair and nuzzled at his ears. His hands slipped down my dress and cupped my breasts. My hand traced the contours of his hips until they found the hardened outline of his masculinity.

I didn't think about what would happen next. I simply assumed that we would make love to each other. I had always been married when this had happened before. And when you are married, you do not wait. So I broke away gently, and thinking about the necessity of some contraception, said simply, "Wait here."

As I hurriedly left, I called back to him, "You can pull out the sofa. It makes into a bed."

I was too enchanted to see the startled look on his face as I left. I did not see how I had shattered the illusion.

When I returned to the room a few minutes later, I immediately saw that something was wrong. But I did not grasp what it was. He stood there, fidgeting. The sofa had not been opened.

"What's the matter?" I asked in genuine surprise. I could not understand how the mellowness of the mood some minutes before could have been so quickly transformed, why our embrace had not faded into instant fulfillment. Ted looked uncomfortable, like he didn't know what to say. "We really should be going to the party," he said nervously.

I felt hurt and rejected, but I didn't say anything immediately. Didn't he want to have sex? I wondered. Why this sudden change? I had no inkling that I was playing by married rules. I did not understand that I had moved too fast. I had skipped all the middle steps. I had not let a fledgling relationship flourish in its own time. And most unpardonably for a romantic heroine, I had taken the lead.

I looked at Ted quizzically, still not grasping what had happened. I reached over to kiss him again, but he drew away. "We really must be going," he repeated again. By now, the earlier mood had been completely fractured. I felt robbed. I also felt embarrassed, as if I had committed a faux pas whose nature everyone else recognized, even as I did not.

"Okay," I said, as I rose to go. "I'm sure the party will be fun." I was trying to put on a cheerful countenance, hoping to redeem what I could of the evening. Perhaps later, after the party, I thought, we can recapture the mood. I took his arm as we walked out to the car. He still looked shaken, but he did not pull away.

The party was a disaster. No sooner had we arrived than Ted fled from me, seeking sanctuary with his friends. When I entered a room in search of him, he would immediately exit it. Hopes of redeeming the evening were quickly evaporating. I didn't know any of the people, but I tried to talk to some of them anyway. All the while, I was wondering what I had done wrong.

The party seemed to drag on interminably. Several times I suggested to Ted that we go, but he only looked alarmed at the prospect, and insisted that he did not wish to leave. Looking back on it later, I realized that he was afraid to return home with me at too early an hour, afraid of the advances that I might make.

Finally, we left. It was 2 A.M. Too late for sex. Too tired for sex. Too sudden for sex. I was finally beginning to understand. We spoke little on the way home. Ted accompanied me to the door. He kissed me, and for a moment our earlier passion was awakened. I clung to him, hoping that I could see him again, hoping that I had not spoiled everything. He seemed to be fighting with himself. I think he really liked me, but I had broken the rules. Finally, he pulled away from me and abruptly said good night. I knew I would not see him again.

Later I expressed my embarrassment and puzzlement to Dr. Lustig. When I described our comedy of errors and my role as the clown, Dr. Lustig laughed so hard that tears formed in the corners of his eyes. Finally, when he could speak, he seemed to empathize as much with Ted as with me.

"Poor fellow," he commented. "He was probably frightened to death by your sexual directness. Take it easier on the next guy, will you? You tried to score a home run without getting past first base!

"It's great to be that straightforward," he continued more soberly, "but you can only be that candid with someone you've known a little longer."

And so, rather painfully, I learned that the rules of marriage do not translate to the single life. Nor could I rely on my experiences of being single at an earlier and simpler time. Social forces larger than myself were forging new expectations and shaping new dreams. One of those aspirations was for sexual freedom, in a context of equal partnership between men and women.

But the dreams, I learned that summer, were far from the social reality. We, my friends and I and the people I met, talked at length of the new order, but in practice, the old order imprisoned our feelings and beliefs.

I had worked in the women's movement before the currents of madness swept me up. Then it had seemed simple—a simple matter of equity. I took the lead on the education committee of our local NOW chapter, approaching the local school boards with demands for curriculum innovations. Our modest efforts had been successful, and we had delighted in our power to effect social change.

In spite of this advocacy, I did not see the women's movement first and foremost as a political force, perhaps because by nature I was not political. For me, it was more like the sounding of an inner bell. Not a call to arms, so much as a call to some long-lost recollection of what I was or what I might be. Its echo was profound in a way that I did not comprehend, then. It called me to consider the issue of my worth.

In this context, I saw my battle with madness as just another, perhaps more extreme, battle for a self-sufficient self. Now, as I stood at the door of society again, I somehow expected the ideals that were being articulated from every street corner to take substantial shape in the relationships at hand. What competence I had, had been forged in the fire. So I expected the men I met to see my worth in my own terms.

That they did not was a surprise to me, although perhaps it should not have been, since my own emotions lagged several steps behind my ideals. I told myself that I was a person of worth, but then was grateful if any man noticed me.

Nowhere, perhaps, was the shifting battleground more evident than at the singles events held at a nearby Unitarian church. There, survivors of divorce and separation assembled every Sunday evening, to participate in group discussions and mingle at a later "social."

The impact of the women's movement was felt in the early evening discussions. There, we talked about the new standards of our times. In order to be equal, should women pay for themselves on dates? Would women respect men if they expressed a gentler, feminine sensitivity? We talked earnestly of such matters and then retired to the drinks and dancing that followed.

But this "mixing" after our discussions suggested a goal more reminiscent of Cosmopolitan than Ms. magazine. The search for equality and sensitivity quickly evaporated into the search for sex. It was a climate of singleness in search of salvation. Since for many, the committed married order had resulted in a fall from grace, many "singles" sought redemption through uncommitted physicality. And the nature of the sexual search was not so far from the traditional sexual roles. I found that any reference to a doctoral degree sent would-be suitors running for cover. Alternately, sexual coyness and passive smiles brought numerous invitations to the one-night stand.

I concurred in all this because I was famished for sex. True intimacy and companionship seemed secondary; simple physical connection was paramount. The desire to be touched became the most pressing need. Committed or uncommitted, my sexual nature demanded fueling. I was willing to play by the new-old rules of the game.

It was at the Unitarian church social that I met Joe. He asked me to dance. After two dances, we retired to "someplace quieter," which turned out to be a vast church hall on the upper floor. We found a sofa there, tucked in one dimly lit corner, and Joe and I proceeded to carry sexual touching as far as was possible in a public room.

From the church hall we retired to his car, where we did not bother to start the engine. Moving shadows of people returning to their cars did not deter us from our explicit sexual goal. Finding the front seat too awkward and cramped, we promptly retired to the backseat, and there consummated our hastily contrived union.

Later we talked. Joe, it seemed, was an auditor, weary of the routine of his life. I thought about telling him of my travails and recent hospitalization, but decided that he would not understand. So we talked of the commonplace, in the absence of a more meaningful intellectual compatibility. But mostly, our relationship took a physical form.

I saw him several times after that, at his house and at mine. Although nothing had been explicitly stated, he seemed to assume that we were going together. It was on our third tryst, the first at my home, that he scared me badly.

He arrived that evening full of smiles, carrying a tote bag under his arm. I asked him what was in it, and he smiled a strange smile. I began to feel uneasy. "I'll show you later," he said mysteriously. I put my vague feeling of unease aside.

Although I had never brought a man to the house when my children were there, Joe began talking about the need for a lock on my bedroom door. He talked about it with a feverish intensity and a certain opaqueness of eye that suggested some deeper concern or meaning behind his words. Again, I felt uneasy. Again, I put it out of my mind.

Later, we retired to the bedroom. Only then did I learn what Joe had brought along in his mysterious bag. With considerable eagerness, he told me to wait in the bedroom while he got it. Reentering the room with the bag, he carefully withdrew its contents and set it on the bed.

It was an electric drill with a long, large bit. He displayed it with excitement, explaining that he had brought it to install a lock on the door.

I panicked. The drill was wicked looking and alarming. The rather crooked way that he smiled when he handled it gave me the oddest sensation that he wanted to use the drill on me.

"Please take it out to the living room," I insisted, the edge of my voice lifting in a newfound fear. "Please take it out of here."

Joe looked bemused and not altogether pleased, but reluctantly did as I requested. When he returned to the bedroom, he looked angry. He grabbed me roughly, as if he had finally put aside any pretense of concern. He pinched my breast as if he wanted to hurt me, and began to force me into anal intercourse.

I suddenly became terrified of the situation. I pushed him away, but that only seemed to make him angrier. No one else was around. I realized that I had to rely on my wits.

I began talking soothingly to Joe. "I really don't feel like having sex now," I said wheedlingly. "I guess I'm just not ready for a sexual relationship now—I'm just too confused."

I started telling him about the hospital and how I had so many problems. I hoped that if it seemed to be my own limitation, perhaps he might go willingly. I talked on and on, in the most calming voice I could muster.

After a while, Joe began to grasp what I was saying. He gathered up his clothes roughly, and slowly put them on. He seemed puzzled by what I said, but satisfied. I told him I was tired and, reluctantly, he said he would go.

As the door closed behind him, I stood shaking for some time. The slice of depravity I sensed in this supposedly normal man had scared me more than the voices of all the lunatics at the sanitarium.

"How are you going to prevent that from happening again?" Dr. Lustig asked earnestly when I told him about it. "What clues were there in the situation that, next time, you'll recognize sooner?"

"I guess the fact that we had nothing in common except our bodies and our loneliness," I replied.

"What else?" Dr. Lustig continued. "Was there a look in his eyes?"

"I don't know," I admitted, feeling inept. "I didn't notice until later."

"Most people give clues about themselves before something catastrophic happens," he said.

"I guess I'd better become a better observer," I acknowledged, understanding in a new way the necessity of a firm grasp of people and events outside myself, rather than so much inner absorption.

"You're ready to do that now," Dr. Lustig affirmed, "and now, as a single person, it's necessary for your well-being."

It wasn't until over a year later, when my divorce was finalized, that I was ready for love. In the meantime I avoided the singles scene, occupying myself instead with the day-to-day business of eking out a living, struggling to be a steady emotional source for Elizabeth and Daniel, trying to transform their tears and insecurities into well-being, encouraging them not to shrink from the world, but to meet it boldly, with confidence in their own worth, showing more confidence and perspective myself so that they could learn from me what they had not before. Especially showing Elizabeth, my deeply sensitive child, how to be sturdier and more matter-of-fact, explaining to her in detail the dynamics of many social situations that she did not naturally understand, how what other people did was not necessarily a response to or criticism of her, how she must make friends if she wanted to have them, how to walk up to other children and ask if they wanted to play, instead of cowering in the background, afraid of rejection. Learning that too much sympathy did not help her, that lessons about getting along in the world were what she needed most. And both of us learning from Daniel, who seemed to have an innate confidence and ability to get along, who seemed to have been born with an even temperament and practical outlook that little could disturb.

And of course, throughout, the business of lawyers, negotiations over child support and future financial obligations to the children for orthodontia, college, other unexpected expenses along the way, parceling out vacation days and holidays, distributing what little property there was, finally settling for fifteen hundred dollars, since Stan had cleaned out all the bank accounts prior to leaving and that was all there was left, and that going to cover my lawyer's fees. Becoming increasingly incensed at the legal system because of its handling of divorce, its adversarial insistence that cost the warring parties time and money, and discouraged compromise.

Somehow surviving it all, sometimes succeeding, sometimes failing, but growing stronger each day, learning to be more observant of what passed outside myself, finding that a self is not given, but must be made by the very attempts to face problems and solve them, by the daily struggle itself that is the fire that forges steel.

Chapter 4

The afternoon, almost a year and a half after Stan had left, when I received my divorce papers was much like any other Saturday without the children, except perhaps for the slight twisting of my heart, the trace of sadness I felt that now it was over. I had expected to feel, at a minimum, a cataclysmic wrenching, but I discovered instead that my mourning was done.

I read through the legalities slowly, noting the transgressions I was supposed to have committed against Stan— how I had humiliated him in public—contrived violations that had allowed the divorce to go through. Our state had no provisions for no-fault divorce, and I had agreed to be the guilty party, just to see it done.

I didn't even feel angry as I read the lies. I just felt tired. Tired to the core after the months of legal wrangling, the distrust, the last savings slipping through my lawyer's hands, the final settlement of meager child support, the court hearing that I, as the guilty party, had not attended, and now these papers, so properly signed and sealed, saying that my marriage was nothing, defining me as a divorced woman.

I stuffed them back into their envelope and put them on the shelf. Later, I would put them in my safety deposit box at the bank, the same one that now held my engagement ring.

I dialed the number of a friend and invited her to join me for a drink. It was not a celebration exactly, but a ritual nonetheless, a public sanctioning of my new unmarried state, just as friends and family had sanctioned my marriage eight years earlier.

My friend, Carol, and I met and drank and talked about our divorces. "How does it feel to be a free woman?" she asked me.

"It feels fine," I said, brushing away the tears that unaccountably sprang up. "I'll manage," I continued, and just as unaccountably laughed heartily, feeling myself expand outward as if to fit the shape of the new freedom my divorce represented. "I'll survive," I summed up both weeping and laughing, knowing that, whatever else was true of me at that time, I would go on.

We drank and talked some more. She recounted the horrors of her marriage, such as the time her husband had thrown a wrench at her head during a marital dispute, missing her by inches and indenting her bedroom wall just above the bed.

As I listened, sadness settled over me. Memories of Stan holding my hand during labor when the children were born, memories of earlier carefree times filled my eyes to overflowing again. I must think about all the other things, I thought. I must remember the reasons why I got divorced. I tried to summon the negative recollections, to remember, to feel the icy disenchantment of the last year. But these thoughts were stubbornly unavailable.

"Why is it easier for me to remember the good times?" I asked Carol. "Why do my reasons for divorce seem now like so many shadows, flitting through the half-light? Why can't I reach out my hand and grab them, so that their presence would make my decision seem right? Why, after all my suffering, do I still wonder if I've done the right thing?"

I wept some more and, this time, Carol wept with me. Then, we got rip-roaring drunk. Near midnight, after short goodbyes, we stumbled back to our respective empty houses.

Stan returned the children the next day. He made no

reference to the divorce papers, nor did I. After all, the legal formality seemed anticlimactic.

That day in particular, I scrutinized the children's faces, to see if I could find mirrored there any sign of psychic damage. I looked to them to find out how we were doing, to gauge whether I should view the divorce as our salvation or our defeat or, most probably, something quite different altogether.

Their faces provided no clues to answer my questions. What they showed me instead was the power of children to survive. For an hour or so, when they made the transition between Stan and me, they seemed unsettled, as if the changing of houses and parents required such an enormous adjustment of feelings and attitudes that their mental gears started slipping. For an hour or so, when they returned, they clung to me more than usual. For an hour or so, they cried and complained about small things. Then slowly, they returned to normal, accommodating to our household as if they had never left it for a weekend trip to another.

That day, when Stan brought the children back, I was reminded of the day he and I had brought Elizabeth home from the hospital. We had spread out a quilt on the living room floor, carefully placing her on it. She burbled and gurgled happily. We looked at her and then at each other. "What do we do now?" we asked simultaneously. Then we burst into laughter.

From that moment of shared ignorance, we had achieved, via the circuitous route of divorce, a newfound shared comfort in our parental roles. Curiously, as divorced parents, we constituted a team. Now, more than ever, we were able to support one another, perhaps because, standing outside of marriage as we did now, our need for support from each other was so much more apparent.

During the year and a half since our separation, both Stan and I had learned much about being competent parents. He now had an ease about him, when he was with Elizabeth and Daniel, that spoke of routines and rituals, security and care. He and I had each become better at drawing the line, and making our expectations firmer and clearer. The children, in turn, had responded with gratitude and affection, had made pictures and signs constructed of "I love you's," hearts in pink and red crayon, rainbows in all the colors of the spectrum.

One critical child-rearing lesson I learned and began putting into practice was how to be the adult in charge, how to be the parent, and how to let the children be children. But confronting their literal-mindedness, from which exceptions to the rules sprang up like Hydra heads, was a Herculean task.

"Stop yelling!"

"I wasn't yelling, I was just talking loudly."

"Well, stop talking loudly!" Humming ensues.

"Stop making that noise!"

"I'm just humming! You didn't say I couldn't hum!"

By simply turning it around, however, as Dr. Lustig suggested, by saying what I wanted them to do, rather than what I did not want them to do, this negative pattern was undercut and order was restored. I did not have to think of all the possible permutations of unacceptable behavior that can make the disciplining of youngsters so exhausting. Although it took effort to think clearly and articulate in advance how I wanted the children to behave, it eclipsed my tendency to react reflexively. I took charge. "Don't do this, don't do that" was replaced by positive commands and expectations.

"I expect you to behave yourselves properly when we go out. You will be polite and well-mannered. That means you will keep your hands to yourself and be considerate of others. Is that clear?"

The children thrived on the newfound order, and I thrived on the newfound simplicity.

I appreciated what Stan did for the children and the appreciation was mutual. Throughout our separation and divorce proceedings, in spite of the bitterness and battles over power, control, and money, we had both instinctively followed one basic rule of decency: We never spoke against each other in front of the children or undermined each other in more subtle nonverbal ways. So the children suffered less, were not pulled apart in their fundamental love or loyalty. Stan and I also benefited, because of all the things to be forgiven in the process of divorcing, the least likely is seeing yourself ridiculed by your ex-partner in your children's eyes.

Because of this fundamental decency Stan and I later could improve our relationship, becoming cooperative parents rather than warring ex-spouses.

AUGUST, 1977

A turning point for Stan and me in our relationship was a conversation we had about five months after our divorce became official. Stan had called me one day and asked if we could meet for dinner. He wanted to discuss the children and ourselves, he said. Seated across from each other at a neighborhood restaurant, we found that the words did not flow smoothly. After some hesitations and a few false starts, Stan began telling me how sorry he felt about my stay in the hospital, and what had happened to me. He regretted that he had not been more helpful, more sensitive to my needs during that time. A tone of guilt infused his words of apology; a note of sadness sounded in his voice. He lamented what we had lost, or perhaps never had, and tentatively suggested that we try again. Perhaps if we made another effort, we might recapture the marriage we had scarcely had.

I did not want Stan to feel guilty about the past—there was no need for that now. Nor did I want him to regret our mutual decision. To me there was no going backward, however appealing the past might appear, set against the backdrop of current loneliness.

As Stan talked, I considered the issue of our relationship.

"The divorce isn't your fault, Stan," I said. "We both contributed to it, so there's no reason for you to place all the blame on yourself. We did the best we could. It just didn't work out."

Stan nodded, but I could see that my words were not taking away the sorrow and regret he felt. I tried again, in a different vein, carefully considering my words.

"Even though we're divorced, Stan," I said, "we're still in a long-term relationship. It's not a married relationship anymore, but because we have children together, we're inevitably involved with one another. Divorce didn't turn you into a monster, nor into a casual acquaintance.

You remain a person of importance in my life—what you do and what happens to you are matters of concern to me.

"Even though we're no longer married," I suggested, "we have a nonsuperficial relationship that demands work and effort on both of our parts. Rather than going over and over the past and our mistakes, I think our energy would be better spent in making our current relationship a mutually cooperative one—the best it can be, for both our sakes, as well as the children's."

Stan listened attentively to me, and nodded.

"Yes, you're right," he said. He reached across the table and, with the lightness of a butterfly, touched my hand.

I realized, then, how often I had been unfair to Stan in my thoughts, painting him and our relationship in the darkest colors, in order to justify so great a loss. I had repeatedly told myself that Stan had not helped with the children, forgetting the many times he had: the daily walks he took with Elizabeth during our nine months' stay in England in 1973, so that I, pregnant with Daniel, could rest in quiet in our tiny cramped flat; the many times he had bathed the children or read them bedtime stories; the way he listened to my concerns about them. And his love for Elizabeth and Daniel—that had never wavered.

Whether or not he had equally shared the child care no longer seemed the issue, for that had not been our bargain. I had chosen that role; he had worked full time to support us.

I told Stan what I was thinking, and he was glad of this more realistic reminder of his former role. Throughout the rest of the meal, our conversation shifted to shared concerns about the children. As we talked, I sensed relief in both of us. We were no longer married, but some continuity was preserved. "You're still like family to me," I concluded as we rose to go.

"I feel the same," Stan replied, as he helped me on with my coat.

From that occasion onward, our relationship was indeed marked by a newfound spirit of cooperation. We both strived to achieve the art of good will, to avoid two pitfalls—the bitterness of continued feuding and the nostalgia for our former married state. We began to direct our gaze away from the past, toward the present and future. We became comrades in the effort of raising our children well. Like an old and valued friend, Stan was there to take the children to the dentist, to ballet lessons, to soccer games. As they grew older, we went together to events at their school, met their teachers at report card conferences, rooted for them at their baseball games.

An ease accompanied our encounters that had never been there before. From the shattering of divorce, we finally moved to a different union—founded on a common commitment to the children we had conceived and continued to share. Our broken spirits slowly mended. Our divorced relationship became, ironically, more successful than our married one had been.

PART V

Looking in a New Direction

Chapter 1

MAY, 1977

Love when it came was unexpected. I was sitting at the kitchen table, sipping coffee, on a May afternoon. From the softness and angle of the sun through the window, I judged that it was about four o'clock. Alone in the house again, on another Saturday, alone because it was Stan's weekend with the children, alone with only the sounds of the kitchen clock for company. I had just woken from a nap and felt thick and heavy. I stared at the clock absently, and then found myself watching it in earnest. I became absorbed by the second hand, methodically ticking away the time—time wasted, gone for good.

I wonder why people say, "Time heals all wounds." That makes no sense, because the wounds I feel are cumulative, an endless string of meaningless encounters with men whose names were forgotten after they never called again, no single one of whom was important enough to be called a wound, any one of whom I could have gotten over easily if he had been the only one. But the wound lay in the pattern of pointlessness—the chance encounters, the bundling into bed after an evening of attention and small favors. Dinner, wine, perhaps flowers. The sense of regret the morning after. Nonetheless, the waiting by the phone. The phone silent for days, just long enough to

253

announce that it was over, without so much as a polite call or meeting to say so directly. Left feeling lonelier than when I was alone.

I would never have left Stan, I reflected, if I had known that freedom amounted to this. Better to be in a marriage, any marriage, however alienated, than alone like this, trailing a string of one- or two-night encounters that spoke of multiple meaninglessness.

I roused myself from the table to prepare a light supper, when there was a knock at the door. I opened it to find Robert standing there, in clean jeans and a pressed shirt, hair trimmed neatly, eyes alight with a smile.

Somehow I was not surprised that he was standing there. I was surprised at the change a year and a half had made. Gone was the haunted look, the desperation that did not lie quietly in the background, the pain of a previous time. He looked well to me in a way that he had not before, as if he had enjoyed the beneficence of some kindly power, or perhaps had himself wrung a new confidence out of the sweat of dismantling a worn-out marriage.

I was glad that he was here, because he was one of those people who make an indelible impression on your life, whether they be friends or lovers, mentors or strangers. They may stay for years, or, like Robert, they may go quickly, but their coming is always an unexpected gift. It matters little whether you have much in common with them or little in common, because you share a secret understanding when you meet.

So it was now, as always, with Robert. As we stood at the door grinning at each other, the year since we had last met dropped away like a shed skin. We resumed our conversation as easily as if it had been interrupted only yesterday.

"I've thought about you often," he said as he slipped his arms around me. "I never could get you out of my mind."

I traced his face slowly with one finger, wondering at my luck that he should have come back. Then we moved to the living room sofa and laughed and talked, again charmed by each other and by the connection that always connected. We spoke of our failed marriages, about his current custody battle for his daughter, about my hospitalization and why we could not have continued before. Later we moved in unison to the bedroom.

Whereas with madness, one feels timelessness as a great divider that isolates the instants and splinters the self, the timelessness of love is a gathering of temporal moments into one cohesive sphere, timeless in the sense of no mechanical division, as if even past and future lay in one another's arms. To love the night away, with no sense of tomorrow, free for the moment of yesterday's limitations, wrapped for the present in the smiles of a spring night, is to know the meaning of luck, or if luckier, of grace. To know the gentleness of a hand that traces the outline of your face, that smooths away the lines that have worried your brow, outlining, still with gentleness, the curve of your breast, sliding down your body to find the places of secret pleasure, bodies stretching and straining in physical attunement, wanting the final release to be soon and in unison, to mirror the enchantment of a rare and instant understanding, to fit the body's pleasures to the ungrasped soul, and when all is accomplished, to lie together with time lifted, is to know for one moment the sweet laughter of the gods.

We made love to each other again and again that night, with a hunger that found no easy appeasement. As we loved each other, I suddenly felt the inadequacy of my physical beauty. I wanted to have a perfect body for him. When I told him my fears, he only smiled and continued his caresses. "You don't have the kind of body that they make statues out of," he said laughingly, "but how you can move!"

Later, in the early morning hours, we returned to the study, where I kept my stereo. Feeling the splendor of our mutual nakedness, we played "Lay Lady Lay" and danced, moving slowly and sensually, our nude bodies intertwining in the center of a room filled with books and other trappings of the intellectual life.

Later yet, just as dawn was breaking, we played Chopin nocturnes and settled on the sofa to watch the first rose-colored light filter through the windows. Robert draped me with a blanket so that I would not be cold.

Finally it was time for him to go. As he was dressing, he suddenly turned to me and said, "Did you notice that we have the same color eyes?" I nodded, and he continued musingly. "They're very unusual eyes," he said, "gray-green." He was quiet for a few moments. "Our kind of eyes are very sensitive to the light."

I smiled in acknowledgment.

Again and again, afterward, I thought of that night with Robert, and of those that followed, as a salutation from the Muses, who understood the simultaneous needs of the flesh and the spirit, the human frailty that can be so touched by its mirror image. Love with Robert was a compelling experience that pronounced the body good and the mind its servant, a step into the Garden of the Happy People that I had earlier only dared to dream. He loved in me what I most admired in myself—not beauty or intellect, but the power to survive, the courage to fight with demons and prevail.

What I remember most about that period with Robert was its beginning and its end, almost a year later. What passed in the middle—stolen hours carefully arranged, glimpses of each other within the confines of our restricted social situation, leisurely afternoons in the country lunching at quaint rustic inns—passed before my eyes with the inevitability of a dream play whose middle is dictated by the playwright's conception of the first scene and the last.

Because of Robert, I learned a little more about loving myself, because I loved him and he was my counterpart. We were both lovers of intensity, seeking the highs and tolerating the lows for the sake of the exercise of our imaginations. He was a person of high temperament, more drawn to the language of metaphor than to the practicalities of the daily round. Like children at play, we strove to be sensible, but our spirits often took the easier road to ecstasy. I told him the lessons that I was learning in my therapy, about how to live better in the middle ground. We would agree on all points, and then, caught up, feed once again on a diet of the senses.

I think Robert left me, finally, because in our alikeness we limited each other. He and I were twin violins, always straining to reach the ethereal timbre. We greeted each other with the same tone color, the union of our sounds echoing some dark and rich and primeval understanding, founded perhaps in the collective unconscious or, as the poet said, in the "wisdom of old stones." But, for all of that, the time came for us to part, to find better balance with more grounded partners.

I often thought afterward of our final meeting. We were sitting in the front seat of his car, having ventured out into the countryside for the afternoon. It was a rainy day in early March of the next year, completing the cycle of the seasons. The wipers of his car rhythmically pushed away the rain, but I could not smooth away the tears in my eyes and the lump in my throat.

As he sat telling me of the new love that he had found, I knew, although I had never met her, that she would be a cello, mellow and grounded. I knew that she would represent the earth and the business of getting along day by day. Even as I brushed aside my tears, I knew that he would be choosing wisely.

"I don't know why you came into my life," he told me as he started the engine to return home. "But I've always thought of you as a bit of grace." I gave him one last look and then asked him to drive me home quickly, because it was the only way I could go.

I knew that it might be months or years before I found another Robert, or better yet, a Robert with more grounding in the practical. But my fledgling sense of worth demanded nothing less. The elementary self-respect that I was building cried out that, first and foremost, I like myself. Better to be alone, than with someone who does not cherish me. Better to build a solid self by myself, than to chase its fleeting shadow in someone else's eyes. There is still much work to be done, I told myself, before you can count yourself among the strong. The foundation to build upon may be in place, but there are still many bricks to lay to build your own house.

Chapter 2

One Sunday in October, I was sitting at the kitchen table, balancing my checkbook. The gray, threatening sky outside filtered a gloomy light over the pile of unpaid bills stacked neatly beside me. Two more weeks until the end of the month, and only fifty dollars left in my checking account. How am I going to get through this month, I wondered not for the first time, and all the months stretching out into the future? I took a sip of coffee, and sighed. Another month, another financial dead end. How to survive?

For years, it seemed, I had been on uncertain terms with existence. First there had been madness to conquer, then depression and divorce. Now the forces of economic insecurity pressed on me like gravity. When I had attempted to ignore them in the past, they had toppled me. I had depended on other people, particularly my family, to pick me up. It's time to stand on your own financially, I told myself firmly, like a football coach giving his team a pep talk. It's time to confront the economic realities. It's time to reconsider the issue of your work.

Somewhere in me, over the past few months had grown the resolve to address the issue of my economic survival.

258

Ignoring this elemental force of nature was an indulgence I could no longer afford.

It's time to reassess your professional goals, I told myself. You started out as a fragmented blue cube. You found the means of sticking the pieces of the cube together. Now you must find the piece that represents your work, and put it into its proper place.

Academic career opportunities, so bright just a few years earlier, were rapidly fading. Tenured positions, the ultimate privilege of academe, were few within the geographical area where I lived, and getting fewer. The part-time teaching that I had done for the past five years was, at best, a stepchild compared to permanent academic work. Even though, this fall, I had been hired full time at a larger university, my position was a temporary one. I was replacing a tenured professor on sabbatical, with no prospects for the following year.

As I surveyed my situation, I regretfully concluded that I must consider an alternative career—one that would allow me to stay within the community where I lived, but would provide adequate financial support for me and my children.

But where to begin? My whole adult life had involved academics—I had worked there, lived there, married and brought my children up there. I knew virtually no one outside this sphere. How do you go about finding another profession, I wondered, when you don't even know what the alternatives are? The prospect of beginning an unstructured search was frightening. I was floundering in the water, wishing someone had thought to give me swimming lessons.

Perhaps because I was an academic by training, I started with a book. *What Color Is Your Parachute?* had been recommended to me as the "must" manual for changing careers. I bought it, absorbed it, and thus inspired, set out on my search for a new occupation. Guided by my self-help manual, I decided that I wanted a career, not simply a job, and that I must be prepared to devote at least six months to establishing it. I also decided that career changing called for a strategy. I would apply my intellectual skills to the problem-solving task at hand.

I began by thinking. What skills do I have that would

be transferable to another occupation? What needs do I
have that I would expect a new career to fulfill?

The first task, I concluded, is to decide what career I
want; the second task is to go about getting it. But I could
not know what I wanted to do unless I knew what options
were available. And I knew no one who could tell me
what they were.

I mused for weeks, wondering how to make a beginning. If I could just figure out some concrete step to take,
then perhaps I could begin to master the art of survival.
But before I could move forward, I had to hurdle a wall
of anxiety and uncertainty. The world outside academe
seemed so scary, because it called for a competence I was
unsure I had. I wondered daily if I was made of strong
enough stuff.

I must find a way to approach that world, I decided.
With a logical approach I can make a beginning. I worried
and thought, until I had a glimmer of an idea. I'll approach
the outside world like an anthropologist confronting a
foreign culture. First I'll learn what its values and language are. Then I'll try them on and see how they fit.

I picked up the newspaper and turned to the classified
ads, not to find or apply for a job per se, but to discover
the cultural values that I would be confronting. I scanned
the newspaper for jobs paying annual salaries of fifty thou-
sand dollars and upward. I noticed that, aside from experience, there were certain key skills that these jobs
demanded—"problem-solving" abilities, "communication skills," "managerial" talents.

I have those abilities, I said to myself. I got out my
résumé and rewrote it, dwelling not on my teaching experience, but on the skills that becoming and being a philosopher had demanded. A common prejudice against
academics, I reflected, is to assume they can *think*, but
not *do*. So I chose my words carefully as I rewrote my
résumé, ensuring that I articulated my abilities in terms
of *action* words. Under the section I titled "areas of exper-
tise," I wrote "analyzing, synthesizing, problem solving,
communicating, managing."

Now that I had some grasp of my skills, I needed to
find a job they would fit. But first, I reflected, I must

decide which of my abilities *I want* to utilize from nine to five, what I want my career to do *for me*.

I thought about that for several days. My children demand my emotional and intuitive side. My artwork demands my creativity. What's lacking, I realized, is a strong analytic component. I primarily want to use my intellect in a career. Using my rationality there will provide me with the best balance in my life, especially in light of the way intuition earlier held sway.

So a rational, problem-solving job is what I need, I concluded. Now, how do I go about finding one? I could rule out certain occupations right away—social work and social services were too demanding on the emotions and too lacking, from my perspective, in an analytic focus. I crossed social services off my list of possibilities. Government and private industry remained. I must explore those spheres, I decided, to try to find my niche.

My book had recommended a procedure known as interviewing for information, as a way to match one's own skills with the skills demanded by particular professions. The idea was to find people doing interesting things, and to ask them not for a job, but about what they did, in order to match one's own skills against that job profile. While it seemed like a good idea, I didn't know anyone to interview.

I began asking around among my friends, "Do you know *anybody* who does anything else besides teaching?" Finally, I found a friend of a friend who did. I had one name to start from. Unfortunately my contact worked in social services. But that did not deter me. At least it was a starting point that could lead me to others.

As I picked up the phone to dial the number of my first contact, fear paralyzed my throat. When I heard the voice on the other end of the line, I spoke with exaggerated boldness to cover my terror. I introduced myself and explained my interest in finding an alternative career.

The voice at the other end of the line was sympathetic and helpful. She would be glad to give me information about her agency's project. They wrote many grant proposals for federal funding. Perhaps they could use my skills. She would see me next Tuesday at one o'clock if that would be convenient. I hung up the phone grinning and leaped into the air, clapping my hands together in congratulation. I've done it, I thought. I've made a start!

My meeting with the social services woman began, despite my pounding heart and sinking stomach. It's just fear, I told myself. You've struggled with that before. Almost miraculously the interview went smoothly. I gave the woman my résumé, in case a job opening materialized in her agency. She gave me several other names to contact.

And so from one name, my "network" grew. I visited several other social-service agencies; I contacted government offices; I got names of potential leads in private enterprise. I told everyone I met, friends and acquaintances, what I was doing. I asked all those I met if they knew anyone else I might contact.

There were many dead ends. I was still teaching full time while conducting my search, so I had to set reasonable goals for myself. If I contacted two people a week, or wrote two letters, I considered that I had done my job. Slowly but methodically I would draw closer to my objective.

The most difficult part of all lay in giving up my professional identity, or rather in changing it for another that, as yet, had no definition. "How do I maintain my identity as a professional," I asked Dr. Lustig, "when I'm losing the only profession I have ever known, and have nothing to replace it with?" I was discouraged and, most of all, I felt very vulnerable.

"Do you remember the story of the Little Prince?" he asked me. "Do you remember the king without a kingdom?... Well, that's what you are, right now," he continued. "You're a professional without a profession."

I clung to that idea in the discouraging days ahead, as I made my way from one interview to the next. I'm a professional, I repeatedly told myself, even though I don't know what my profession will be. I'll try on an identity at every opportunity. Surely, one of these days, I'll find a profession that suits me.

So I continued my search, from one contact to another. Nothing captured my imagination, however, until May 20, 1978, the day that I ran into my friend Carol at the local office-supply store. We chatted and I told her of my job search. She suggested that I visit her at her center-city office. She offered to introduce me to some people there. Carol worked for a marketing-research and consulting company, she told me, as a field supervisor. However, most of the professional staff were Ph.D.'s. "It's a good place to work," she said. "There's a good feeling about the place." It sounded promising, so I eagerly arranged to meet her there on the following Tuesday. "Wear a suit," she told me. "This is the business world."

I took my last bit of savings, and bought a navy-blue suit and a light-blue blouse for the meeting. As I surveyed myself in the mirror, it seemed a different person looked back at me. My new clothes felt uncomfortable. I felt too dressed up, like a child playacting. But what I saw in the mirror was an image of a bright young business professional. I found myself taking the suit off and then, later, putting it back on, letting the mirror tell me what I might be. I walked back and forth before the mirror, holding imaginary conversations with interviewers, telling them about my skills, trying to sound confident as I did so.

Tuesday arrived and my suit felt less uncomfortable. I met Carol at her office, résumé in hand, and she led me upstairs to meet with a member of the professional staff, a study director named Sally. As I walked through the strange halls past office after office, I felt excitement replace fear. Something about the place and the pleasant-looking people I passed made me feel at home. My meeting with Sally confirmed that feeling.

As she described the work, it seemed heaven-sent. "Marketing research," she explained, "is like a halfway house between business and academics. The clients, mostly large businesses, have specific marketing problems. Our company customizes research to meet their needs. That means designing a study, implementing it in the field, processing the data, and, finally, analyzing the data and writing the report. You need good analytic skills," she told me, "and you also must be able to write."

She was amused when I told her that my Ph.D. was in philosophy.

"We mostly hire Ph.D.'s in the social sciences," she explained, "but a Ph.D. is a Ph.D. What I think you need for a job here is further background in quantitative meth-

ods or marketing. Perhaps you should learn statistics,"
she suggested, "or take a computer or marketing course.
Also try to get some research experience."

I left the meeting feeling that I had found my profession. It was not just the match between my skills and the
work that intrigued me. It was the total feeling about the
place. I want a job in marketing research, I decided on
the way home. And in particular, I want a job at that firm.
It seemed to have a social element that was missing from
academics. These professionals worked together as a team.
The efforts they made, it appeared to me, were cooperative as well as individual. Theirs was a society I felt I
would enjoy.

I had a month left in my teaching job. I'll go on unemployment, I decided, and take some statistics courses and
a computer course. Then I'll ask my academic friends if
they have any quantitative research projects that I can
do gratis. I'll get some research experience, and then go
back to the company and apply for a job.

I promptly enrolled in the courses at the university
where I had been teaching, and went on the unemployment rolls. It was a paradoxical summer. On the one hand,
I was stimulated by the courses and what I was learning.
On the other side, I had hit rock bottom financially. Standing in the unemployment line, I patiently waited for the
surly clerk to process my unemployment check as if it
were a personal beneficence that she somehow begrudged
giving. At that moment the outer world mirrored the profound discouragement I would feel from time to time. That
was when I relied on Dr. Lustig to keep me focused on
the possibilities of a better future.

I saw him every two weeks during this period. He
reduced his fees in light of my shaky financial situation,
and, with some financial help from my parents and brother,
my therapy could continue. I continued to take my medication, although at a much smaller dosage.

In August, when my courses were completed, my friend
Elaine offered me the chance to do some data analysis
for a research project in which she was involved. With
three A's in my statistics and computer courses boosting
my confidence, and with that bit of analytic experience
behind me, I approached the marketing research firm again

in October, 1978— this time to interview for a job, not simply information.

I was passed from one professional to the next, until an interview with the president of the company was arranged. Dressed once again in my sole blue suit, which now felt like it belonged on me, I entered his office. The interview was a most unusual one.

After scanning my résumé, he tossed it onto his large desk and exclaimed, "You don't have any of the experience we're looking for."

I started to speak up for myself, but he silenced me with a wave of his hand. I said nothing more, just sat there, staring straight back at him, while he looked at my résumé again. After what seemed like an eternity of silence, he finally spoke.

"I see that you have the problem-solving and statistical background," he said. "Do you, by any chance, write poetry?"

I was more than startled by his question, but I quickly replied that I did occasionally. "There's some evidence that people with a quantitative background who can also write poetry make excellent marketing-research professionals," he told me. "So I'm willing to consider you. But how do I know that you can do the work?" It almost seemed as if he was musing out loud.

"Give me a project to do," I suggested. "I'll do it for free. Give me a chance to show you what I can do."

"Perhaps," he replied as if he was still thinking. "I'll let you know if any project turns up that you can do." He shook my hand, and I was dismissed. I returned home and wept, sure that I had missed my opportunity.

I waited a full month, but heard nothing from him. In the meantime, I had done other interviewing and had been offered a job with a telecommunications firm. I decided not to go through intermediaries anymore. On impulse, I picked up the telephone and called the president of the marketing-research company that was my first choice.

"I haven't forgotten you," he told me. "You're high up on our list of potential candidates."

"I'm still interested in a position at your firm," I assured him, "although I do have a concrete job offer that I must decide on." He promised to get me a trial project right away. Two weeks later, I was writing my first marketing-research report.

Although my analysis was occasionally shaky, it must have shown promise, because I got the job. I agreed to take an entry-level position, with the understanding that I could work my way up rapidly within the company. We negotiated my salary, and it was done.

To celebrate my new career, I promptly bought a simple gold pinky ring as a present to myself, and as a reminder that I was wedded to a new way of life.

Chapter 3

I spent the next year honing my competence at my new job and directing my children along the path of common sense. By the end of this time, my madness had become a memory, but one I remained on uneasy terms with. Alone at night, after a full day's activity, I would find myself wondering about it all.

Why had it happened, where had it sprung from? Was it an unspoken stigma that I would always carry with me? Not content to simply set it aside, I searched out a reason for that unspeakable, ultimate irrationality.

I found my thoughts turning to my past. Perhaps somewhere in my childhood lay the seeds of later sorrow; perhaps the madness had been mandated by my distant youth.

Images from my past flickered across my mind, slippery as shadows in Plato's cave, trying to speak and tell me where I had come from and what forces had made me, yet always elusive, first dark and then light. My past, which only recently had appeared fixed and irrevocable, was susceptible, I was finding, to countless interpretations. My memories changed like the colors of a chameleon, blending into the environment of thoughts they rested against.

267

Memories of my father had grown more compassionate lately. I had put aside my earliest recollections of feeling deserted because he had gone to war. Instead, I remembered the later, grade-school years—how he had helped me with my report about geysers in Yellowstone Park. Not content to use the encyclopedia, he had drawn me pictures of the geological stages by which geysers are born, from a crack in the ground to jets of shooting steam. When finally I had stood trembling in front of the class, drawing the pictures on the blackboard, I had remembered the look of confidence and pride on his face when we had worked together, and that memory had wiped away my fear.

What about my mother? My mind closed up around that thought, and then ever so carefully opened up again. Why do I find myself so often angry with my mother? Why is it easier to blame her than anyone else, to accuse her in my thoughts of having been unloving, when in spite of her faults, I know that she always did love me? Is it some part of me that doesn't love myself, that wants an excuse, wants to pretend that it was really someone else's fault? It's almost as if I *wish* that there were somebody to blame for what had happened to me. Why my mother? Because we're so alike? Because I feel her vulnerability more than anyone else's, and I despise that very same vulnerability in myself? Why do I have trouble seeing my mother as strong? Is it just that her strengths are of character and feeling, rather than worldly competence?

Why do I remember the trace of fear in her voice whenever she answered the telephone, as if she must be shielded from some alien and potent and potentially dangerous outsider? Why was it, is it, so important to me that she should not be afraid of the outside world? Is it because, somewhere in me, I believe that if her fear was gone, mine would go too? Do I want her to fight that particular battle for me?

Why do I keep remembering the time in my earliest childhood—I couldn't have been more than three or four years old—when I picked some flowers early one Sunday morning, flowers from a sprawling pink hedge of our neighbors' yard?

I had taken the flowers with delight to my mother,

thinking them an especially auspicious gift of the early spring. But instead of being joyful, she had been angry and ashamed, angry that I had "stolen" the neighbors' flowers, ashamed that a child of hers could do such a misdeed. She insisted that I go immediately to the neighbors' house and apologize to them for my theft.

The memory of walking into their cheerful, wood-paneled kitchen is indelibly etched in my mind—the parents, the two twin girls a year or so older than I, another older girl finishing breakfast. Telling them shamefacedly, stumbling over the words, that I was sorry, hearing them laugh uproariously. I thought, of course, that they were laughing at me. Somehow or other, I exited the house.

Anger welled up in me as, once again, I remembered that day. Why had my mother shamed me so? Was it not, after all, a natural impulse toward beauty that had prompted my action? Why was my mother so fearful of social censure? Why had she not sided with me?

To make matters worse, when, later that day, I had told her I was angry, she had refused to hear of it. "No, you aren't angry," she had said. "You're my good girl, and good girls don't get angry."

A week later, another neighborhood friend and I pulled up an entire row of tulips skirting our neighbors' front drive. The punishment I got for that, I felt I deserved.

I talked about my anger at my mother with Dr. Lustig.

"If somebody says, 'You're not angry, dear,' when you know that you are, they're taking away your *power*," he said. Intrigued, I asked him to continue.

"We cannot always control what goes on outside of us," he went on to explain, "but what is *inside* of us, belongs to us—we *create* it; we *control* it. If I want to feel an emotion, I'm going to feel it, because I'm in charge of me. That's my way of exercising my personal power. But if somebody says that something I possess inside, something that I created, doesn't *exist*, denying my experience of my emotion, then I become the victim of the ultimate robbery—the loss of my personal power."

An enormous sadness welled up in me as I thought about that loss. "That's probably my single overwhelming feeling about my childhood," I said quietly. "Powerlessness." I stopped there, overawed by that single word. "I remember," I went on slowly, "I remember having the very strong sense from the time I was very small, maybe two or three, of wanting to control my own fate—wanting to decide for myself what I would do. I even remember saying to my father, who was a very impressive and imposing man, 'You can kill me if you want, but you can't *make* me do anything.' I was only about two or three when I said that—but that's how strongly I felt about it."

"If you're willing to say, 'I'd rather let myself die, because I'm going to be in charge of me and nobody else is; I'm going to keep my power and I'm not going to give it up'—when you're that *clear* about it, it makes a big difference in the world," Dr. Lustig said.

"But where did I lose it—that determination?" I asked miserably. "Somewhere along the way, I lost it."

"Well, you traded it for love," Dr. Lustig promptly replied.

"That's right," I answered, relieved that he should understand. "I felt that to stand up for myself, and to have self-respect and be self-determining, was to be denied love."

"Well, that's where you were had," Dr. Lustig replied. "You gave up your power in order to be . . ." There he paused and thought for a moment. ". . . *imperfectly* loved."

"In order to belong," I said.

"Yes, to belong," he replied.

We sat for a while, then, in silence, each thinking our own thoughts. Where is the line, I wondered, between proper parental control and autonomy for a child? Was it just that I had sought independence too early, or was it that I had sought it at all, being a girl, that is, in a time when self-determination of females was not the norm? I thought about all the girls I had known, and how many of us had so understandably, but so foolishly, given away something that was best about ourselves—how I had given up my self-determination, a part of my integrity, inch by inch, so that finally I didn't know that I had lost it. I didn't know what Dr. Lustig's thoughts were on that occasion, but the look of sadness on his face suggested that he also had some regrets of his own.

Finally, I broke the silence. "Yes," I said, thinking it out, "I can see how losing autonomy is losing personal power. But there's still something missing in the equation."

"Well," he said, "when you lose personal power you also become angry at the people who are telling you to give up your power, and at yourself. And if you're *angry* at yourself, you can do *mean* things, *destructive* things. And if you want to, you can even hide them, so that nobody will ever know. But inside you're constantly being flagellated in some way."

I thought about the way that my anger would devour me, and I understood the other price that I was paying for not acknowledging it.

"How do I stop, then?" I asked quietly.

"By acknowledging what's going on inside of you, by letting yourself feel it, but still having enough self-control to use it only for the benefit of yourself and others."

I thought about the story of the flowers again, and I felt petty even as I felt angry. After all the wonderful things my mother had done for me, how could I blame her for such a minor thing? She made a mistake, that's all. I know I've made worse.

"I know how my mother felt," I said. "Her feeling was shame. She felt ashamed of me that I would take the flowers. She felt that it made her a bad mother—that is reflected badly on *her*."

"That's losing sight of the limitations of the child. Children need opportunities to learn. And every time a child does something to indicate some confusion about a rule, it means that the parent has to make sure that the child learns the rule correctly. It isn't a punishable misdeed. It's an opportunity for the child to learn some subtlety about the rule. However," he went on, "once the child knows the rule, has followed it, and then breaks it, that's a different story."

I didn't say anything. A tear rolled silently down my cheek. "I'm afraid I've done the same thing to my own children." I spoke quietly, as you do at those rare times when you trade an imagined fault for a real one. "My daughter will say to me, 'You said do so-and-so, and I did *exactly* what you said,' and I get angry at her and I say, 'Well, you knew perfectly well what I *meant*!'"

"No," Dr. Lustig said softly, "it's *your* obligation to

tell your kids what you mean—not for them to attempt to figure it out. It's the obligation of the person communicating to communicate *exactly* what they intend."

We sat some more in silence. I felt a new empathy for my mother; I felt empathy for all mothers, including myself. Like my own mother and the chain of mothers stretching back before me, I regretted the distance between my desire to protect my children and my ability to do so, between my intentions and my actions, between my love and my limitations.

If the memory of the flowers was the worst memory from my childhood that I could summon up, I realized, then I'd been pretty lucky. Certainly here was no explanation of my illness. With a curious irony, it was almost as if my childhood had been too good—too protected and warm; too honest, loving, and kind. And my parents, although not society at large, *had* encouraged my autonomy at what they considered a reasonable age. So, I had been surprised and unprepared for the injustice I had found in the larger world, and had raged against the pain and unfairness of life. It would have been convenient to find something long buried that would have made sense of the madness I had endured, that would have provided an excuse, so that I need not blame myself. But perhaps there's no need to locate blame anywhere, I reflected. Perhaps madness remains a mystery to be survived, not explained.

And then, like an unexpected gift, another memory of my mother and flowers came to my mind. It was when I was in grade school, maybe nine or ten. Easter was coming soon, and my mother had not bought a new Easter hat. When my sister and I asked her about it, she said that she didn't need a new one. But we knew that the real reason was that she didn't have the money. So my sister and I pooled our allowance and the money we had earned from odd jobs, $9.56 in total, and walked to town one day to buy our mother a hat. We finally settled on a bonnet that was covered with pink and white flowers. It met our budget and our tastes, so we bought it and brought it home.

When we gave it to Mother, she almost wept. She

immediately tried it on, pronounced it most becoming, and proudly wore it to church the next Sunday.

Many years later, Mother fondly recounted the story, telling us that she, of course, would have worn the hat to church no matter what it had looked like. "But how did you know it would look good on me?" she asked us. "Oh, I tried it on myself, and it looked good on me," I replied. We laughed about it, at my assumption that what looks good on a nine-year-old will suit her mother.

I smiled to myself as I thought about the Easter hat. Does the character of one's memories mark the stages of one's life? Is the secret of well-being to put painful memories in their place, and if possible to transform them or replace them with more kindly remembrances? Whenever I think of my mother and flowers, I decided, I'll think of her Easter hat.

Chapter 4

So often, the best gifts are small, ordinary things. We may miss them amid the clutter of complexity; we may dismiss them because they are so near at hand. During that year I came to recognize them, one by one. My profession offered me order and rationality and the grounding of quantitative measures. Numbers were no longer mysterious and powerful and secret and contradictory. They were straightforward and ordinary, and could be dealt with.

My children became a pleasure rather than a burden, as they shared with me my growing up. My responsibility for them firmly fastened me to the world, so that I did not again drift into magical or mad waters. Family and friends offered real connection, banishing my former need for companions of the mind. And Dr. Lustig, my healer and adviser, continued to clear away the cobwebs from my psyche, replacing them with skills that solidified a new self.

My madness was gone, was put behind me, but I had yet to find a place for it in my thoughts, to discover how it would continue to define me, how to accept it but not as part of my current self. As I was pondering

on its place and its effect on the rest of my life, I had
a dream that pointed the way to a new acceptance. Even
a crazy person, I discovered, may have gifts to give.

NIGHT OF DECEMBER 1, 1979

*A crazy person is standing on a hillside overlooking the
ocean. A man appears. The crazy person points to the
ocean and the vast expanse of horizon beyond. "For
the price of five pence, which is healing," the crazy
person says to the man, "I will give you a piece of the
sky." The crazy person pauses and gestures toward the
sky. "But for the price of ten pence, which is wisdom,
I will give you a perfect sunset at the end of a perfect
day." So saying, the hands of the crazy person frame
the sunset, and offer it to the man.*

My dream set me thinking, put madness in a new
light. If the crazy person has gifts to offer, then perhaps
I needn't feel shame at that just-passed portion of my
life. Perhaps someday, I will be able to speak of it to
others, if I myself can understand the nature and price
of that journey: its illumination but also its humanless-
ness; its destination: a place enchanting but grudging of
comfort, most terrible finally because of its nonhuman
scale. Perhaps it is a place to bring something back from,
I reflected, a source of gifts that can be given only by
turning away, by returning to the cave and looking in a
new direction, free of shackles, but warmed by a mortal
fire.

I have been crazy, I said to myself, but I am still a
human being. I drew myself up just thinking of the
dignity of it.

A few days later, I redreamed my first dream.

NIGHT OF DECEMBER 15, 1979

*I am back in the house on the hill overlooking the ocean,
the house of my first dream with all the interesting windows and rooms. This time, however, I go directly to the*

*lone dark room. I open the door. The room appears gray
and gloomy and ominous, although it is no longer black
and terrifying. I walk through the dimness of the room to
the large window on the other side. I open the curtains.
Light floods into the room. I see that it is empty, and that
it is a perfectly ordinary room. There is nothing frightening about it anymore. I walk throughout the house.
Light is everywhere. The heart of the house is no longer
dark.*

Several days later, as I was driving to see Dr. Lustig,
eager to tell him the symbolism of my changed dream, I
idly switched on the car radio. It was tuned to a station
that I had never listened to before. Someone was speaking
about the jester in literature. "The court jester was mad,"
I heard a man saying. "He was inappropriate, but considered by some to be divine. And he was exempt from
the usual rules of the court, because he constantly
reminded the king of his own humanity."

I remembered the jester of my first dream. It seemed
natural that I should be reminded of the jester now. The
king and the jester—two sides of myself—no longer at
war, but reconciled. I knew with the certainty of attuned
intuition that my earlier drama was now resolved—that
peace lingered in that dream kingdom, that the king and
the jester were now each more complete.

By the time I arrived at Dr. Lustig's, a smile was
securely fastened on my face. An answering smile quickly
appeared as I told Dr. Lustig the details of my new
dreams.

"The dark room is now empty and light, calm and
serene?" he reiterated in amazement. "Wonderful!...
How long has it been since you dreamed that first
dream?"

"Five years." I was struck with the symbolism. In my
lexicon 5 was the number of healing.

"Perhaps that's what the dream about the crazy person's gifts is saying," I said. "Perhaps the dream is about
the five years it has taken to achieve some degree of
healing." Perhaps it will take ten years to muster some
wisdom, I added to myself, although I did not presume
to speak this thought out loud.

Dr. Lustig nodded. "I've come to greatly respect the timetable that each person has for his or her own life," he said softly, as if he was marveling at the ability of all people to guide their own healing. "It doesn't surprise me at all that it would have taken five years for you to come full circle in a healthy way."

I thought again about the dark room that had been transformed into light. Then I remembered that Dr. Lustig, in all those five years, had never interpreted my first dream.

"I've told you many dreams in these last five years," I continued musingly, "and you've never really interpreted them. I wonder why."

"Your dreams are *your* creations," Dr. Lustig answered. "My interpretation of your dreams would be imposing my forms on your creativity. And I'm reluctant to do that. But I'm very interested in what *you do* with your dreams, especially with the elements that are problematic. I'm interested in how you change those elements, so that they become productive and helpful."

Perhaps it's better to redream a dream, I reflected, than it is to interpret one. Whatever was dark, in that room in my first dream, has now been transformed into light. Better to achieve the light now than to continually delve into the infinite origins of the darkness.

"I do have the sense that many things have come together for me," I said, feeling a quiet sort of peace creep over me as I spoke. "Yesterday, for example, I had a day with a perfect sunset. It was a special, peaceful day with the children. We were a family together. I didn't feel the absence of anyone, not of a man or anyone else. We went out in the early morning and bought a Christmas tree, came back home, and put lights on it. Then the children strung popcorn and cranberries, just as I had so often done in my childhood. It seemed like an old-fashioned Christmas. For the remainder of the day, we all stayed together in the living room, around the tree. The children didn't quarrel, but played quietly. We just stayed in the room together, because we felt so comfortable and good there. It was the nicest day I can remember in a long time."

"That's lovely," Dr. Lustig said. "And it only cost ten

pence? . . . There was a time when you feared that it would never happen."

I nodded in acknowledgment. "It seemed like the three of us were a family—whole together."

I sat quietly, steeped in the remembered sense of peaceful purpose. Life seemed good. Then I recalled those other days, also part of my current life, when nothing was easy, when I worried about my job and whether I did it well, when I felt less than adequate as a parent, when I felt alone and discouraged in spirit.

"That's not to say that I no longer have any anxieties or fears," I said aloud for Dr. Lustig's benefit, not wanting him to think that I had found a magic talisman. "The fact that I sometimes have those old feelings makes me wonder if I really *am* all right now, if I ever *can be* totally well."

"Are you talking about being well," he countered laughingly, "or are you talking about being *perfect*?"

I granted that I might be confusing the two, that I did now have more tools to cope with life's strains.

"Before you had *some* tools, but not *all* of them," he affirmed with his usual precision. "And the ones that you didn't have were costing you a great deal, in terms of what was happening to your mind and your life. But now you have all the ones you need. I certainly do hope, Carol, that you use them and enjoy them, because I'd much rather have you as a friend than a patient."

Friendship with him was something I had long coveted, but now that it was being introduced as a real possibility, I felt unaccountably unsure. What if I still needed Dr. Lustig as a therapist? What if I wasn't well enough yet to be his friend? He must have guessed some of my uncertainty from my awkward smile, because he quickly added, "Whenever you're ready, it's fine with me if we become friends. *You'll* be the person who decides that."

I sighed comfortably, glad that he had left the timetable for friendship to me, just as he had let me set my own course of healing. He never takes away a grain of my freedom, I realized, grateful that the price for a whole self had not been a loss of volition.

We sat in silence then, both occupied with our own

thoughts. It seemed to me that we had arrived at a turning point, that something had changed, although I could not at that moment state precisely what it was.

"You know, Carol," he resumed musingly, "your story is almost a universal one. Look at all you've been through—marriage, getting divorced, going mad, being hospitalized, reorganizing yourself, keeping your family together, switching careers, and now succeeding in a way that you never expected. Have you ever considered writing about it?"

It was as if a half-formed idea at the back of my mind had suddenly jumped forward. I was surprised and flattered at his suggestion, while another part of me was hesitant.

"I wonder..." I said aloud. "I've kept journals throughout the course of my therapy. I've written down many of our conversations."

"More than what you gave me?" he asked astonished. I had never mentioned the journals before. "You have more material than what I've seen? I still have a whole file full of writings that you gave me when you were going crazy."

"Yes, I have five notebooks," I replied with a smile, realizing that once again the 5 of healing had crept into our conversation.

But the thought of writing had its drawbacks. Wouldn't it be too painful to write, to have to go back over that experience again? Wouldn't it be better to stay solidly fastened in the present?

"It would be painful," I said.

"What would be painful about it?"

"Having to go back over the experience, having to relive it," I answered, thinking about the price that must always be paid for creativity.

"You don't have to go crazy again to write about going crazy," Dr. Lustig replied. "You'll be able to intimately examine the experiences of your past from your present perspective as a healthy, normal person. It might not be pleasant to examine them, but it certainly won't be dangerous. It could even be a final step in your process of healing. It would allow you to harness those elements in your past that had wounded you, had caused you to go mad. In writing about them, you could return to those old places and view them exactly as they were, but with the light of wholeness, just as you returned to the dark room of your original dream and found that it was no longer frightening, because you had let the light in."

His reference to a wound reminded me of "the wound and the bow," the literary theory that the artist is more wounded than other people, and that the wound is the source of creativity. I explained the view to Dr. Lustig.

"The people who write about that theory make one mistake," he responded. "They look at the surface of things. The wound is not the issue. The issue is the fact that the wound has made an *opening* into another world, which the artist now has an opportunity to explore. The truly creative person is someone who has explored that world as *safely* as possible, and has become *familiar* with as much of it as possible. Then the other world is available to that person all the time, without it having to be costly. It is not necessary to be wounded in order to create. It is only necessary to establish a permanent safe passageway to the other world through your experiences, a *door* that only you can open. The other world is accessible to everyone. It is neither good nor bad—it's just dark, that's all."

We said no more on the subject of writing that day, beyond my statement that I would think about it. But an idea was left germinating in the back of my mind. Perhaps if we become friends, I thought, we might someday work together to write my story.

We fell into another comfortable silence. Soft strains of Christmas music from the nearby shopping center filtered into the room. The music recalled me somewhat, reminding me of the gift that I had brought for Dr. Lustig, partly because it was Christmas, but mostly because it marked our five years of work together. I drew a small gold-wrapped box from my sweater pocket and handed it to him. "For all you've done for me," I said.

He accepted the package with a smile and some eagerness. He quickly pulled aside the wrapping paper, drew out the enclosed velvet case, and opened it. Inside was the gold pocket watch I had chosen for him, because time to me had always been the symbol of reality, and reality was what he had given me. On the cover of the watch, I had had his initials, H.S.L., inscribed, and inside the words, "Because you made time golden."

As he read the inscription, it was clear that he was moved. His eyes moistened and he seemed momentarily at a loss for words. His voice somewhat choked as he finally said thank you. He continued to hold the watch carefully in his hands, turning it this way and that in the light, opening the case again to reread the inscription.

"A lovely watercolor, a lovely haiku, and now a beautiful watch with a beautiful inscription," he said. "Are you sure that you haven't been shortchanged?"

Images from the last five years flickered past my mind's eye, as they are purported to do at the moment of death. But I am alive, I thought, alive and well. And it is only this man, and the determination in myself, that has made it possible. How do I say thank you for all of that?

"I don't know how to say thank you, except to say thank you," I said.

"I don't know how to say thank you, except to say thank you," he echoed.

We both smiled.

Sitting at my desk in my new office several days later, I was quietly greeting the morning with a fresh cup of coffee. Natural light from the winter sun streamed through the window to my left, casually defining my place. Sitting in the middle of my new beginning, I was thinking about my madness and its end. I did not waken from my nightmare in Emerald City. There can no longer be such transcendent realms for me. I have put aside wizards and magical red shoes. I must discover the comforts of dwelling in Kansas. Amid the problems and trials of everyday living, I will seek some grain of sanity, some sense of achievement, some impulse toward health. I will learn what the Greeks always knew—that to be well and do well is happiness.

Psychiatrist's Note

This book is an accurate chronicle of Carol Allen's mental disintegration and reconstitution. It is also a testimony to her personal courage, faith, and determination.

Although each of us, during periods of intense mental stress in our lives, might have had one or some of the behavioral, cognitive, or sensory disturbances that Carol experienced, it does not mean that we have, or might develop, the same illness. It just means that we all share the condition of being human, and that our responses to an extreme situation are sometimes selected from the same menu of mental symptoms, but usually to a lesser degree.

In this book, we have purposely refrained from giving a clinical diagnosis of Carol's illness—although a mental health professional should be able to infer one—in order to avoid incorrect and agonizing attempts at self-diagnosis by our lay readers. Carol's symptoms indicate that her illness was severe, one that would have rendered most people nonfunctional. Surprisingly, Carol did function, albeit in a diminished manner sometimes, during the events of this book. This is due, I believe, to several factors. Carol kept voluminous and detailed notes about her daily activities, mental life, and therapy sessions. These allowed her to maintain a modest perspective, even during the active phase of her illness, and helped to form and order her chaotic experiences. Carol also used the intellectual discipline of philosophy, in which she had been thoroughly trained, to help balance the specter of intuition that was threatening to overwhelm her. And finally, Carol had a good family—one whose unity, solid values, and emotional stability served as a permanent anchor to the real world of loving people.

The psychiatric treatment that Carol received from me consisted of psychotherapy and the prescription of a standard psychotropic medication. Because we are all unique, the particular combination of mental symptoms that we might come to produce is very special. For this reason, Carol's psychotherapy was designed and customized specifically for her. The therapeutic style that I used with Carol evolved during this period, having had its roots in more traditional methods of intervention, and in my personal appreciation for the efficiency of altered states of consciousness and skill mastery in the healing process. A different psychiatrist might well have used a different approach.

Although Dr. Wainwright's sexual activity with Marion was professionally unethical and personally painful to me, Carol and I reluctantly deemed the inclusion of the episode necessary, in order to explain Carol's further deterioration and subsequent hospitalization.

This book publicly confirms my cherished belief that competent and compassionate psychiatric treatment of people with mental illness is a reality. It also confirms the reality of the mind's ability to restore itself, and of the power of healing with the spoken word. For this, I thank a former patient and current friend.

—HERBERT S. LUSTIG, M.D.

About the Author

Carol Allen is a native of Idaho, attended Carlton College and Bryn Mawr, and is the mother of two children. Formerly a professor of philosophy, she has begun a new career as a business consultant. She lives in suburban Philadelphia.

Herbert S. Lustig, M.D., is a nationally and internationally respected psychiatrist. For more than a decade, he has maintained a private clinical practice for psychotherapy and hypnosis on Philadelphia's Main Line and in suburban New Jersey.